The Medieval Economy and Society

The Medieval Economy and Society

An Economic History of Britain in the Middle Ages

M. M. Postan

Weidenfeld and Nicolson
5 Winsley Street London W1

First published 1972 by arrangement
with Penguin Books Ltd.

ISBN 0 297 99543 X

Printed in Great Britain by
Willmer Brothers Limited, Birkenhead

Contents

Preface

Some of the features of this book may require an explanation, or even an apology. To begin with, the book omits several important topics. It does not deal with medieval economic doctrines, for the simple reason that in my view the discussion of medieval economic doctrines should not be detached, as it usually is, from that of the general doctrinal and intellectual developments of the time. An adequate discussion of these developments, however, would be beyond my competence, and would also greatly change and possibly even distort the balance of the book. The second omission is that of the economic policy of the Crown. I have touched upon taxation in so far as it affected the position of different social groups, more particularly the landowners; but to have dealt with state finance and with economic policy in all their ramifications would have required retelling the whole of the constitutional history of medieval England. This again would have made the book into something different from what I have been commissioned, and have felt myself competent, to do.

As it is, the balance of the book, measured by the number of words devoted to individual subjects, may appear to be unsymmetrical. My object has been to present an account of medieval economy simple enough to be read by the uninitiated, yet capable of reflecting the state of knowledge at its most up-to-date. This two-fold objective has compelled me to allow more room for subjects on which text-book knowledge has been greatly outrun by recent researches and to be rather laconic on subjects well-represented in current literature. Hence the relative length of chapter 2 dealing with reclamations, chapter 4 dealing with land use and technique, and chapter 11 dealing with landlords; and the brevity of most other chapters. The disproportionate attention to individual subjects has also affected the treatment of evidence and of footnote references. Generally speaking I have tried, in keeping with the character of the book, to be as sparing as I could in my references to sources, and also to confine the evidence cited in the text to that available in published books or articles and to limit my footnote references accordingly. But on some subjects, such as landownership, reclamations, land use, or agricultural technology, the story as presented here is so fresh from the researcher's oven that I felt compelled to make occasional reference to original sources and to results of researches, including my own, not yet available in published form. In general I have also tried to avoid reference to foreign literature. One or two subjects, however, such as the rise of the manor or early foreign trade, are so closely related to developments abroad that some reference to foreign authorities had to be made both in the text and in the footnotes.

1 Roman Heritage

I

It is the accepted convention of the university curricula to commence the story of the middle ages—more especially that of medieval society and institutions—with the settlement of Anglo-Saxons in England. This convention must not be accepted unquestioningly. Was the Anglo-Saxon era—the invasion and the occupation of Roman Britain between the fourth and the sixth centuries—the real opening point in English social and economic history? In other words was the world the Anglo-Saxon invaders found, or the world they created by the invasions, so virgin that economic life and social organization—sites of settlement, villages and farmsteads, rural institutions and social ties—all had to be created from the very beginning, and that in creating them the Anglo-Saxon settlers had nothing to inherit and nothing to continue?

The academic inclination, near consensus, is to answer all these questions in the affirmative even if rowadays the affirmative is becoming somewhat less categorical than it used to be. In the past the attitude to pre-Saxon survivals followed the ideological assumptions of medieval historiography. In the nineteenth and the early twentieth centuries English medieval scholarship, especially when it concerned itself with state and society, shared its intellectual bias with medieval historiography on the Continent and more particularly in Germany; and in Germany the underlying bias was Germanic. It owed its origin and its strength partly to the political and emotional involvement of young academics of the early nineteenth century with the rising German nationalism, but partly also to the nature of the evidence available to German medievalists. The most important sources of early German history were laws of Teutonic tribes and early medieval records of land titles and conveyances. German scholars found it therefore both easy and tempting to seek the roots of medieval institutions in German tribal societies. Their disciples elsewhere, more particularly the constitutional and legal historians in England and Scandinavia, were similarly taught to trace the history of medieval institutions to the tribal past of their Germanic ancestors.

The belief in the Germanic origins of medieval civilization would not of course have been tenable except on the assumption that in central and northern Europe the Roman civilization made little impression on the culture of indigenous peoples. The prevailing tendency among medieval scholars was to take it for granted that in the period immediately preceding the invasion of the barbarians Roman influences in lands beyond the older provinces of the Empire were feeble and shallowly rooted. Influences as feeble as these could easily be obliterated in the course of the invasions. For the invasions were accompanied by wholesale destruction, displacement of native population, reoccupation and the settlement of lands by Germanic newcomers. The transition from Rome to the middle ages was thus a true break. The word the Germans use to describe it is *Caesur*: a sharp and clean cut.

These presuppositions appeared to apply with special force to Roman Britain. The prevailing view was that the Roman influences were weaker and more transient in Britain than in most other parts of the Empire. Britain was on the very geographical fringes of the Roman world, late to be occupied and among the earliest to feel the retrenchments of the imperial rule. The rule itself was half-hearted: certainly not backed by a mass settlement of Roman or Romanized people or by a fully developed network of Roman institutions. The people, their mode of life, the administrative framework of their government, remained Celtic and tribal.

This being the prevailing view of Roman occupation, historians did not find it surprising that the Roman elements of Roman Britain should have been unable to survive the Anglo-Saxon invasion. What made the destruction and replacement of Romano-British civilization all the more certain is that the invasion itself proceeded stage by stage and took nearly two centuries to complete. The Roman towns, such as there were, were emptied of their Roman or Romanized population and in many cases physically destroyed. In the countryside the effect of the invasion was to exterminate or to replace the indigenous Celts. In the end the surviving Romano-Celtic people, presumably their retreating warriors and refugees, were driven beyond the furthest limits of Anglo-Saxon occupation: the River Tamar in the south west, the Severn and the Welsh hills in the west and the Cheviots in the north. The country they had abandoned was resettled anew by Germans who were themselves wholly new to the land they occupied.

Hence the purely Anglo-Saxon character of the economy, society and culture which developed in this country between the fifth century and, say, the tenth. To students of Anglo-Saxon history, including so recent and authoritative a historian as Sir Frank Stenton, the novelty and the Anglo-Saxon purity of the early middle ages appear to be incontestable. The forms of settlement, indeed the place names themselves, especially names of fields, bore hardly any marks of a Celtic connection. The social and legal customs of Anglo-Saxon England, the principles and procedures regulating the occupation of land, the titles to holdings, the rules of succession to heirs, the communal rights over waste and pasture and the collective arrangements of open-field cultivation, were all characteristic of the laws and rules which had governed the lives of the invading tribes in their continental homelands. Even where the Anglo-Saxon society diverged from this general pattern, as it did in certain regions of England, the divergences themselves reflected the tribal differences of the separate branches of the Anglo-Saxon peoples. Jolliffe has argued that the ways in which property was held, managed and inherited in medieval Kent faithfully reproduced the laws and customs of the continental Jutes who invaded and occupied Kent. Professor Homans has produced a similar argument to apply to East Anglia, especially to Suffolk. According to him the peculiarly East Anglian rules governing tenures and successions merely carried over to this country the customs of the Frisians who occupied the plains of East Anglia. Jolliffe also offered a corresponding hypothesis concerning the northernmost regions of Anglo-Saxon settlement, those of Northumbria.

Such were until recently the views of medieval historians; and to some extent they still prevail in current historical discussions and writings. Their continued prevalence is not however to be accounted for solely by the strength of the professional bias, since their underlying basis of facts has not been wholly destroyed by more recent researches. Nevertheless more researches have brought up some new facts, which differ sufficiently from the information previously available to make it no longer possible to hold the older view of Roman rule and of Anglo-Saxon invasion in all their erstwhile simplicity. In the first place the economic and social influences of Rome, however shallow and unstable, appear to have spread more widely and affected lives more deeply than the Germanists had once upon a time believed them to have done. In the second place Anglo-Saxons—some Anglo-Saxons—had been coming to these shores and settling, as Roman soldiers, long before their invasions in force had commenced. The invasions themselves, however traumatic and innovating, need not have been accompanied by an utter destruction and displacement of pre-Anglo-Saxon elements. Altogether the continuity in the material and even cultural history of pre-medieval England was greater than the historians writing in the nineteenth century were prepared to admit.

Recent archaeological researches and the critique of the surviving literary sources have done nothing to dissipate altogether the prevailing impression that the physical occupation of English land by Romans and Romanized persons was anything but scattered and very thin. Nevertheless the evidence reveals the rise of wholly new Roman communities, as where the Romans established settlements of retired legionaries. Some high imperial officials came from metropolitan areas of Rome and some of them may have established themselves in country villas as owners of large estates or in some of the British cities.[1]

It also remains true that the Romans were not able and probably did not attempt to displace the tribal systems of government and to reconstruct the native society and government in the Italian fashion. *Gleichschaltung* of this kind was not attempted by the Romans and certainly was not carried out by them in any of their other outlying provinces, not even in northern Gaul. Britain under the Romans remained a collection of tribal units ruled by the native princes and aristocrats and continuing in the main to conform to their ancient tribal customs in all matters legal and social and agrarian. Such institutions as the Romans imported, their civil service and their villas and even their military organization, were merely superimposed on a society and an economy which remained largely native and Celtic.

It will nevertheless be wrong to underestimate the weight and the impact of this superimposition. Its economic impact, in a purely material sense of the term, was bound to be very considerable. How much the population itself grew in the shelter of Roman rule and peace we do not know, but if the area under cultivation is a guide to the numbers of men cultivating it, population must have grown very considerably between the second century and the fifth. Some of the additional acreage must have come from major pieces of reclamation. There are clear signs of such reclamations on the fringes of the eastern Fens, in the marshes of Kent and Essex, in the Somerset marshes of Sedgemoor. Additional arable and pasture were also cleared in the more accessible regions of England's forest plains, which, according to the prevailing views of historians, had been largely shunned by the pre-Roman agriculturalists. It is indeed quite possible that these plains had been broken into even earlier; probably with the coming of the Belgae—the latest wave of Celtic invaders before the Roman conquest.[2]

Generally accepted and easy to demonstrate is the effect of the Roman occupation on overland communications. Roman roads have always been there to bear witness to the Roman achievement, even if some of these roads, such as Icknield Way or the local roads in regions like Sedgemoor, had probably been made and maintained some time before the Romans came to this country. Roman engineers and road builders also established other overland arteries of traffic. Above all, dykes and canals, such as the Cardyke or the Fossdyke in the eastern provinces of England, served the double purpose of drainage on the one hand and the lines of communication on the other. The Romans must also have done a great deal to improve and maintain the traffic on rivers. The Thames, with London at its head, was obviously an important channel of communication and so apparently were the other principal estuaries of the rivers flowing into the North Sea.[3]

The Roman roads and waterways were largely designed to serve the military needs of the occupation: to supply the legions guarding the frontiers and garrisoning the fortresses. They were nevertheless bound to help the civilian traffic whether they were designed for that purpose or not. What we know of the long-distance trade of Roman Britain suggests that it was quite active, though not perhaps as abundant as England's foreign trade was to become in later centuries. Britain's exports mentioned in sources were mainly metals. Tin had been mined and exported from Cornwall long before the Romans occupied Britain. Silver was mined and exported from Devonshire and Derbyshire and so also was lead which was a by-product of silver mining. Copper may have been exported from North Wales (it was certainly mined there); and a little gold may have come from north-east Cornwall. Iron works and mines were to be found in the Weald, the Forest of Dean, in Northamptonshire, Lincolnshire and North Yorkshire, though we do not know whether any iron goods were actually exported. We possess one reference to a large quantity of grain taken out of England in the third century. But the reference stands isolated and is presented in a way which some historians interpret as a single isolated shipment of food to Roman legions in Germany provided not by way of trade but out of the proceeds of the Roman taxes in kind. There is also at least one documentary reference to cloth exported from Britain —*burrus Britannicus*. The reciprocal traffic in imports may well have exceeded (in theory it should have done so) the movement of imports. From across the Channel there came wine, miscellaneous manufactured products including pottery and metal work, and above all coinage.[4]

Indeed nothing testifies better to the strength of Rome's economic impact or enables us better to follow these fluctuations than the record of coinage in Roman Britain. Roman coins or local coins imitating the Roman ones had circulated in pre-Roman Britain as they did in the various Barbaric principalities bordering upon the Roman Empire but not actually occupied by the Romans. With the establishment of Roman rule several official mints were established in Britain: among them one under Caransius (287–93), another under Alexius (293–6), and two others under Magnus Maximus (383–8) and Constantine (287–324). In addition, coins minted on the Continent, in Rome, Lyon, Trèves, or Arles, continued to be imported until the very end of the Roman occupation. The flow was, needless to say, very uneven. It appears to have ebbed from the middle of the second century to the second half of the third, but the end of the third and the fourth centuries witnessed very large issues of coins of small denominations, including the profuse bronze coinage of Valentinian the First in the second half of the fourth century; and it can be reasonably argued that it was the small coinage rather than the coins of large denominations that testify best to the spread of exchanges and the commercialization of economic life.[5]

Where the Roman influence ran shallowest was in the human relations and institutions which overlay the material substratum of economic life. In agriculture the *villas*, which in historical writings and in popular notions are commonly identified with Romanized agriculture, were to be found all over Britain. Only about 40 of these Roman villa sites have been excavated, but many more sites of villas have been identified. Judged by this evidence alone, it might therefore appear that British agriculture was as closely fitted into the network of large estates of the Roman type as it was in other more ancient and more fully Romanized parts of the Empire.[6] These appearances, however, may be misleading. To begin with, there is a great deal of evidence of other types of agricultural enterprise which lay wholly or largely outside the system of Romanized estates. There were individual farmsteads, some quite large, others quite small, which did not appear to form part of any villa organization. There were also villages of humble peasant cultivators like the one in Cranbourne Chase excavated by Pitt-Rivers, some of which may have been attached to or dominated by a nearby villa but others of which may have led as independent an existence as they had done in pre-Roman times. In the second place the villas themselves differed in size, use and function. Some of them—like Fishbourne near Chichester or Chedworth in Gloucestershire in its fourth-century form—acquired all the superficial characteristics of a Roman patrician villa: a large built-over site on a courtyard with a residential nucleus equipped to house a wealthy family and provided with farm buildings large enough to serve as the managerial headquarters of a substantial agricultural estate. Estates of this size and type could comprise satellite villages such as that near Cirencester described by Professor Finberg. Other villa-estates may have conducted larger agricultural enterprises directly as home-farms or, to use a German term, as *Gutscherrschaften.* On the other hand some villas, like that of Fishbourne, were country residences of men of great substance, possibly Roman. Others still, like Cotesgrove in Somerset or Langton in Yorkshire, were on a scale no greater than that of substantial peasant farmsteads. In the closing century of Roman rule some erstwhile villas, which may previously have been run in a manner close to the Roman prototypes and had housed resident families of important estate owners, lost their residential character and became little more than the business headquarters of agricultural enterprises run presumably by bailiffs for their absentee owners. It will thus be too much of a simplification to take the existence of Roman villas or the numbers of sites in Roman Britain as evidence of a well developed or deeply rooted system of Roman estates.[7]

In this respect, however, conditions in Roman Britain were not exceptional. In many other parts of the Roman Empire outside Italy the Roman villa and latifundia was superimposed upon the pre-existing rural society without wholly absorbing it or doing away with its local and native features. In general, in Roman Britain as in many parts of Northern Gaul, the pre-Roman agricultural organization persisted throughout the Roman period under the superficial crust of villa and villa-like units.

The same conclusion is suggested by the evidence of Romano-British towns. Settlements described and ranking as urban were quite numerous, and some of them may have been quite large. London may well have had a population of 50,000: comparable in size to the population of medieval London. Some historians have estimated the size of Camulodunum at 108 acres, which was a figure not much inferior to the estimated size of contemporary Cologne. By the end of the third century some towns also acquired the superficial insignia and amenities of Roman cities: regular street plans, as in Isea Dumroniorum (Exeter), Caleva Atrebatum (Silchester), Corinium Dobunorum (Cirencester), Camulodunum or Verulam and London (Londinium); somewhat later, towns like Londinium, Viroconium (Wroxeter) or Verulamium could boast of piped water supplies or of communal buildings of a Roman type such as baths and temples and arenas. Judged by the numbers and the superficial features of its towns and town-like places, Roman Britain appeared to be as fully urbanized as most other outlying provinces of the Empire.[8]

Viewed more closely, however, the urbanization was to say the least superficial. Hardly any of the numerous Romano-British towns occupied a position and played a function of a typical Roman *civitas*—a near-city state gathering to itself the top layers of the population and dominating the administration, the commercial activities and even the agriculture of the countryside. To begin with, very few of the Roman British towns owed their rise and development to the role they played in commerce and industry. In this and in so many other instances Roman London was something of an exception. Its development and importance were due to its exceptionally favourable geographical position at the estuary of Britain's most important river and athwart the shortest lines of communication between southern England and the Continent. But in addition London also grew to become the administrative focus of the entire country, as well as the largest agglomeration of urban inhabitants, which eventually grew to occupy an area of over 300 acres, or more than almost any other Roman city north of the Alps. Other towns would claim one or some of the urban functions. Some were centres of regional administration: in fact the *oppida* like Venta Silurum (Caerwent) or Venta Icenorum (Caister-by-Norwich) were centres of tribal administration and continued as such in Roman times. Others, like Camulodunum or Lindum (Lincoln), were settlements of *coloni*: residential townships housing newly settled veterans. Others still enjoyed some commercial importance as centres of regional or inter-regional trade, and some traders and artisans were apparently to be found quite early in most urban or urbanized centres of population. Some towns also provided places of residence for families of substance. Above all, towns—especially those immediately behind the northern borders, such as Corbridge, old Penrith, old Carlisle or Catuructonium (Catterick Bridge)—housed the rear headquarters of the legions from which the military units guarding the frontier were supplied and administered. In short, by comparison with the typical Greco-Roman city-state which gave the Roman civilization its characteristic, most Romano-British towns were only part-cities. Their hold over the country and the influence over the people's lives in it was correspondingly partial.[9]

II

An economic and social organization so formed could not therefore possess the same capacity for resisting the irruption of barbarian settlement as it did in southern Gaul or in Italy where its strength and hold over the countryside were far greater. This should not however be taken to mean that it disappeared without a trace in the course of the Anglo-Saxon invasions and that no trace of it survived into the early middle ages.

The continuity of the material sub-stratum could be taken for granted. The roads which the Romans constructed, the dykes they put up and, needless to say, the areas which the ditches and dykes drained and reclaimed could be, and in fact were, taken over and used in later centuries. The same is in general true of the sites of agricultural settlement. In all probability the places cultivated by Romano-British landowners and husbandmen continued to be cultivated in the Anglo-Saxon period. It is even probable that most of the agricultural sites occupied by the Anglo-Saxons in the first flush of their occupation, in the fifth, sixth and seventh centuries, were on sites previously occupied and cultivated by the Roman and even pre-Roman agriculturists. The drier parts of Sedgemoor, where Roman and pre-Roman roadways and paths and village sites were continually occupied since pre-Roman times, is perhaps one of the best known instances of topographical continuity.[10] Until many more early Anglo-Saxon sites have been excavated it is difficult to be certain how many of them similarly reached back to Roman and pre-Roman settlements. But the few which have so far been explored reveal signs of pre-Anglo-Saxon occupation. If the signs are to be trusted it would appear that the early Anglo-Saxon settlement was in a large measure concentrated in regions previously cleared, occupied and cultivated by the Romano-British husbandmen and their Iron Age predecessors.

The continuity of sites need not of course signify the continuity of actual settlement. Much of it may merely reflect the predilection of conquerors for areas and places into which capital and labour had been sunk, and which were therefore capable of immediate exploitation. Above all the continuity of sites may mean little more than a similarity in the evaluation of land by the different waves of occupiers. Archaeologists and historians no longer confine the location of pre-Roman and Roman agriculture to hilltops and river beds, since some Romano-British sites have been found on land which was neither open downland nor river gravels. Yet on the whole it is bound to be true that the sites of the first preference were on land which, given the existing technology, were those best suited to agricultural use. And these were, as a rule, the light, well-drained and well-watered loams which were easy to work and yet retentive of nutrients. That the sites were occupied by the Romano-British agriculturalists, by their Iron Age predecessors and by the first generations of Anglo-Saxons does not prove anything more than a similarity of technological conditions. In each of the successive waves of settlement the settlers may have had the same preferences and the same standards of evaluating the agricultural qualities of land.

The continuity of sites could thus be reconciled with the presumption that the Anglo-Saxons did away with the human and social superstructure of Romano-British agriculture. It may even be reconciled with the belief that the entire rural population was expelled and displaced and that none of the pre-Saxon settlements survived. There are however some *a priori* reasons and a certain amount of evidence to suggest that continuity was not confined to sites alone. The notion that the entire rural population was exterminated and expelled runs counter to what we must assume to have been the main motive of Anglo-Saxon invasion, as well as to the experience of other conquered and occupied territories. Except where the occupation of the land was the result not of a military conquest but of a mass migration of agricultural settlers, as in the middle west of USA, or in the northern borderlands of modern China, it is seldom the object of the conquerors and new occupiers to possess themselves of land and get rid of men cultivating it. Where and when land is relatively abundant acres have little value without labour to work them. Conquering settlers of new lands would as often as not be expected to keep at least some of the conquered population either as independent cultivators or land-working slaves. On these purely *a priori* grounds we cannot take it for granted that the Anglo-Saxon conquerors were so perversely destructive, and so indifferent to purely economic considerations, as to expel or to exterminate the Romano-British manpower throughout the 150 years of their military progress towards the west.

These, so to speak, theoretical doubts are strongly reinforced by such little evidence as we possess. The most direct and most relevant evidence at our disposal is the reference in the earliest Anglo-Saxon documents in Kent to groups of villagers, perhaps entire villages, composed of Wealhs, persons who, judging by the name alone, must have descended from the Romano-British or Welsh natives. Their abject social status—they ranked among the most servile sections of the Kentish population—provides a further indication of their having descended from the conquered aborigines.[11] And it is quite possible that the Kentish Wealhs were not the only men so descended. In the fifth and sixth centuries, but also in 1086, Kent possessed large numbers of slaves; but slaves were at that time also to be found in other counties, as were also villages with the 'Wealh' element in their place names. Would it then be too fanciful to assume that the slaves, like the Wealhs, found themselves in that condition merely because they had been subjugated by conquest? The regions in which slaves were especially numerous in the tenth and eleventh centuries were the western provinces of Anglo-Saxon England, those bordering upon Wales; these were also the regions most recently occupied by the Anglo-Saxons and most likely to contain the largest admixture of native Celts. And if slave status, or the social and personal condition nearest to that of the slave, are to be accepted as indirect indications of subjugation by conquest, it is possible to argue (though of course impossible to prove) that some of the lowest ranks of medieval villeins, those described as serfs in medieval documents and subject to the greatest restrictions of personal freedom, owed their abject condition to their descent from conquered natives.

Too much must not of course be read into the purely terminological accident that in many cases men in the lowest ranks are described in our document as 'natives'—*nativi* in Latin, *neits* in Anglo-Saxon. The words may have denoted nothing more than the heritable nature of the servitude, or may have no discernible etymological derivation of any kind. In some places, however, the men of the lowest rank were also described in terms which—at least phonetically—bear a strong pre-Saxon flavour such as the name of 'Enke', by which servile tenants of the lowest rank are designated on some of the westernmost estates of the Bishop of Worcester.[12]

The problem of human and social survivals in the English countryside is thus much more speculative and uncertain than the Germanic school once upon a time assumed. It may be, though it is in my view unlikely, that so utter was the destruction and displacement of population during the Anglo-Saxon conquest that with the arrival of the Anglo-Saxons the social history of rural society began wholly anew. On the other hand the presence in the earliest phases of Anglo-Saxon history of wholly or almost wholly servile groups, and the great antiquity of slavery and of the lowest forms of serfdom at the time of the Domesday Inquest, could also be considered as an after-effect of a conquest: a conquest in the course of which a proportion of the aboriginal population was subjugated by the conquerors into their agricultural organization and social system. If so, we may be justified in concluding that continuity from Roman Britain was not confined to sites and even technologies but extended also to matters human and social.

But even this is not the end of the argument. The most potent reason why human and social continuity from Roman Britain is so difficult to accept and is not commonly accepted is that it appears to be difficult to reconcile with the general impression conveyed by the evidence of life, society and culture in the closing stages of Anglo-Saxon history. At that time everything was thoroughly and uniformly Anglo-Saxon. English was the universal language of discourse. Not only the place names but also personal names were in the main also English; and not only the laws and customs governing the management of land, the succession to property and legal titles to land, but also the criminal and civil liabilities of persons were English and not Romano-British in origin and character.

However, this evidence, powerful as it may seem, is not as conclusive or relevant as it may appear at first sight. In the first place it is very general and impressionistic, for it is not based on any concrete and detailed information about the actual conditions in individual localities. Secondly, it is all very late. It represents the conditions in England as we find them a short time, at most a century or two, before the coming of the Normans at the end of the eleventh century. The period of five or six hundred years separating the two conquests was not only very long (it was in fact longer than the entire life-span of Roman Britain) but also witnessed remarkable changes in religion, culture, government and economy. The five or six centuries of cultural evolution and above all of material growth were bound to overlay and to submerge the fabric of the culture and society as they came out of the Anglo-Saxon conquest. Considered as part of the latter-day mixture the ingredients taken from Roman Britain were bound to seem much weaker and much more difficult to detect than the 'input' of the intervening centuries of change and growth. More particularly the economy and the social organization of England on the eve of the Norman conquest are much easier to understand in the light of the six centuries of Anglo-Saxon growth than in that of the events which accompanied and immediately followed the invasions of the Anglo-Saxons. Some of the consequences of this later growth will be surveyed in the next chapter.

References

1. I. A. Richmond, *Roman Britain*, 2nd ed. (1963), pp. 63 ff. and *passim.*

2. Sheppard Frere, *Britannia: a History of Roman Britain* (1907), p. 24 (pre-Roman settlements on heavy soils); H. C. Bowen, 'The Celtic Background', in A. L. F. Rivet (ed.), *The Roman Villa in Britain* (1909), p. 18.

3. Frere, *Britannia*, pp. 275 ff., 173.

4. Richmond, *Roman Britain*, pp. 118–28; Frere, *Britannia*, p. 371.

5. Richmond, *Roman Britain*, pp. 141–8.

6. A. L. F. Rivet, 'Social and Economic Aspects', in Rivet (ed.) *The Roman Villa in Britain*, pp. 174 ff.; Richmond, *Roman Britain*, pp. 87 ff.

7. A. L. F. Rivet, 'Social and Economic Aspects', *passim.*

8. Frere, *Britannia*, pp. 239–41; Richmond, *Roman Britain*, pp. 55–63.

9. See note 8 above.

10. Frere, *Britannia*, pp. 375, 380.

11. For 'wealhs' in place names and other evidence indicative of surviving 'Welsh', see A. H. Smith, *English Place-Name Elements* (1956), Vol. I, pp. 119–20, Vol. II, pp. 242 ff. Cf. Glanville Jones, 'Basic Patterns of Settlement Distribution in Northern England', *Advancement of Science*, 1961; Laws of Ine (688–694), paras 23, 32, 33, 46, 74, in D. Whitelock (ed.), *English Historical Documents*, Vol. I (1953), pp. 364 ff.

12, Marjorie Hollings (ed.), *The Red Book of Worcester*, Worcestershire Hist. Soc., 1934–50, pp. 100, 156–7 and *passim*.

2 The Land: Settlement and Reclamation

I

Great as may have been the material inheritance of Roman Britain, the economic and social physiognomy of medieval England, as it emerges to our full view in the twelfth century, derived most of its characteristic features not so much from the conditions before or immediately after the Anglo-Saxon conquest, as from the developments of the following 500 or 600 years. In these centuries medieval England grew manifold in area, population and agricultural output; and her growth brought with it fundamental changes in her economy and society.

How much the sheer area of agricultural settlement grew in these centuries was not fully realized by historians until very recently. In judging the extent of the growth it is important to recall how small was the area of the initial Anglo-Saxon settlement. We must assume—and such evidence as we possess supports the assumption—that most of the oldest sites on which the Anglo-Saxon invaders settled were on lands previously occupied and cultivated by their Romano-British and pre-Roman predecessors. These sites, however, could not suffice for the needs of expanding Anglo-Saxon settlement. If the area under plough were to grow much beyond the limits of the initial Anglo-Saxon occupation, settlement had to spill over, as a few Roman-British settlements had already done, into much more abundant but also more difficult land of the second choice. Second-rate land, still largely unreclaimed, was mostly to be found on England's inland plains. As a rule, it carried trees and scrub, and the initial effort of clearing was bound to be great; as was also the subsequent labour of cultivating it. Yet it provided the most accessible supplies of colonizable sites and was gradually occupied and brought under cultivation between the sixth century and the twelfth.

The pace of this colonizing activity cannot be measured, but its magnitude could be judged by the result it achieved. In the late eleventh century, the end of the Anglo-Saxon era, the work of occupying the better lands of second choice appears to have been all but completed, and the completion was clearly reflected in the evidence of the Domesday Book.

The Domesday Book, its compilation and contents, have figured so prominently in historical discussion that readers may be excused for assuming that it has little to disclose beyond what historians have known for generations. Yet in taking its evidence it is important not to consider it, as it often is, solely as a fiscal survey compiled in order to organize the levying of royal taxes. The great survey was nothing less than a cadaster: a description of England's land and the people occupying it. In fact economic historians, and, more recently, historical geographers, have been able to derive from the Domesday Book a view of England's agrarian economy more comprehensive than any available in any other country before the coming of modern agrarian statistics.

Indeed the possibility of using the Domesday Book as a starting point for English agrarian history is so inviting that in the past some economic historians were almost imperceptibly led to treat the Norman conquest itself as a starting point of English economic history. It is only recently that historians and geographers have come to realize how much of England's area had been cleared and occupied by the time the Normans came to these islands. From the economic point of view the Domesday Book was much more an epitome of past performance than the announcement of achievements to come. In Mr Reginald Lennard's words England of the Domesday Book was an 'old country'.[1]

The length to which the clearing and the occupation of the land had gone by 1086 is revealed by at least three sets of Domesday entries. One is that of named settlements. Broadly speaking the numbers and the distribution of places recorded as occupied by men and their ploughs in the Domesday Book were not much different from the numbers and the distribution of named settlements in later centuries, not excluding our own. Divergences between place names of 1086 and those of say 1800 are bound to exist. But in general there were about as many settled places in 1086 as at the end of the eighteenth century, and most of them were to be found on the same sites and under the same names.

The second body of evidence is that relating to ploughable lands as measured by Domesday 'ploughlands' (*terrae carrucae*). Of all the conventional units of measurement employed in the Domesday

Book that of *terrae carrucae* is probably the one nearest to economic reality. Doubts still attach to the exact dimensions of the ploughland unit, but it appears highly probable that the average area of a ploughland was equivalent to that of the 'ideal' fiscal hide, i.e. about 120 acres or more. If so, it is highly important, and at first sight surprising, to discover that the aggregate acreage represented by the Domesday ploughlands was at least as great as, and in most Midland counties greater than, the areas under plough during the periods of high farming in the nineteenth century.

The third and most important testimony to England's old age in 1086 is provided by the distribution of Domesday settlement and ploughs over the soil map, as described and mapped in recent studies by historical geographers. Even the most superficial comparison of that distribution with the variations of geology and surface soils would be sufficient to show that by 1086 the Anglo-Saxon settlers had fully occupied not only the lands of their first preference, i.e the lighter and outer loams best suited to the mixed husbandry of that age, but also most of the lands which in contemporary estimation must have ranked as lands of second choice.[2]

Needless to say the eleventh-century rating of soils was not quite that of modern agriculturalists. The Anglo-Saxon apparently avoided the very light sandy and gravelly earths liable to dry up and to leach. Most of the areas in which such soils predominated —the Bagshot sands of Surrey, Berkshire and Hampshire, the sandy soils of the New Forest, the sands of Norfolk Breckland and the Suffolk Fielding, the sterile gravels and sands of patches of some of the Cheshire forests—figure on the maps of the Domesday settlement as empty or nearly empty patches. It was not until the late seventeenth or eighteenth centuries that artificial fertilizers made it possible to use very light land profitably, and rank it high for its ease of working. Such land was apparently shunned by the husbandmen of the eleventh century and carried very few agricultural settlements in 1086.

Consistent with this aversion for sands was the eleventh-century husbandman's partiality for the more benign claylands like the boulder clays which covered so much of England's plains, or clays with a large mixture of flints of a kind to be found frequently on limestone rock. Clays were retentive of moisture and of nutrients; and in an age which—as we shall see presently—was increasingly short of natural manure, the ability of the soil to resist the leaching of its mineral nutrients was all-important. Furthermore if we accept some of the recent climatological argument that the period of Anglo-Saxon and medieval settlement coincided with one of Europe's cold cycles, we must take account of the further possibility that in the earlier centuries of the middle ages more frequent and harder frosts helped to break up the heavy clods of clay tilth into fine seed-beds.

Whatever his reasons, the medieval Englishman's willingness to occupy and to work the better of the strong clays is unmistakable. In almost every Domesday county the areas of boulder clay were second only to those of light and fertile loams in density of their population and in the numbers of ploughs they employed. Here and there, however, the Anglo-Saxon may even have gone some distance beyond the limits set by the supplies of easier clays. There were some signs of arable cultivation on the London clay areas in north Middlesex, on the Oxford and London clays of north Buckinghamshire, on the heavy gaults of north Oxfordshire and south Bedfordshire, or the almost equally badly drained clays over the coal measures of the West Riding. Some other soils, not clayey but equally third-rate, had also begun to be broken up for ploughing. There was some settlement on such soils as the river sands near London or the waterlogged alluvia at the north end of the Vale of York or the infertile 'carrs' of the Vale of Pickering.

In the aggregate, the area of such soils occupied by 1066 was not, as yet, very great, but their very presence among the settled areas shows that settlement had begun to overflow into lands worse than those ranking as second-rate.

II

With the colonizable land so fully drawn on, reclamation and settlement in subsequent centuries was bound to be increasingly restricted. Yet in spite of these limitations reclamation did not stop in 1086. For at least another two centuries new lands continued to be broken up for arable cultivation or for improved pasture. In that period documentary evidence of reclamations, mostly described as 'assarts' and 'purprestures', abound in all the sources of agrarian history. Indeed if the prevalence of reclamations were to be judged by the amount of surviving evidence it would be only too tempting to conclude that in these two centuries, especially the thirteenth, the movement of internal reclamation was more active than in any previous period at peak. This temptation must be resisted. In a country as 'old' as the England of 1086, all subsequent reclamation was bound to be something of an aftermath. Closer attention to the geographical distribution of the latter-day reclamations or to the soils on which they were made would easily reveal their marginal nature. They were marginal in several senses.

As we shall presently see, most of these lands were 'marginal' simply because they were, to use a humdrum adjective, poor. And yet it would be something of a simplification to assume that all the marginal lands yet unreclaimed in 1086 were poor in the simple physical sense of the term. Some had been neglected because their reclamation was beyond the technical resources of medieval men. Others had remained unreclaimed because they had been kept out of cultivation by legal and administrative impediments. Others were still available for colonization in the twelfth and thirteenth centuries because they happened to be situated on the geographical periphery of medieval England. Each of these three categories of lands, which were marginal though not necessarily poor, may be worth considering in some detail.

The first category, that of soils on the 'technological' margin, was mostly to be found on the wet lands, the marshes and fens of medieval England. Given medieval technology the difficulties of draining and protecting from floods such permanently submerged areas as those of the Deep Fen in the Eastern Counties or the Hatfield Chase in the West Riding were unsurmountable. These areas therefore remained submerged and stayed neglected until the settlement of easier and drier lands had been nearly completed.

The potentialities of these wet reserves were very considerable. Measured in acres, the flooded and waterlogged wastelands of the twelfth century may have represented but a small portion of England's surface, but their total area was nevertheless very large. England's geography with its broad rim of coastal lowlands and slow rivers, was highly favourable to the formation of silted up estuaries and of flooded maritime marshes. Such marshes, both great and of middle size, lay at frequent intervals all round the settled interior of medieval England

Of the marshes of southern England, those of Kent were probably reclaimed earliest and are best known to historians. The great Kentish marsh along the coast between Hythe and Rye, i.e. the Romney Marsh proper, had been reclaimed long before our records begin, in part at least in Roman times. It is also probable that elsewhere in the county, especially in the Isle of Thanet and south of the Stour, several thousands of acres of wet lands had been reclaimed before the middle of the thirteenth century. Yet on the whole, the old Romney Marsh apart, none of the Kentish marshes had by the end of the thirteenth century been reclaimed in their entirety.[3]

The same probably holds good also of the marshes of East Sussex (Pevensey and Winchelsea), which were still at the mercy of flood waters in the later thirteenth century. In the west of England a large 'wet' area under reclamation in the twelfth and the thirteenth centuries was that of Sedgemoor, more particularly round the great colonizing manors of the Glastonbury Abbeys: Brent, Zoy and Ham.

The state of marshlands—or at least the greater marshlands—in the eastern half of the country can be reconstructed with somewhat greater precision. The most northerly wet lands figuring in medieval records are those of Holderness. References to marshlands both drained and undrained become even more numerous as we cross the borders of West Riding into Lincolnshire. There, just across the border, the River Ancholme was fringed with marshes which were apparently to remain unreclaimed until the end of the middle ages. The great marshes of Lindsey, bordering on the Hatfield level of West Riding, were apparently drained on a large scale in the thirteenth century, though much of this land was still under water at the beginning of the eighteenth century.

It is in the eastern fens proper that reclamations had by the end of the thirteenth century achieved most. Modern studies agree with the impression given by the chroniclers that within the memory of the men of the twelfth century the Great Fens still stretched wholly intact over an area which, not counting the fens of Axholme and North Lindsey, covered more than 350 square miles. Except for occasional islands and peninsulas of higher ground and a band of villages on silt land skirting the Wash, the area was mostly watery marsh, or at best woodland and pasture periodically submerged by floodwaters.[4]

Throughout the earlier centuries of the middle ages, the owners and inhabitants of the *terra firma*, above all the fenland monasteries of Peterborough, Crowland, Ramsey and a host of smaller houses, conducted a continuous war of conquest against the wet lands nearest to them.

Medieval reclamation of wet lands was thus quite extensive;

and, when drained, these lands could provide arable and pasture of the highest quality. This may not be equally true of the other large reserves of reclaimable land, those from which the medieval reclaimers were kept back by law and administration. These were mainly lands comprised in the Royal Forests.

The King's Forest was primarily a legal and administrative, not a botanical or an ecological, concept. It referred to areas placed under a special forest law designed to preserve game and keep them for hunting. There was thus no necessary reason why the lands within the King's Forest should invariably have been less fertile than some of the land already under cultivation. Yet in general it remains broadly true that most 'forests' occupied areas inaccessible or uninviting to the farmer.[5]

To this extent the settlement of the Royal Forest need not have differed much from the settlement of other marginal lands. Where it differed most was in its timing. From the late twelfth century, mainly in the period following Henry II's drastic afforestations, the issue of the Forest becomes a burning political issue, figuring prominently in almost every presentation of baronial grievances and in every statement of royal concessions.

The issue however was not necessarily that of conflicting claims to hunting ground. By the beginning of the thirteenth century, if not earlier, the main value of the Royal Forest lay not in the game it harboured but in its reserves of land available and tempting to colonizers, at a time when such reserves were dwindling elsewhere. In fact these reserves were being actively exploited in many forest areas in the late thirteenth and early fourteenth centuries. Evidence of the thirteenth and fourteenth-century reclamations of the Forest comes mainly from an important class of document which has fortunately been preserved in the records of the Crown. These are the proceedings of the Justices of the Forests: officials who sat in periodic courts in each county containing large royal forests to adjudicate breaches in the forest laws. These proceedings indicate that, in general, the reclamations in royal forests gathered momentum later than reclamations elsewhere. But though untypical these dates are by no means unaccountable. Settlement had been kept away from the forest by the action of the forest law for a whole century and more: so when in the thirteenth century the rigour of the law was relaxed, the colonizable lands within the forest were still sufficiently abundant to attract the reclaiming husbandmen and to provide for them for a long time to come.

The other, the third, land reserve not wholly made up of the poorest lands was to be found in the peripheral regions of medieval England. Beyond the ancient core of English settlements lay large areas late to have been reached and settled by the Anglo-Saxons. The existence of the peripheral regions is clearly reflected in the Domesday Book, which records sparse settlement, if any at all, in the counties on the Scottish border, in Devonshire and Cornwall, in north-west Staffordshire, north-western Cheshire, the western and northern parts of Shropshire, the west of Herefordshire.

The causes of this sparse and belated settlement are not far to seek. Some of the peripheral areas were remote or inaccessible, or separated from the rest of the country by barriers, geographical or cultural and ethnic, while some border lands, both the Welsh and the Scottish, suffered also from being continually disturbed by raids and military campaigns. To the disturbances and destruction of frontier wars the opening decades of the Norman rule added troubles of their own. The conquerors' armies devastated much of Yorkshire and some areas of Staffordshire and Cheshire while repressing the anti-Norman risings and unrest of 1169 and 1170.

The settlement of all these areas appears to have been relatively sparse even where soils were comparatively good. Thus in 1086 the density of settlement in Staffordshire, Herefordshire, Shropshire, Cheshire or Derbyshire was considerably lower than on soils of comparable qualities in Wiltshire, Hampshire, Suffolk, Northamptonshire or Oxfordshire. In other words, the peripheries of England could also provide, even in the thirteenth century, some reserve of fairly good land.

To sum up: on wet lands, in the peripheral areas, and perhaps also in some of the Royal Forests, the supply of land for reclamation in the twelfth and thirteenth centuries need not have been greatly restricted in either quantity or quality. But in the older fully occupied regions continued reclamation and the breaking up of the waste had to be confined to lands which, compared to the land taken up in an earlier age, were little suited to arable or mixed farming. Much of it was to be found on clays more intractable than the clay lands occupied before 1086. The other type of inferior land which men in the twelfth and thirteenth centuries were compelled to occupy was that of thin overlays on top of chalk and impermeable rock, as a rule avoided by reclaimers and settlers before 1086.

Examples of new settlement on each of these types of soil could be found all over England's more anciently occupied counties: in the heavily wooded wet and heavy clay of Hertfordshire, the heavy clay lands in the weald of Sussex, and above all on the poorest of the chalk downlands.[6] The Domesday evidence suggests that the downlands, carrying thin soil over chalk, were still very sparsely furnished with people and ploughs in 1086. In the thirteenth century, however, the arable farmers in the downland valleys began to take over the high and the thinly covered chalklands previously given over to permanent pasture. It was at that time that St Swithun's Priory of Winchester established a mixed farming manor among the downland pastures pertaining to the large village of Preston. The soils on which the new manor stood were thin and hungry, and judging from the surviving accounts the crops they bore were correspondingly meagre. Somewhat similar were the conditions on most of the Bishop of Winchester's manors on the downs north of Winchester. Much of the land belonging to these manors stretched over what later came to be known as the Longbarrow Warren, a belt of barren and exposed chalk which some 500 years later struck Cobbett as one of the most infertile areas he encountered on his rural rides. Some of the Bishop of Worcester's manors on the uplands of the western Cotswolds, or the new fields on the Templars' manors in the central Cotswolds, or the Bishop of Winchester's possessions in the eastern Cotswolds provide characteristic examples of arable fields recently carved out of soils equally poor over rock even less hospitable than the chalk of the downs.

Needless to say these examples cannot, and are not intended to, give a true measure of reclamations on marginal lands. Medieval evidence being what it is, examples are all a historian can produce, but in this case the examples are both widespread and unanimous. Taken *en masse* the surviving evidence leaves the student with an impression bordering on certainty that in the older parts of England the lands taken up for the first time by the arable farmers in the thirteenth century were as a rule of the lowest possible quality; too forbidding to have tempted the settlers in earlier centuries, and some of them too unremunerative to have been maintained in cultivation by farmers of a later age.

III

The spread of arable cultivation to lands as marginal as these was bound to affect the nature of the rural economy and its development. Its social and economic penalties were very high and mounted as time went on. The worst penalty of all was the deleterious effects of excessive reclamation on yields; another penalty was the precariousness of crops or the impermanence of some of the newly reclaimed lands. The penalty of low yields I shall have to take up in discussing the productivity of agriculture. But the penalty of impermanence must be considered here in some detail, since it forms an essential part of the history of reclamation. This nemesis of impermanence is easiest to observe and to account for on thin and hungry soils: the poor sands, or the shallow overlays. The exploitation of such lands in the initial stages of their arable use was essentially a mining operation; it could remain profitable only until their stored-up fertility had been worked out. After that their cultivators were increasingly punished by the leaching of their minerals and by denudation.

Medieval agriculturalists and manorial clerks were not of course in the position to observe this physical process, and still less to describe it. But the history of the fields themselves as revealed by the cropping returns in manorial accounts bears witness to fields, mostly of recent origin and often on thin and light soils, disappearing after periods of regular cultivation.

It is also possible to detect signs of impermanence on other types of land, more particularly on the worst of clays. Medieval husbandmen would not be conscious of, and if conscious not sufficiently articulate about, the reasons why some of their clay lands deteriorated. But judging from what we know about the behaviour of similar soils in modern times, their morbid history in the middle ages is easy enough to reconstruct. Continuous ploughing and regular cropping for grain could punish heavy clays in two ways. In the first place their physical composition could deteriorate and turn into a pasty mass impervious to moisture and air and hard to reduce to sowable tilth. The other process of deterioration would be the formation of 'pans'. Heavy land ploughed regularly and shallowly was liable to form water-tight platforms underneath its tilled surface. Such platforms or 'pans' once formed impeded the drainage of the upper soils and increased the risks of waterlogging.

The deterioration of the physical structure of clays could be remedied by liming and underdraining. These remedies, however, were not generally available or widely used. The deterioration and the depletion of the lightest and the heaviest soils remained an inescapable penalty of marginal reclamation and was bound to slow that reclamation down and even arrest it altogether.

IV

The impermanence of marginal assarts revealed itself at the time when the whole movement of reclamations slowed down, and thus aggravated the resulting penalties. The slowing down itself is well exhibited in our sources, though it cannot be dated uniformly or precisely since the dates were bound to differ from place to place. In general, as the thirteenth century drew to its close, one manor and one village after another ceased to add to its acreage until at some point in the fourteenth century the age-old movement of internal colonization comes to a halt almost everywhere: everywhere except for a few untypical areas, mostly on the peripheries of medieval England. In the second half of the fourteenth and the fifteenth centuries the area under plough in the country as a whole, so far from expanding, actually began to contract. By the middle of the fifteenth century the contraction becomes sufficiently marked to justify our describing it as 'decolonization'.

The slowing down of reclamations and their eventual cessation cannot of course be accounted for solely by the impermanence of arable fields won from marginal lands. Other, more obvious and perhaps more powerful, forces were at work. One of them was the pressure of population: mounting in the earlier centuries, declining in the later ones. The other, equally obvious, factor was the dwindling of land reserves, a process whose working has been assumed all through our discussion of reclamations.

The geographical distribution of internal reclamations in the fourteenth century brings out the logic of events behind their chronology. Where these reclamations still continued, they were largely confined to marshes, to the King's Forest, or to marginal soils. Now and again, we find instances of reclamation even in the fifteenth century. This is not surprising. Considering the intensely local character of agriculture and of rural economy in general, occasional reclamations could occur in a few places at the most unpropitious moments. These exceptional instances do not detract from the overall impression that in England as a whole reclamations came to an end in the thirteenth or the early fourteenth centuries. In many places the area under plough not only ceased to grow in the late fourteenth and fifteenth centuries but even began to contract. The story of the contraction or 'decolonization' will be told later.

References

1. R. V. Lennard, *Rural England, 1086–1135* (1959), Ch. I.

2. H. C. Darby, L. B. Terrett and others, *The Domesday Geography*, I–IV (1952–1962) (second editions now in progress), Sections on ploughlands and *passim*. See Appendix 1 below, p. 247.

3. For 'wet land' in general, W. Dugdale's classic *History of Imbanking and Drayning* (1662), 2nd ed., ed. C. N. Cole (1772), is still the only survey. For Romney Marsh, cf. R. A. L. Smith, *Canterbury Cathedral Priory: A Study in Manorial Administration* (1943); M. Teichman Derville, *The Level and the Liberty of Romney Marsh*, 1936. Some references to the reclamations on the Pevensey Marshes of Sussex will be found in P. F. Brandon, 'Demesne Arable Farming in Coastal Sussex during the later Middle Ages', *Agric. Hist. Rev.*, Vol. 19 (1971). L. F. Salzman, 'The Inning of Pevensey Levels', *Sussex Archaeological Collection*, Vol. 53 (1910); F. J. F. Dulley, 'The Level and Port of Pevensey in the Middle Ages', *Sussex Arch. Coll.*, Vol. 104 (1900).

4. H. C. Darby, *The Medieval Fenland* (1940), *passim*; H. E. Hallam, *Settlement and Society* (1965), Chs. I–V; N. Neilson, *A Terrier of Fleet*, Brit. Acad. Rec. IV i (1920), Introduction.

5. G. I. Turner, *Select Pleas of the Forest*, Selden Soc. (1901), Introduction. M. L. Bazeley, 'The Extent of the English Forest in the Thirteenth Century', *Trans. Roy. Hist. Soc.*, 4th Ser., IV (1921). N. Neilson, 'Early English Woodland and Waste', *Journ. Econ. Hist.* II (1942).

6. For the settlement of 'denes' on the heavy clays of the Sussex Weald, see N. Neilson, *Cartulary and Terrier of the Priory of Bilsington* (1928); Eleanor Searle, 'Hides, Virgates and Tenant Settlement at Battle Abbey', *Econ. Hist. Rev.* 2nd ser., Vol. XVI (1963); P. F. Brandon, 'Demesne Arable Farming', p. 124; and above all the forthcoming history of the estates of Battle Abbey by Eleanor Searle.

3 Population

I

Behind most economic trends in the middle ages, above all behind the advancing and retreating land settlement, it is possible to discern the inexorable effects of rising and declining population. As in most under-developed countries of our own day, the numbers of people on the land determined not only the performance of the economy as a whole, but the wellbeing of individuals.

Unfortunately, our evidence being what it is, a close and a clear view of demographic trends is impossible; least of all is it possible to measure the total size of the population at any given point of time. This has not, however, prevented antiquarians and historians —a continuous succession of them, beginning with Matthew Hall in the sixteenth century and ending with J. C. Russell in our own day—from attempting to estimate the totals at different periods in the middle ages. What has tempted them into this undertaking is not only antiquarian curiosity about the total size of the English people but also the seemingly promising nature of certain pieces of English evidence. At first sight medieval England, unlike any other medieval country, happens to possess at least two sources capable of yielding estimates of the total population. One of them is the great Domesday Book which appears to list all the tenants of land in almost every county in 1086; the other is the Poll Tax returns of 1377 which purport to tax, and in the process of doing so to record, the entire adult population of this country. With these two sources available, the temptation to construct estimates of England's population in 1086 and 1377 has been very great, and few historians interested in population problems have been able to resist it.[1]

We must resist it here. The reason for doing so is that a closer look at the evidence will make it quite clear that it will not yield reliable measurements of this nature. What the Domesday Book and the Poll Tax returns contain are not true enumerations of the people, but numbers of certain sections of the population. Before a true population aggregate is derived from these numbers, they must be supplemented by estimates for the missing sections; or, to be more exact, they must be multiplied by co-efficients representing the proportion by which the numbers fall short in the total. And unfortunately the construction of the co-efficients is fraught with uncertainties and errors so great as to make the whole enterprise worthless.

Let us take the Domesday Book estimates. What the great survey enumerates are the individual tenants-in-chief and the tenants who held of the tenants-in-chief. If these figures are to be converted into totals of England's population in 1086 we must be able to estimate the proportion of the total population, if any, which did not happen to hold land directly of the tenants-in-chief and therefore remained unrecorded in the Domesday Book. In the second place we must know the size of a household or family represented by one tenant's holding. On both these points unequivocal information is lacking and the range of possible assumptions is immensely wide. At one end of the range is the presumption that every household in the middle ages held land of one manorial lord and that consequently there were as many households, neither more nor less, as there were tenancies in the Domesday Book. At the other end is the presumption that the numbers of landless people or of tenants' tenants (undersettles) or joint tenants of holdings, which the Domesday Book assigned to only one of them, were quite common. If they were approximately as common at the end of the eleventh century as they were to be in the thirteenth, the total numbers of households in 1086 might be as much as fifty per cent higher than the numbers of tenants actually listed.

Equally wide are the possible divergences in the guesses about the sizes of individual households. In his pioneering study of medieval population Professor J. C. Russell came to the conclusion that not only did the Domesday holdings support no more than one household each, but that an individual household contained on the average not more than 3.6 persons. He based this figure on elaborately constructed estimates of mortalities and generation tables of medieval population derived from various, mostly thirteenth-century, sources under the assumption of an all-but-stable population. On the other hand the evidence presented by some other historians will justify an estimate of an average household considerably larger than 3.6. Certain direct evidence, such as the surviving thirteenth-century enumeration of individual households on the Lincolnshire estate of the Priory of Spalding, support a figure of nearly five per household, which was also the estimate previously formed by Maitland. It may be higher than that in the families which comprised, in addition to the householder and his wife and their children, also their retired parents and resident household servants, as they frequently did in the thirteenth and the fourteenth centuries.[2]

These variations could result in enormous differences in the total estimates. On Professor Russell's assumptions of the identity of tenures and the size of households, the total of Domesday population would be just under one and a quarter million. But if we were to assume that the number of households was 50 per cent higher than the number of tenants, and that the average family was five strong, our total estimate would be between two and three millions. In other words, the possible gap between the minimum and maximum estimates could be as wide as 150 per cent.

Margins of errors on a scale similarly heroic attach to all attempts to estimate population at peak from the returns of the Poll Tax of 1377. Before these returns can be converted into those of the total population we must correct them by an allowance for under-enumeration, i.e. for the extent to which the tax was avoided. The allowance which some historians, including Professor Russell, have made is 2½ per cent, or about half the allowance which most statisticians would nowadays make for the avoidance of income tax in our own day. Considering the inefficiency of medieval administration, the novelty and the unpopularity of the Poll Tax itself, and the general lack of scruple in popular attitudes to state impositions, a more realistic co-efficient of evasion and under-statement would have to be pitched many times higher than the avoidance of modern British taxes. Indeed such few comparisons as are possible between the enumeration of inhabitants in the Poll Tax returns, and the comparable evidence of contemporary manorial documents, invariably reveal disparities well in excess of 25 per cent. To assume a similar gap between the taxpayers and the totals of population would not therefore be too great an exaggeration.

The other allowance to be made is that for the proportion of population below the age of fourteen who were exempt from taxes. The figure of 35 per cent which some historians have suggested depends on the birth-rates and death-rates corresponding to those estimated by Professor Russell. But if in a population, even if it be as stable as Professor Russell believes the medieval population to have been, expectations of life could be lower while birth-rates were higher than those computed by Professor Russell, such a population would contain a proportion of the young greater than 35 per cent. An allowance of 45 per cent would on these assumptions not be excessive.

Finally, in order to derive from the figures of 1377 the estimate of English population at peak, we must form some judgment as to the point of time at which that peak was reached, and the extent to which the population had receded between the date of the peak and 1377. Most historians now assume that the peak occurred some time before 1377, but whereas some would place it at 1347–48, i.e. the eve of the Black Death, others believe that population had reached its highest point and begun to decline in the 1320s. The gap between these two dates may make a very considerable difference to our computation of the fall of population between the peak date and the Poll Tax. This computation would also be affected by our estimates of mortality in the Black Death. Some historians, including Professor Russell, put the mortality at 20 per cent, but we shall see presently that the mortality may have been as high as 40 per cent. Moreover, the fifty years between 1328 and 1377 saw the recurrence of the plague on at least two, and perhaps even three, occasions. If further allowance were made for these outbreaks, the decline of population resulting from plagues could well have exceeded 50 per cent.

The difference this alternative set of assumptions could have made to the total is very great indeed. If population declined between 1320 and 1348 even by as little as 10 per cent; if the mortality of the plagues was at least 50 per cent; if the evasions of the Poll Tax were, say, 25 per cent; if furthermore the proportion of untaxed under-fourteens was about 40 per cent of the total, the estimate of the population at peak would be somewhere between six and eight millions. On the other hand, if on each of these points we accepted the minimum estimates, i.e. a population at peak in 1347, the underenumeration of only 2.5 per cent, the numbers of juveniles at 35 per cent, and the mortality from the plague at 20 per cent, our estimates of the population at peak could be very near Professor Russell's estimate, i.e. 3.7 millions, or about 50 per cent of the possible maximum.[3]

Where the estimates can vary so much, their worth as historical facts is, to say the least, doubtful. Fortunately, economic historians in search of demographic factors may console themselves with the thought that for most periods in the past very little meaning could be read into total figures of population, no matter how accurate and generally accepted they be. Global figures of population are economically significant only if and when related to the other factors, above all to capital equipment or the standards of technology. From the historical and economic points of view, much more significant than global numbers of population is its dynamics, i.e. the speed and direction of its movements and its changing relation to other economic factors. Did it grow or decline? Did it in growing or declining move towards or away from its point of overpopulation, i.e. the point beyond which the well-being of individuals or the aggregate wealth of the country could no longer grow at a rate commensurate with the population increase?

Fortunately on these points our evidence, although still incomplete and uncertain, is sufficiently abundant and unanimous to support a clear impression of the directions in which the total English population moved. It makes it certain that the numbers were mounting all through the earlier centuries and began to decline or sagged at some time in the fourteenth century.

II

The evidence of the early growth is manifold though largely circumstantial. The most obvious even if indirect sign of continued population growth will be found in the continuous expansion of land settlement and reclamation throughout the seven or eight centuries separating the Anglo-Saxon conquest from the beginning of the fourteenth century. We have seen that, to begin with, the area occupied by agricultural settlers was very small, not much greater than it had been under Roman occupation, and that the greater part of the English plain was reclaimed in later centuries. It is of course impossible to assign a precise enumerator to the total additions made to the occupied land before 1300, but we can be certain that it had grown manifold.

Our demographic deduction from this fact is that population must also have grown by at least the same rate. In theory it is possible to assume that an agricultural population, even a wholly settled one, would try to expand the acreage of its land and continue to do so indefinitely merely in response to the insatiable desire of individual peasants to add and to go on adding to their holdings. This is not, however, what in fact took place in most of the rural societies in the past, and it is certainly not what happened in medieval England. On the contrary, such evidence as we possess —and it will be recalled again later—makes it quite clear that the average size of family holdings between the eleventh century and the fourteenth declined. If so, the population must have increased at a rate even faster than the areas reclaimed for arable and improved pasture.

The evidence of reclamation is the most comprehensive, but also the most indirect, measure of population growth we possess. We also possess some other evidence which is more direct even though more restricted. For a few places such as the Bishop of Winchester's manors of Taunton, or certain manors in central or western Essex, we possess the records of local *per capita* taxes which appear to be sufficiently full and continuous to enable us to reconstruct the changes in the total numbers of inhabitants over long periods. Thus, on the Bishop of Winchester's manor of Taunton, the annual records of the 'hundredpenny' show that in the Vale of Taunton population increased uninterruptedly from 1209 to 1348 at the compound annual rate of growth of above 0.85 per cent. The rate was low compared with say modern Ceylon or Taiwan, but higher than in Russia or indeed the whole of eastern Europe in the eighteenth and early nineteenth centuries; and high enough to have raised Taunton's population nearly two and a half times between 1209 and 1311. An increase of population at somewhat similar rates and equally continuous could be traced on some Essex manors so far studied. The total increases of the population on the estates of Glastonbury Abbey were of a comparable magnitude even though the surviving records are not sufficient to demonstrate the continuity of the growth.[4]

A testimony of large numbers of population in thirteenth-century villages which is almost equally direct, although unfortunately not equally continuous, will be found in the totals of villagers presenting themselves on various occasions in manorial courts, and also in the numbers of men called up by the manorial lords for the great annual 'boon works'—usually harvesting services—in the autumn. These numbers are sometimes surprisingly large. On many of the manors of the Bishop of Winchester, the Abbey of Glastonbury, Peterborough and Bury St Edmunds, the numbers appear to be greater than the corresponding village populations were to be in the eighteenth century or even at the time of the earliest population census, in the first decade of the nineteenth century. If so, they justify the conclusion of a great expansion of the rural population in the preceding centuries.

The same conclusion emerges from the decline in the average size of holdings to which I have already referred, and particularly from the large and increasing numbers of cottagers with diminutive holdings or of landless men. The ratio of men to acres was obviously changing. Indeed the change was sufficiently dramatic to bring about eventually a veritable land hunger.

By the end of the thirteenth century the land hunger revealed itself in innumerable ways. One of its signs was the long and lengthening queues of men seeking land. In some places the queues had become so long as to disrupt the traditional routine of succession from father to son on the former's death. So valuable was the land, and so numerous were the men willing to take it up, that sitting holders were frequently tempted to sell long before they died. Purchase was becoming a common method of acquiring land. On the Glastonbury estates in the second half of the thirteenth century more than a third of the sitting tenants had acquired their holdings by various forms of open or disguised purchase, and sometimes over the heads of the legal heirs whom they frequently bought out. Another, and increasingly common, means of acquiring land was to marry well-endowed women, more especially widows with land. What made widows especially attractive was that in most villages the spouses of customary holders were allowed to keep the whole of their deceased husbands' tenements. On some manors, such as Taunton, men marrying widows with land could retain the land on the wives' death and were thus able to contract second marriages destined to produce later a further crop of marriageable widows.

The transmission of land by purchase or by marriage, and the declining proportion of transmission by ordinary inheritance, was merely one of the signs of the increasing land hunger. This hunger was the most obvious consequence of an overgrown population, and its principal economic penalty. Society was paying for its growing numbers by moving ever nearer to the margin of subsistence. It is because the margin was so close and getting closer that the death rates were high and may have been getting higher.[5]

Needless to say, in some years the high death rate resulted from severe epidemics or bouts of severe weather. But it is highly revealing to find how frequently death rates rose in years of bad harvest. The bad harvests themselves may have become more frequent because the quality of the land was declining. But even if we make full allowances for possible deterioration of the weather (the catastrophically bad harvests of 1290 and 1315–17 were obviously due to unusually wet seasons), the high mortality in years when crops failed would not have been as high as it was had not the population been especially sensitive to bad harvests. Its sensitivity manifests itself in our documents in various ways. In years of very bad harvests we find manorial bailiffs pleading an inability to carry out this or that operation, or justifying the high cost of the operation by the dearth of labourers (*caristia operariorum*) caused by bad crops. In other words, when harvests were very bad labourers died off and were scarce. In a more general way the steeply increasing death rates in years of bad harvest are revealed by the upsurge in heriots, the manorial death duties. Moreover, on the estates on which these records of heriots are abundant and are capable of being correlated with the total number of tenants, they frequently bring out not only the connection between harvests and deaths, but also that between death rates from starvation and improverishment. For on these estates poorer sections of the population were the ones to succumb most frequently to privations following the failures of crops. It is obvious that large and growing sections of the population had been reduced to a condition in which they could keep body and soul together only in years of moderately good harvests.[6]

The dynamics of medieval population before the first half of the fourteenth century is thus unmistakable. Population grew but could not have gone on growing for ever. By the beginning of the fourteenth century, and perhaps even earlier, the relative overpopulation was so great as to push the death rates to a punishing height. In theory over-population could also have brought the birth rates down, by reducing the ability of the young men to set up households and to marry. Our sources being what they are, this theoretical possibility cannot be convincingly demonstrated; but even if, for lack of evidence, the changes in marriage rates and ages of marriage were disregarded, the behaviour of the death rates would by itself have been sufficient sooner or later to prevent the population from continuing its growth.

III

The evidence of the population ceasing to expand, and even starting to decline, begins to accumulate in the first half of the fourteenth century. Some such slowing down is indicated by a corresponding slackening of internal colonization. In a few regions such as the Weald of Sussex or the uplands of the West Riding or north Lincolnshire a trickle of assarts and reclamations could persist throughout the late fourteenth and fifteenth centuries. But we have seen that over the greater parts of England, and more particularly in its older arable areas, lands under plough not only ceased to grow, but appear to recede from the limits that were previously reached. We have also seen that one of the reasons why in England as a whole reclamations were ceasing is that the reserves of reclaimable land were giving out. It is obvious however that the passing of the land reserve was not the only operative cause, and that the reduced demographic pressure was to a large extent responsible for the downturn in internal colonization. Reclamations dwindled or even ceased altogether in the Sedgemoor vills of Glastonbury Abbey, the Derbyshire or Staffordshire manors of the Duchy of Lancaster, and a number of other localities which still contained lands no worse than those colonized a generation or two earlier. The evidence of contracting reclamations would by itself have been sufficient to demonstrate that the ratio of men to acres was changing. Such evidence as we can cull from manorial records makes it highly probable that acreages were contracting because the numbers of would-be tenants declined and the demand for land weakened. Vacant holdings appeared in large numbers; villages on the furthest frontiers of cultivation—such as the hamlets at the head of some Yorkshire Dales or the poorer chalk lands of Hampshire and Wiltshire—contracted: some of them to the brink of total demise. A proportion (though not the majority) of deserted villages which nowadays lie hidden under overgrown mounds and trenches dates to the fourteenth and fifteenth centuries, bearing witness both to the deterioration of some of the marginal areas, and to the shortage of men willing to take up inferior lands.[7]

The slump in land values supplies an even clearer testimony of the weakening demand for land, since on most estates land values —rent, prices of freeholds, entry fines—began to decline some time before 1348, and the decline rapidly accelerates after 1348.[8] We are thus driven to the conclusion that the ratio of men to acres was changing, and the conclusion is also supported by the evidence of wages. While the values of land were falling the values of men—their wages—were rising. It will be shown in a later chapter that at times when the supply and demand for labour changed very drastically, the customary wage rates broke down, and wages changed accordingly. Similarly when the supply of manpower and the demand for it changed very persistently over long periods, a gradual change in wage levels would also take place. In the thirteenth century as a whole the supplies of labour increased continually, with the result that real wages, i.e. wages measured in amount of food they bought, probably declined, even though money wages remained stable. In real terms agricultural wages on the estates of the bishops of Winchester, the abbots of Westminster or the abbots of Glastonbury may have fallen by about 15 per cent between 1208 and 1225 and by another 10 per cent between 1225 and 1328.[9]

It is therefore highly significant that on most medieval estates the trend of wages should have turned upwards some time in the first half of the fourteenth century and pursued its upward course for another 150 years. It is possible to argue that wages could have risen as a result of increased investment and of a general expansion in the labour-intensive arable farming. Many, perhaps most, historians of the later middle ages also appear to believe that wages were boosted by increased industrial employment, above all by the expanding cloth manufacture. These various hypotheses will be discussed at greater length later where it will be argued that the factors they invoke could not have operated, or at least operated strongly enough, to overlay or to neutralize the underlying demographic trend. If so, the rise in wages must be accepted as a clear evidence of a declining population.

What may still cause some doubt is the chronology of the decline and its underlying cause. Both the timing and the explanation of the decline are greatly involved with the part played by the catastrophic Black Death of 1348. The plague was a disaster so unprecedented and so great that it has engraved itself upon the collective memory of Englishmen for many generations to come and has coloured the interpretation of the later middle ages by historians of all ages. The coming of the plague and its baleful progress across England are well known and have frequently been told. The bubonic plague hitherto endemic in the Near and the Middle East came to Italy in the spring of 1348 and reached this country by

May of the same year. Having broken out, it then spread far and wide ravaging the population almost uninterruptedly for a period of eighteen months. The extent of the ravages, though defying all exact measurement, must nevertheless have been enormous. One or two recent attempts to play down the mortality of the Black Death, and to put it as something in the neighbourhood of 10 to 12 per cent, need not be taken seriously. They are as a rule based on medical arguments of no great cogency, and are greatly at variance with the opinion of contemporaries to whom an increase in mortalities of 10 to 15 per cent would not have seemed an unusual or a catastrophic event: the mortality in the bad harvests of 1315–17 was as high as this. Above all they are greatly at variance with the evidence we possess. While some villages may have escaped lightly, most of the villages and all the towns for which we have evidence suffered grievously, and historians will have no difficulty in citing numerous villages in which population had been reduced to a pitiful remnant. What we know of the mortalities of separate groups of population, above all the monks and the secular clergy, suggests a rate of mortality approaching and sometimes exceeding 50 per cent. Among the better-informed historians some would put the mortality from the Black Death at 20 per cent, others would put it near 40 per cent; but 50 per cent would also be not wholly improbable.[10]

Moreover, as I have already suggested earlier, the Black Death, though the first and the greatest of outbreaks of the plague, was by no means the last. There were at least two such outbreaks in the late fourteenth century, in the early 1360s and the mid 1370s, both sufficiently great to impress the chroniclers who still remembered the great plague of 1348. Indeed, but for those memories, the two plagues might have earned for themselves the ill-repute and the name of Black Deaths. The records have also preserved the evidence of repeated smaller and local outbreaks of pestilence throughout the fifteenth century. The cumulative effect of these pestilences on a population must therefore have been enormous. No wonder most historians agree in ascribing to the pestilence the main responsibility for the down-turn in the demographic trend in the later middle ages.[11]

Impressive as this near-consensus may appear, it cannot however be accepted without some questioning and reservations. In the first place most of the indirect evidence of declining population we have cited here betrays a break in the underlying trend much earlier than 1348. Reclamations began to peter out at or soon after the turn of the thirteenth and fourteenth centuries even in the areas where colonizable land was still to be found. In places where they rose, wages also began to rise in the first quarter of the fourteenth century. Land values ceased to mount and began to decline at about the same time. If all these movements are, as we believe them to be, true indications of the demographic trend, they compel us to conclude that the true turning point must have occurred at least two decades before the outbreak of the pestilence, or perhaps even earlier.[12] The outbreak must greatly have aggravated the slump in population, even if the latter had been triggered off by other factors. But however aggravated, the slump may well have begun much earlier, and, if so, was due to causes other than the Black Death or the Black Death alone.

What these causes could have been, and probably were, has been repeatedly suggested here. The demographic expansion went to the point of relative over-population. Beyond that point the amount of land available for population, and its produce through good years and bad, were insufficient to sustain large sections, perhaps the bulk, of medieval population; but this very insufficiency was in the end bound to bring about its own cure. The cure was, of course, a punishing one, and the punishment took the form of recurrent famines, high and rising mortalities, and perhaps also of low and declining marriage rates and birth rates. The record of a population similarly over-reaching its own powers of maintaining itself is by no means an unusual one. We find it restaged manifold in pre-industrial societies of almost every continent and every age. But whereas in present-day Africa, South America or South East Asia, modern medicine, social services and technological progress make it possible for the increase to continue unabated, in medieval England the population could not have continued to increase and must have begun to decline even had the Black Death by-passed the country altogether.

The part which the Black Death played in this decline was greatly to aggravate the mortality in the late 1340s, and to delay the recovery from the demographic decline in a subsequent century or century-and-a-half. In ordinary circumstances the decline in population due to the increasing mortalities and declining birth rates, which were in their turn due to an insufficiency of land, could be expected to correct itself by its own inherent momentum. For as population declined the ratio of land to men could improve and the ability of men to raise enough food to sustain themselves, to marry and to breed, would accordingly be enhanced. This in effect should have happened, and for brief periods appeared to take place, in the second half of the fourteenth and in the fifteenth centuries. Superficial signs of a dramatic recovery appear on the very morrow of the Black Death. Where the evidence is available, it reveals the numbers of marriages and births at the very end of the 1340s suddenly rising. The rise was not however sustained for long. By 1370 or 1375 its visible signs pass away, and throughout the greater part of the fifteenth century, more particularly in the middle decades, the numbers continue to decline or at best to sag. In the last quarter of the century the population may have resumed its upward trend, though if we are to trust some recent researchers into the economic conditions of the sixteenth century the real recovery was not to come for another two generations.

Until the 1470s or the 1480s, the recovery was probably held back by a variety of causes. The continued malfunctioning of the field-metabolism which we discussed elsewhere, and the continual inability of men to repair the damage done to the land in previous centuries, may have been one of the causes of delayed recovery. The recurrent plagues were undoubtedly another cause. But whatever the cause, the low and perhaps also sinking levels of population continued to dominate the economic situation.

References

1. Josiah Cox Russell, *British Medieval Population* (1948), pp. 6–14 (previous estimates).

2. Russell, *British Medieval Population*, pp. 34–54; Russell, 'The Pre-Plague Population of England', *Journal of British Studies*, Vol. V (1966). J. T. Krause, 'The Medieval Household large or small', *Econ. Hist. Rev.*, 2nd ser., xi (1958). M. M. Postan, 'Medieval Agrarian Society in its Prime', *The Cambridge Economic History*, Vol. I, 2nd ed. (1960), pp. 560–70.

3. Russell, *British Medical Population, passim*; Postan, 'Medieval Agrarian Society'; J. Z. Titow, *English Rural Society* (1969), pp. 66–73.

4. J. Z. Titow, 'Some Evidence of the Thirteenth Century Population Increase', *Econ. Hist. Rev.*, 2nd ser., xiv (1961); H. E. Hallam, 'Population Density in Medieval Fenland', *Econ. Hist. Rev.*, 2nd ser., vii (1963).

5. M. M. Postan and J. Z. Titow, 'Heriots and Prices on Winchester Manors', *Econ. Hist. Rev.*, 2nd ser., xi (1959); a revised and enlarged version is in preparation.

6. See note 5 above; also J. Z. Titow, *English Rural Society* (1970), pp. 73–8.

7. M. W. Beresford, *The Lost Villages of England* (1954); Maurice Beresford and John G. Hurst (ed.), *Deserted Medieval Villages* (1971).

8. For a discussion of rising and falling entry fines see B. F. Harvey, 'The Population Trend in England between 1300–1348', *Trans. Roy. Hist. Soc.* (1966); and J. Z. Titow, *English Rural Society*, pp. 73–8.

9. See below pp. 243–5.

10. J. Z. Titow, *English Rural Society*, pp. 70–1.

11. J. Saltmarsh, 'Plague and Economic Decline in England in the later Middle Ages', *Camb. Hist. Journ.*, Vol. VII (1941). J. M. W. Bean, 'Plague Population and Economic Decline in England in the late Middle Ages', *Econ. Hist. Rev.*, 2nd ser., xv (1962–3).

12. M. M. Postan, 'Some Economic Evidence of Declining Population in the later Middle Ages', *Econ. Hist. Rev.*, 2nd ser., ii (1950).

4 Land Use and Technology

I

Agricultural technology should be, but seldom is, treated as one of the dominant themes of medieval history. Readers familiar with present-day discussion of economic development, more particularly that of pre-industrial societies, need no convincing of the effect of agricultural technology in the widest sense of the term—the management of fields as well as the choice of implements and the related flow of investment—upon agricultural output and consequently also upon the wellbeing of agriculturists. Technological changes can be expected to have exercised a similar influence in the middle ages. Our knowledge of medieval agricultural technology may still be very rudimentary, but enough is known about it to provide a general retrospect of medieval agricultural technique and to bring out the principal changes it underwent in the course of centuries.

The retrospect will not abound with incident and fact, for in general the most distinguishing attribute of medieval technology was its immobility compared to the technology of modern times. Changes took place; more particularly, at the beginning of the middle ages, in the initial period of Anglo-Saxon settlement, England probably went through a sequence of revolutionary innovations in the use of land and implements. It is also possible that the agricultural crisis of the later middle ages compelled lords and peasants to adopt a somewhat more experimental attitude to inherited agricultural practices. On the whole, however, it remains true that throughout the middle ages proper, and above all during the period best covered by evidence, i.e. the twelfth, thirteenth and a great part of the fourteenth centuries, methods and implements changed very slowly, and such changes as we can discover were mostly confined to the management and use of land.

For this technological stagnation many reasons have been adduced. The one most fashionable a few decades ago ascribed the technological inertia of the middle ages to their traditionalist outlook. The historically oriented sociologists of the Weber-Sombart school viewed the middle ages as an era when the methods of production were as tightly bound by inherited custom as the habits of consumption were in their own day. The *rationale* of the productive processes—the proper relation of means to ends—was not questioned by medieval peasants any more than the *rationale* of dress, food and general deportment were questioned by the German middle classes at the end of the nineteenth century. The fact that certain methods of production were generally practised was sufficient reason for continuing to practise them.

Thus put, the argument is less illuminating than it purports to be. It reduces the problem to psychological attitudes as if they were final and residual determinants of economic behaviour, requiring no further analysis or explanation. It should however be possible to propound the idea of the essential traditionalism of medieval technology without wrapping it up in the sociological mysticism of culture patterns. Students of the middle ages could think of more concrete and simpler facts of medieval life capable of fostering a traditional attitude to methods of production and of inhibiting the will and the ability to change the prevailing technology.

Not all these simple facts will be found among the explanations sometimes offered. The most obvious of these simple explanations is the paucity of new technical ideas. Medieval peasants and landlords simply did not possess sufficient knowledge or understanding to be able to conceive important improvement in agricultural technique. Regarded in its broad historical perspective the insufficient flow of ideas would have made impossible technical achievements comparable to those of modern agriculture. Plausible as it is, this explanation is neither complete nor wholly relevant. As I shall have to emphasize over and over again the real problem of medieval technology is not why new technological knowledge was not forthcoming, but why the methods, or even the implements, known to medieval men were not employed, or not employed earlier or more widely than they in fact were.

Other historians draw for their explanation on the medieval institutions. Some of them have blamed the communal organization of agriculture and the common-field system for the inability of medieval agriculturists to change it. The assumption underlying this argument is that technological change is, as a rule, brought about by the break-away action of adventurous and non-conforming individuals, and that communal regulations and restraints impede the enterprise of such individuals. This notion of a conflict between communal regulation and technical progress underlay most of the historical accounts of the enclosure movement in the eighteenth and the early nineteenth centuries.

The view of the common fields implicit in these explanations is simplified to the point of being crude, but may nevertheless contain a grain of truth. A grain of truth, however, may be more than can be claimed for the explanations ascribing the technological immobility of medieval agriculture to its feudal and manorial background. We are told that on holdings which were not owned by their holders in permanent or secure title—and most manorial holdings were not—all incentives and means for technological improvements were lacking. What makes this argument difficult to accept is that not all medieval husbandmen were serfs, and that it is not at all certain that technological progress was any more conspicuous on free holdings, or on average manorial demesnes, than it was on the land of the unfree villagers.

If the manorial regime impeded technical innovation, it is more likely to have done so through its stultifying effect on investment. In modern economies most innovations are closely linked with investment. Every time a new piece of equipment is installed some technological improvement takes place; and almost every time additional investment is made some improvement or innovation is introduced. These links between investment and new methods could not have been as close in the middle ages as they are now since in the middle ages a much larger proportion of new investment was, to use the jargon of modern economists, 'in width', i.e. it merely added to the stock of productive resources some further increments wholly identical to those already in operation. Nevertheless it remains true that even in the middle ages a number of improvements—they will be named presently—required an expenditure of funds. Such funds were not, however, forthcoming as freely as they would have been in a technologically progressive economy, and as we shall show elsewhere, the flow of investments into agricultural improvements was very sluggish.

Greater use of capital was obviously not the means which medieval agriculturists *en masse* consciously adopted to raise the productivity of their arable fields. Was the remedy found in greater investment of labour? Arguing on *a priori* grounds and by analogy with other pre-industrial societies a more abundant use of labour would have provided not only a remedy for land hunger but also an obvious way of increasing output per acre. Historians have in fact been able to assemble a certain amount of evidence showing now in certain respects medieval agriculture was becoming more 'labour intensive'. More frequent ploughing could be one such 'labour intensive' improvement; better weeding of growing crops could be another. Manorial accounts frequently record expenses incurred in the wages of weeders or in labour services expended on this work, though they very seldom tell us what proportion of the demesne lands was thus treated.[1]

So much for investment in manorial improvements. Investment into innovations was probably scantier still on the land of the villagers. Unlike the landlord, the peasant often lacked the financial resources for investment, and more will be said about this later. But he was certainly not short of manpower. Labour was abundant and was becoming more abundant in the course of the thirteenth century. From this point of view there does not seem to be any reason why in localities where the lords considered better weeding worthwhile the villagers should not have done likewise. There is however little evidence that they in fact followed the lords' example and there is certainly no evidence to show that they were becoming more 'labour intensive' in their agricultural practices as the century advanced.

In short, no matter how we account for it, the inertia of medieval agricultural technology is unmistakable. Some progress there was, but it was, so to speak, 'bunched' into certain periods at the beginning and the ends of the era. Over the middle ages as a whole it was slow and uneven, and far greater in the management and arrangement of fields than in the implements employed in cultivation, or in the actual processes of planting, manuring, weeding and reaping.

II

Both from the point of view of implements and that of land-management the Anglo-Saxon era was all-important. It was probably during that era, and most certainly in its concluding centuries, that techniques characteristic of medieval agriculture first came into general use. One of the technical innovations of the Anglo-Saxon era was to change, indeed to revolutionize, the field systems and with them the use of land; the other was to bring about equally radical change in the principal implements. For the convenience of exposition the two innovations—that in field systems and that in implements—will be discussed separately; but their separate treatment must not, and I hope will not, obscure the link between them. They were both induced by the same necessities and opportunities and were from some points of view but different manifestations of the same fundamental change.

The implement most characteristic of the technological innovation of the Anglo-Saxon era, indeed dominating the entire technology of the age, was the heavy plough, the *carruca*. The heavy plough as it emerged in the middle ages was a larger and more efficient instrument than the lighter plough employed in most parts of the Roman Empire including Roman Britain. In its fully-developed form it had an iron share, whereas the lighter plough in earlier use, the *aratra*, had a wood share at best tipped with iron. In the second place it had a coulter knife fixed in front of the share to incise the furrow and to direct the movement of the cut. In the third place it had a moulding board fitted in parallel with the share whose function it was to turn the cut and to lay it on its side. In addition, a fully-developed plough had to be provided with wheels.[2]

Needless to say, the individual features of the *carruca*, taken separately, could be found in local use before they were adopted by the Anglo-Saxons. They may have been incorporated in the improved ploughs which the Belgic invaders are said to have brought into this country in the period immediately preceding the coming of the Romans. With a certain amount of imagination it should even be possible to piece together a case for the pre-medieval origin and use of the *carruca* and to credit with its invention such pre-medieval agents as the Belgae of north-western Europe or the Slavonic inhabitants of the east-European plains. None of these attributions can claim incontestable support in the available evidence, but the fact that they could have been suggested and taken seriously should be a sufficient warning to us not to assume that innovations like the medieval *carruca* resulted from wholly new and indigenous inventions. Indeed from the truly historical point of view it does not much matter whether the *carruca* was invented at the time or in places in which it first came to be generally used. What is important is not by whom and at what precise point of time was the new implement conceived but what were the circumstances which made it possible and necessary to introduce it into common use. The record of technological progress at all times is to a large extent made up of innovations which represented not wholly new discoveries or designs but the earliest instances of the widespread use of devices and methods previously available but not generally employed.[3]

From this point of view the most significant feature of this particular medieval innovation is that it was 'induced', made possible and necessary, by concomitant changes in the economic and social conditions. One of these concomitant changes was the reclamation of England's clayey plains described in the previous chapter. A number of writers have shown, and nobody has done it more convincingly than Marc Bloch, how inter-related were the light plough of Roman agriculture and the Roman preference for lighter soils. But once cultivation had to cope with heavy soils, above all heavy soils requiring deforesting and breaking up, the light plough was obviously inappropriate. The heavier plough, whether previously known or not, was an essential pre-requisite of the kind of reclamation that men were compelled to carry out in the Anglo-Saxon and early-medieval periods: it was their technological reaction to the demands of heavy soils.

The *carruca* was not however their sole reaction. The need to work difficult soils and to use the heavy plough for the purpose went together with a whole complex of other innovations, some purely technical, some social in the broadest sense of the term. The most obvious requirement was for improvements in animal traction appropriate to the needs of the heavy plough. The latter had to be drawn by a team of animals more powerful than the one or two beasts (sometimes one or two human beings) which sufficed for the light *aratra* of the Romans. A team of eight, and on some occasions of six or ten, oxen became an essential concomitant of the *carruca*. And with the large oxteam came also the improved ways of harnessing it. Some time ago Noëtte de Lefèvre argued that the Roman method of harnessing animals to the carriage and the plough by a collar to their necks was highly inefficient, wasteful of animal-power and wholly unsuited for use with large teams. The Celtic and Germanic settlers of Northern Europe accordingly replaced it with the much more efficient harness which hitched the draught animals from their shoulders and did so by means of a yoke linked to the plough by traces tied to a whipple tree.

This version of the facts has recently been challenged by some students, who have shown that the medieval method of harnessing had been known and occasionally practised in pre-medieval, indeed pre-Roman, times. This argument is not however strictly relevant to our present theme. It may be of great interest to historians of technology considered as an intellectual process, or to antiquarians unconcerned with the social implications of historical facts. But, to repeat, what interests an historian, especially an economic and social one, is not so much the discovery of a new process or device as its adoption for general use. And from the point of view of its adoption the improved harnessing of plough-animals was a true innovation of the Anglo-Saxon age.

What made the innovation so important was its manifold links with an even wider range of contemporary innovations. The *carruca* and its use in reclamation and cultivation and the employment of the large oxteam went with changes in the dimensions and shapes of fields, in the general routine of agricultural operations and in the ways in which land was occupied and managed.

Historians have always known or assumed that ploughing with the *carruca* and a large team of oxen was bound to effect the shape and the size of the fields. The pre-medieval *aratra*, light and easy to turn at corners, was well suited to the small square fields of the Romano-Celtic countryside. On the other hand, the heavy *carruca* with its large team, so efficient in other respects, was cumbersome to turn and was at its best only when it could be used to cut straight and long furrows. The fields appropriate to it would therefore be as long as the lay of the land would permit; and fields so formed would on the average also be large.

The introduction of the heavy plough and the formation of large fields also necessitated changes in the economic and social setting.

The larger fields appropriate to the new ploughing techniques would as a rule be too large to be held and cultivated by single peasant households. They were therefore frequently managed by several families or households working together. In fact some such co-operation would be made necessary by the very use of the *carruca*. For not only was the *carruca* itself too costly to be owned and maintained by a single peasant household, but the team of eight oxen was also much larger than a single peasant could provide. The plough and its team therefore came to be organized as co-operative equipment to which several peasant households contributed their shares of beasts and other resources.

Co-operation was not however confined to ownership and management of the plough and the oxteam. Once new tools and the appropriate techniques were adopted, some co-operation was also required for working the land. It is of course quite possible that the very task of initial reclamation and settlement frequently compelled the settlers to work in groups larger than the single small family of no more than two adults. Where the 'extended', or 'sib' family combining several collateral couples of adults under the authority of a common parental or grand-parental head, was to be found (as we shall see presently it may still have existed at the beginning of the Anglo-Saxon era) it could perhaps command human resources sufficient for some reclamations. But where settlement required the clearing of large areas, especially areas which had to be excoriated of trees and scrub or drained by ditching and dyking, even the resources of an extended family might not suffice, and the work had to be done by several families banded together.

The needs of co-operative reclamation and co-aration may help to explain the tendency of Anglo-Saxon settlers to establish themselves in clusters of households or villages. This tendency to 'club' can be accounted for by other reasons as well. It may have conformed to ancient patterns of custom and behaviour no longer serving immediate social ends; but it may also have been favoured by some social function or another. Above all we must not take it for granted that clustered settlements, any more than any other great innovation of the time, were wholly new devices conceived by the Anglo-Saxons. There had been some clustered village settlements in Roman and even pre-Roman Britain and, as we shall see further, some non-nucleated settlements could be established in Anglo-Saxon and medieval times in places where conditions were unsuited to clustered villages. Nevertheless, it would still remain true that in the early middle ages men were more prone to occupy and cultivate land in co-operative groups of households than they had been in earlier times and were to be in the modern era; and that this propensity most naturally followed from the ways in which land had to be cultivated and managed. Thus considered the nucleated village was an Anglo-Saxon innovation and was part of a technological 'mix' of which the *carruca* and the large team were the most important ingredients.

Another important ingredient of the 'mix' was the composite nature of most village holdings. As every schoolboy knows the typical holding was made up of several strips dispersed all over the arable fields. That the strips themselves should have been of the shape and size in which we find them need not occasion any surprise, since both the size and the shape were clearly related to the common field and their co-operative plough. As I have already suggested, the typical strip in the common fields was long and narrow. It usually went the whole length of the field so as to reduce the frequency with which the plough had to be turned and the direction of the furrow reversed. It was also narrow since it was as a rule formed by a day's or half-a-day's ploughing.

What is not so easy to account for is the reasons why the strips were dispersed all over the village fields and so frequently lay in a strict order. Some historians, notably Professor Homans, have accounted for the dispersal, above all for the regular order in which strips of individual holders were arranged, by the surviving influence of ancient custom, such as the Scandinavian custom of *Skolskift*. Other historians have emphasized the part which subdivision of property among heirs played in the breaking up into strips of holdings which began as compact plots. But of the explanations so far offered the simplest, the most convincing and the best capable of accounting for the universality and the regularity of the composite holdings derives the make-up of village holdings from the requirements of collective landholding and co-operation. Both the logic and the ethics of the common field demanded that every holder should have his share of good and bad land; similarly the logic of the plough-and-team partnership demanded that every partner should have a portion of the tilled land corresponding to his contribution to the team. And presumably the best way of allotting the shares accurately would be to measure them in units representing the amount of land the plough could turn over in a working day. It is for these reasons and in this sense that the dispersed composition of holdings must be considered as yet another ingredient of the complex of innovation linked with the *carruca*.

The communal ownership of fields, the dispersal of holdings over them and the employment of a co-operative plough were largely the social and economic attributes of Anglo-Saxon and medieval husbandry and were true innovations in the sense in which this term is used here. But apart from the design of the plough and its harness the other purely technological attributes of the system were not equally novel or equally bound up with the essential features of the Saxon and medieval landholding. Of the various technological characteristics of medieval agriculture none are better known or more frequently discussed by historians than the 'two-field' or the 'three-field' systems which are commonly taken to embody the medieval rotation at its purest. The technical idea underlying the rotation was not by itself very new, since some rotation of crops must have been practised in pre-Saxon times. Nor was it an intrinsic part of the common-field system since it could be, and was, practised on holdings owned and cultivated in severalty. In practice however the requirements of rotation were bound to influence the management of the common fields. More particularly, the rules regulating the routine and the time-table of rotation had to be made to fit into the collective ownership of land, the dispersal of holdings, the common use of pastures, the co-operative employment of ploughs, and also the physical qualities and the lay of the land itself.

The terms 'three-field' or 'two-field', as commonly applied to medieval agriculture, designate the management of land and of agricultural operations under which crops followed each other in regular sequence broken by equally regular periods of rest or fallow. In medieval practice, or to be exact in the current descriptions of the practice, the system functioned in two alternative ways distinguished by the proportions of the land left fallow and the frequency of the fallow periods. Under the two-field-system half the land lay fallow each year, while the fields sown—the other half of the total—carried all types of grain they were capable of growing—wheat and rye as well as barley, oats and various minor crops. Under the three-field-system not more than one third of the land was left fallow while the rest was apportioned into winter and spring fields—the former sown with wheat or rye, the latter with oats and barley. The winter crop, being more exacting as well as more valuable, was grown on land fresh from the fallow, while the spring crops were grown on fields which had in the preceding year carried a winter crop.

Depicted in this way, the system may appear to be highly regular and symmetrical, especially in its three-field variant; but in actual practice it was much less rigid, and certainly much less symmetrical, than is commonly depicted in textbooks.

To begin with, local differences in the choice and proportions of different crops were unavoidable since local soils and even climate varied, as did also local transport and markets. What is however very significant is that changes in crops grown could also be made in the same villages from time to time, more especially in the fourteenth and fifteenth centuries when landlords and villagers tried to adapt themselves to a slump in the fortunes of agriculture. We shall see presently that not all these changes were able or were designed to raise the aggregate output or the productivity per acre; they were nevertheless undertaken with rational objects in view—mostly that of reducing the costs or raising the quality of the product—and must therefore be considered as technological improvements.

A cropping change which deserves to rank as an improvement was the substitution of wheat for rye as the principal winter crop. Our manorial sources may be too late to catch sight of the substitution in its earlier stages, but most of them are able to show wheat continuing to gain at the expense of rye. What lay behind the substitution is difficult to say for certain. All it may signify is a growing preference of medieval consumers for wheaten bread; or else it may reflect the rapidly growing competition of Baltic rye which was beginning to flow into Western Europe during the second half of the thirteenth century.

Another change in crops commonly regarded as a technological improvement was the expanding use of legumes. This has frequently been described as an innovation of the later middle ages, i.e. of the fourteenth and fifteenth centuries, anticipating the use of legumes as soil-improvers in the seventeenth and eighteenth centuries. In actual fact, however, leguminous crops featured in crop accounts of much earlier periods, though they may have become more widespread in the late fourteenth and the fifteenth centuries. On at least one group of manors, the composite Sedgemoor Manors of Brent and Zoy, beans were one of the principal crops throughout their recorded history. There were as many as 400 acres under beans in Brent in the middle of the thirteenth century, and the area, though still large, did not expand but contracted somewhat towards the end of our period.

Where beans and peas were sown on portions of the fallow fields, as they were occasionally on the Glastonbury manors in the Sedgemoor, they could be regarded as a remarkable technical advance over the older methods of fallowing, and a presage of the revolutionary innovations of the seventeenth century. In many cases, however, beans and peas were grown merely because they were an important constituent of popular diet or good cattle fodder. The contribution which legumes could make to the success of other crops by replenishing the nitrates in the soil may or may not have been realized. It certainly could not have figured as an important incentive in the minds of the husbandmen who sometimes grew beans on ground on which they were not immediately succeeded by any other crops, as was obviously the case on some of the furlongs of Brent in the late 1250s, or on the St Swithun's Priory Manor of Chilbolton, and elsewhere.

Much less doubt attaches to the other and the more widespread changes in spring crops in the later middle ages, more particularly to wholesale shifts from and to oats which occurred on a large number of estates. The progress of reclamation was probably responsible for most of these shifts. Generally speaking oats, the least demanding of crops, was better suited to cold and wet soils than any other grain grown in the villages. It is therefore not surprising that wherever heavy, cold or wet soils were being broken up, the acreage under oats should have expanded. On the Bishop of Winchester's demesne of Whitney, which I have already cited as a typical colonizing estate, the acreage under oats in 1209 formed 80 per cent of the total sown in that year.

The link between reclamations and oats worked both ways. If the area under oats expanded as the occupation of land advanced, it also declined as the reclamation ceased and the occupation of land retreated. The area under oats in Whitney fell sharply in the late thirteenth and the early fourteenth centuries—and so it did in most other places where larger oatfields had been created in the process of reclamation. Indeed so sensitive did the output of oats appear to be to the expanding and contracting reclamation that the acreages under oats can sometimes be used as a rough and indirect index of internal colonization. But whether so taken or not, the changes in acreages of oats can be regarded as proof that medieval farming practice was less custom-bound than we sometimes imagine it to have been.

III

More widespread than the changes men rang on the types of grain they grew, and much more far-reaching in their economic effect, could be the local differences in the actual lay-out and management of the fields, and the transformation which their lay-out and management underwent during the middle ages. Of the local variations none diverged more radically from the prevailing system than the use of land as closes, i.e. compact plots which their occupiers held and cultivated in severalty, outside the framework of the common fields. In some areas of England the closes could represent the prevailing form of landholding and cultivation, as they often did in pastoral uplands. Such arable activities as the inhabitants of these regions carried on alongside of their pastoral pursuits were frequently conducted in enclosed crofts and in severalty.

Such units could however exist in the arable areas as well. There is much evidence to suggest that some of the land 'purprestured' by villagers, in the course of the reclamations of the thirteenth and the fourteenth centuries, was sometimes enclosed and cultivated in severalty. The practice was not, of course, universal since most additions to common fields also originated in recent reclamations, and our documents contain numerous references to newly assarted pieces of lands employed as common fields, especially in marshlands and royal forests. Nevertheless the progress of reclamations in the thirteenth and fourteenth centuries doubtless added to the total area of enclosed plots all over medieval England, and accounts for the prevalence of enclosures in such recently settled regions as the interior of Devonshire or the Bockland half of Warwickshire.

Finally, scattered enclosures appeared all over England as a result of occasional arrangements between landlords and some of their tenants by which the latter were allowed for special payment to enclose their land and to cultivate it apart from the common fields of the village. Such arrangements apparently become more common in the later middle ages, when a great deal of erstwhile demesne land was let out to tenants. As a result of the new lettings and the changing distribution of land among the villagers, the latter showed a growing inclination to consolidate their holdings and to cultivate them in severalty. These inclinations were symptomatic of the late fourteenth- and fifteenth-century changes and anticipated similar changes in later centuries, but were not sufficiently widespread to have altered the predominantly open-field character of medieval agriculture. They are mentioned here because they represented a departure from the typical conditions radical enough to warn the historians against an excessively generalized view of medieval landscape and agriculture.

Excessive generalization must also be guarded against in representing the layout and management of the common fields themselves. In current historical accounts the division of the village lands into component fields and furlongs, and also the relative order in which the fields and furlongs participated in rotation, have been simplified to the point of distortion. The over-simplification can in part be accounted for by the nomenclature of our sources. The documents, mostly surveys of manors, frequently distinguish between two or three 'great' fields and describe them by such names as the Southfield, or the Norfield, or the Middlefield. The distinction and the nomenclature must not, however, be taken as evidence of the way in which fields were divided and grouped for the purposes of rotation. What their names frequently indicate is their topography and location. It is therefore not surprising to find in manorial cropping accounts some portions of the individual 'great' fields under winter crops and other portions in the same fields under spring ones.

Even greater deviations from the symmetrical plans of open-field-husbandry could result from the requirements of fallowing and the variations in its frequency. The object of the fallow was to maintain the fertility and the good heart of the soil. It was not therefore required in places where fertility could more efficiently be maintained by other means or where it could not be maintained at all. The former situation is as a rule to be found on the small pieces of land adjoining the peasant houses, the house 'tofts' which would now be classified and described by their modern name of garden. We know very little about the crops grown on them and the ways in which they were managed, but judging from contemporary testimony of continental villages it appears highly probable that the gardens were cultivated very intensively: lavishly manured and thereby made to bear produce without fallow breaks.

The other extreme is represented by the so-called 'outfields'. Where land of inferior quality abounded, and while it abounded, the village husbandry would as often as not be conducted under the 'infield-outfield' system of intermittent or shifting husbandry. Under this system a part of the village land would be run as 'infields', where two- or three-course rotation was followed, and crops succeeded each other in a fixed order and alternated with fallow at regular intervals; while other lands, usually poorer or more distant ones, would be run as an 'outfield'. In most years it would be used as pasture, even rough pasture. But now and again the villagers would break up a plot or plots within it and take from it a crop or a brief succession of crops and then allow it to revert to waste, either for good, or for a long period of rest and recuperation.

On purely general grounds it would be legitimate to assume that in the initial phases of Anglo-Saxon settlement, when poorer lands not yet reclaimed for arable were more abundant than they were to be later, the infield-outfield practice was more general than in the later centuries. It is however remarkable how widespread it still was in the thirteenth and the fourteenth centuries. We find clear evidence of it in the parts of Devonshire studied by Professors Finberg and Hoskins, in the Norfolk Breckland described by Mr Saltmarsh, in the Dales of Yorkshire, or the Hampshire downs; in fact in most areas where poor lands not fully exploited as permanent arable were still to be found.

The co-existence of an intermittently cultivated outfield with a regularly rotated infield was not the only departure from the uniform two-field and three-field systems. In the middle of the thirteenth century, when the grange accounts of some medieval manors began to record in full the annual crops furlong by furlong, we do not always find in them the same order of rotation followed all over the manorial fields. Some, perhaps most, of the furlongs might be subjected to a three-fold rotation, others to a two-fold one, as for instance on some manors of St Swithun's Priory and Glastonbury Abbey. Some lands diverged from the general cropping sequences by concentrating on only one of the crops, such as oats. There is therefore little doubt that at the height of its economic expansion medieval arable farming, while in the main following the routine of two-course or three-course rotation, had acquired a field system much more complicated and much better adapted to the local variation of soils and topography than the conventional accounts of the open field systems imply.[4]

The field systems could thus vary from village to village or even within the same village. And they could also change from time to time. The one important change in the field system in the course of the middle ages about which we hear most was the change-over from the two-field system to the three-field one. Professor H. L. Gray, who has done more than anybody else to explore this hypothesis, was able to cite a number of villages and manors where the three-field system was introduced anew in the thirteenth century and later. His evidence consists mainly of decisions of manorial courts or village assemblies ordering village lands to be re-grouped into three common fields. These and similar records are quite numerous and seem to be unambiguous; some historians have accordingly concluded that the three-course rotation, and with it the common field system itself, were innovations of the later middle ages and even of the early modern era, when they were brought about by conscious endeavours of rural authorities to rationalize and reorganize the management of the fields.[5]

In a certain sense, narrow and special, this argument will carry conviction. The common field system could be defined very precisely to apply only to cases in which it happened to be uniform, wholly symmetrical and above all comprehensive, or in other words embraced the village lands in their entirety, imposed upon all the holders the obligations of common pasture on the stubble and held all waste, meadow and pasture in collective ownership and under communal management. Very few of the manorial and village fields in the earlier middle ages would satisfy a definition as rigid and as restricted as this. Historians adhering to the definition would therefore be quite justified in concluding that field systems rigorously and symmetrically organized—and, with them, the very principle of common fields—were a late medieval or even a modern product of a deliberate administrative reform. On the other hand if we are prepared, as I have been here, to accept as 'common' all communally held and managed fields even if the communal control over them did not happen to be as perfect and as all-embracing as that decreed in latter-day regulations, we shall have no difficulty in finding common fields in existence, indeed prevailing, in most parts of England throughout the earlier centuries of the middle ages and in the Anglo-Saxon era. In that case a verdict of a village community to organize the fields on a three-field system must be taken at its face value, i.e. not as a decision to bring in a wholly new principle of landholding and land management, but merely as a changeover from less intensive methods of exploiting the land to the more intensive ones.

This simpler and more modest interpretation of the evidence accords well with what we know were the economic necessities of the time. There was every economic reason why, in many places where two-course rotation had prevailed, men should have now been impelled to go over to the three-field system. The two-course rotation with half the fields lying idle every year was obviously wasteful of land. It is therefore not surprising that in the thirteenth century, when land was getting exceedingly scarce, the three-field system should have commended itself to villagers.

The change-over was therefore something to be expected. Yet even then it may not have been quite as general as a superficial reading of Gray's account may suggest. The records of the later middle ages show that much of the land which had been under two-field rotation in the twelfth century and earlier continued to be under it in the thirteenth century and after, as on some of the Yorkshire estates of the Duchy of Lancaster or the 'Fielding' estates of Bury St Edmunds Abbey.

IV

A change in the composition and use of village lands more widespread and, in the end, more important than the movement towards three-course rotation was the changing ratio of arable and pasture. In no sense was this an innovation; in the end it did not turn out to be an improvement; above all, it was not deliberately imposed by reforming villagers or landlords. It was a mere by-product, unpremeditated and often unwanted, of the centuries-old process of reclamation. The areas under corn could grow only at the expense of the areas under grass, and most of the reclamations necessitated the taking in of communal and manorial wastes, previously used for pasture, however rough. The resulting reductions in pasture were bound to affect the entire economy of villages.

Presumably they were felt least of all in the purely pastoral areas of England, among her uplands, marshes and forests, given over exclusively or mainly to cattle and sheep. But in areas where mixed farming prevailed and where men depended for their living on the grain they grew—and such areas yielded most of medieval England's produce and carried most of her population—the continuous reduction of pasture could threaten the viability of arable cultivation itself.

The threat was inherent in the very nature of mixed husbandry. In the latter the pastoral element not only provided a direct source of food and income but also served certain essential needs of grain growing. Some grass was needed to maintain the animals employed in ploughing and cartage; but in addition arable farms needed animals as their only source of manure.

Animal manure was not the only additive to soil in the middle ages. In some places and at some times minerals or chemicals were also added. Lime was one of them, marl was another. In some places sea-sand, or rather shells broken up fine by the action of the sea, was used on land near the sea. Now and again villages and landlords also indulged in the ultimately wasteful practice of 'burning and beating' the top turf and thereby adding to the potash in the soil. How widespread these practices were is difficult to say, but they were certainly not universal since lime and marl were not available everywhere. And even if and where used the various mineral additives did not fertilize the soil but merely helped to condition it: to keep its physical composition and its acidity under control.

Dung was the only real fertilizer, but the extent to which it was employed is somewhat uncertain. The manorial accounts contain regular references to its employment. Above all they bear witness to the oppressive privilege of the 'fold', which compelled the villagers to pasture some or all their animals on the lord's arable in order to manure it. The regulation for the communal folding of animals on village stubble after the harvest was designed with the same purpose in view. There is thus little doubt that men made such use of manures as their knowledge and their resources allowed. The main restriction on the use of manure—a restriction which got tighter as time went on—was imposed by its paucity. The abundance of manure depended on the sufficiency of animals; the latter depended on the adequacy of the pastures. And we have seen that pasture was continually invaded and reduced by reclamations for arable.

For very obvious reasons pastures were not reduced to the same extent and at the same speed everywhere. We must nevertheless accept that what Professor Beresford describes as the 'frontier' between grass and corn was moving away from grass towards corn all over the areas of mixed farms throughout the middle ages. How far the movement had gone is shown by the early spread of mixed farming into regions not nowadays considered as such. We have seen that by the beginning of the thirteenth century and even earlier arable farming had become the mainstay of local agriculture in areas which throughout English history have ranked as pastoral. In the Breckland and the Fielding in the eastern counties, the slopes and valleys of the Wiltshire and Hampshire and Dorset downs, in parts of the eastern and southern Cotswolds—in all these pastoral areas corn was not only grown at the turn of the twelfth and thirteenth centuries but in fact appeared to form the main source of agricultural incomes.[6]

So inherent was the shifting frontier between grass and grain in the very process of medieval growth and reclamation that most readers will be prepared to take it for granted. What is less self-evident is that in the course of the thirteenth century and perhaps even earlier the frontier not only approached but in many places crossed its limits of safety, and that by the end of that and the beginning of the following century, in corn-growing parts of the country taken as a whole, pasture and the animal population had been reduced to a level incompatible with the conduct of mixed farming itself.

The evidence in support of this contention is mostly indirect, though direct evidence is not altogether lacking. Now and again manorial records enable us to relate the size of a manorial flock or herd to the area of its arable; and where such comparisons are possible they very frequently reveal a provision of animals much lower than that which appears to have been made in the same localities in modern times, or that which the experts of the eighteenth-century Board of Agriculture considered desirable in their time.

The same conclusion emerges from the few surviving assessments to royal taxes, above all those for the double Hundred of Blackbourne in Suffolk. All these assessments are unanimous in recording fewer animals than in 1868, the year in which the Board of Agriculture series of livestock statistics begin and which happens also to have been the highest point in the expansion of English arable farming in the nineteenth century, and consequently also the lowest in the fortunes of local sheep farming and cattle grazing.

The evidence of the taxation assessments is well supported by what we can learn about the animals in possession of individuals. Almost all the available sources reveal the existence of large numbers of peasants without any animals or with no more than one head of cattle per family. Of these sources none are more revealing than the records of heriots, i.e. of manorial death duties. The heriot usually took the form which the Germans describe as *Besthaupt*, an animal taken as payment at the lord's choice. It is therefore significant to observe how often the English landlords were compelled to take small money payments instead, merely because the deceased tenants possessed no animals.[7]

We have so far assumed that it was the shortage of pasture that kept the numbers of animals down. That the assumption is right and that the shortage of pasture was great and widespread is revealed by the high and rising rents and by the prices of pastures as given in manorial surveys, custumals and similar manorial valuations of land. Some of these valuations might at first sight appear very curious. Normally we could expect arable acres to be more valuable than pasture—otherwise reclamation of pasture for arable use would have no sense since it could not offer any economic inducement to the reclaimer. In most of the earlier surveys pasture other than meadowland was in fact valued lower than arable land. But in the thirteenth century and more especially in its second half we begin to come across surveys and accounts in which an acre of pasture—ordinary pasture, not mowable meadow, and sometimes pasture frankly described as poor—commands a higher rent or price than arable land. When, in an early fourteenth-century inquisition of the manors in the Honour of Clare, we read that in the Suffolk manor of Hundon arable land was rated at 4*d* an acre but pasture, not meadow, at 1*s* 6*d* per acre the disparity may appear to be too great to be taken at its face value. But in the same and other parts of England inquisitions frequently report disparities equally striking. On an Essex manor of Bardfield, where the arable was large and good and was rated at the unusually high figure of 7*d* an acre, poor pasture of which we are expressly told that it was not mowable (*non possunt falcare*) was rated at 1*s* per acre.

More indirect still, yet even more suggestive, is the evidence of the rents of meadowland. Meadow, i.e. grassland so good and well-maintained that it could be regularly mown for hay, was always highly rated in medieval England, and there was no time when it did not command prices equal to or even higher than those of arable. But in most of the arable areas the price of meadow appears to reach its highest at the turn of the thirteenth and fourteenth centuries. These high and rising values of meadow must be taken as a sign of its great and growing scarcity, for in places where meadow was abundant its rent did not exceed that of arable by a large margin, while in places where the allowance of meadow was very small their rents and prices were many times those of the best wheatfields. Thus on the Priory of Eynsham's manor of Charlbury in Oxfordshire, where arable was extensive but meadow exiguous, the latter was rated at some twenty times the value of cornland: 6*s* and 3½*d* respectively. But on the same Priory's other manors where pasture was more plentiful the rent of meadow could be little more than twice that of arable land. Similarly on a Derbyshire estate of the Earls of Lacy with only 6 acres of meadow the latter was rated at two to three times the value of arable, but in another of the manors in the same group, that of Belper, where meadow was relatively large and, in addition, mountain pasture abounded, the corresponding rates were 10*d* and 1*s*.

In view of these contrasts in valuations it is significant that the values of meadowland in the late thirteenth and fourteenth centuries should have been on the whole higher than they appear to have been earlier, and that relatively cheap meadows should have been confined to the pastoral regions and localities where grasslands were still relatively abundant.

V

On *a priori* grounds the probable consequences of contracting pastures and dwindling supplies of manure would seem to be obvious. One of the possible consequences has already been mentioned. Where shortage of manure compelled men to reserve it for their better and nearer fields it would make it impossible for them to maintain their marginal lands indefinitely in arable use. On such lands, as well as better lands more regularly manured, the shortage of dung would manifest itself through its effect on yields. The average yields could be expected to decline, though it is still arguable that the decline would not be, so to speak, endless. Yet even if it could be expected to lose its momentum it was bound sooner or later to reduce the yields below the level at which land would still be worth cultivating.

So much for the *a priori* argument. How far, it will be asked, is it borne out by the evidence of actual yields? The difficulty of answering this question does not arise from any shortage of evidence. The evidence is short for the last 150 years of the middle ages. As a result of manorial decline in the late fourteenth and the fifteenth centuries, the records of manorial crops peter out, and the discussion of yields at the end of the middle ages must revert to a mere play with balances of probabilities. But fortunately the period preceding the Black Death and even more particularly that of the thirteenth and the early fourteenth centuries has left behind returns of crops and yields more numerous than any available to agrarian historians of other countries or other periods in this country before the coming of the modern series of agricultural statistics. And it so happens that the behaviour of yields in these earlier centuries may hold the key to the main problems of medieval agriculture—its aggregate product, its output per man and acre and the part which the changes in the product and the productivities played in shaping the economic trends.

Needless to say the study of the thirteenth- and fourteenth-century yields is fraught with great difficulties, mostly on account of their local variations. The very abundance of the data merely helps to bring home the range of local differences. Thus a few years ago Professor Finberg cited returns to seed on some of the manors of Tavistock Abbey in Devonshire very much higher than the similar returns elsewhere. But, in general, a study of yields, be it never so mindful of local variations, cannot help bringing out their low general level. On the estates of the Bishop of Winchester the yields of all the types of grain during the whole of the thirteenth and the first half of the fourteenth centuries were between 6 and 8 bushels per acre, compared with at least 40 to 50 bushels in the same localities in our own time and possibly 20 to 30 bushels in the middle of the nineteenth century. No other medieval estate has left behind figures of yields equally numerous and equally amenable to historical analysis, yet it is highly significant that on most of the estates—those of Glastonbury Abbey, Crowland Abbey, the Priory of St Swithun's, the Abbey of Bury St Edmunds, the Earls of Lancaster, the Suffolk and Essex manors of the Honour of Clare—would be found within the range of Winchester figures. To put it in more technical terms, 6 to 9 bushels per acre was the statistical 'mode', i.e. the figure representative of the largest number of instances in the entire collection of returns.

The very low yields of the thirteenth century can very plausibly be accounted for by the action of several convergent factors: the low quality of the seed, the shallow ploughing, the absence of proper underdraining of the heavier and more fertile soils, the inability of the fallowing routine to deal properly with weeds, and, of course, the insufficiency of manure. But at the risk of some untestable speculation it is also possible to think of a more truly historical, time-conditioned, cause: the results of a long drawn-out, perhaps several centuries long, decline in the yield of the more anciently cultivated lands.

Yet even if, for lack of sufficient data, the secular decline of yields in the six or seven centuries preceding the thirteenth could not be convincingly demonstrated, the decline of yields in the centuries for which the evidence is available, the thirteenth and the early fourteenth, is now fairly certain. Until very recently the tendency in historical studies has been to interpret the few figures hitherto published as evidence of wholly stable yields. This impression of a stable trend of yields is no longer tenable. A more recent and a very detailed study by Dr Jan Titow of some 20,000 returns of crops extracted from the accounts of the Bishop of Winchester's estates (the largest collection of medieval statistics yet published) exhibits the decline of yields very clearly. The trend was bound to differ from manor to manor, but broadly speaking the thirty-six Bishop's manors fall into three groups. On one or two manors the yields may have been buoyant during the greater part of the period. On a large number of other manors, some eighteen in all, yields declined in either the first or the second half of our period. On most of the demesnes on which yields declined in the first half, they were stabilized in the course of the early fourteenth century; but on most of those on which they had happened to be stable or buoyant in the earlier decades of the thirteenth century a decline as a rule set in at the turn of that century or in the following one. In addition, a number of manors, some eight to ten, appeared to suffer a continuous decline in yields during the whole or nearly the whole of the period. All in all the manors on which the yields per acre declined, either all the time or for spans of time as long as half-a-century, were in an overwhelming majority: twenty-eight out of thirty-two.[8]

Figures from certain other estates exhibit the same trend. None of the other series are anywhere near as full or continuous as those of the Winchester estates, nor do they reach as far back into the thirteenth century. Their combined evidence however tallies well with that of the Winchester estates. Where the figures are sufficient to reveal a trend—as some of them are for the later part of the period—the latter resembles the one displayed by the contemporary Winchester figures: gently sagging if unrelated to areas sown or to other economic changes, declining more markedly if so related.

In this way the most direct evidence available to us, that of demesne crops, bears witness to yields declining in the thirteenth and the early fourteenth centuries, and to the underlying presumption of the deteriorating quality of arable lands. This deterioration is also borne out by other, mostly indirect, signs, above all by the valuations, i.e. the rents and prices, of arable land. On general grounds we could expect that in the thirteenth and the early fourteenth centuries, when internal colonization was increasingly restricted to lands of ever lower quality, newly reclaimed plots of inferior land would command lower prices than the older and presumably better lands. Yet it is not what we always find. Over and over again the surveys of estates in the mixed-farming areas and the entries of rents in manorial accounts record what could anachronistically be described as a 'reverse gap': higher rents for assarts than for much of the older arable.

The presumption is that the older lands, though situated on what should have ranked as better soil, were worth less because their productive power had been sapped.

VI

The possibility of arable land aging and decaying, once admitted, might suggest a tentative explanation for several agrarian phenomena otherwise difficult to account for. It may help to account for the unusually high yields on the Tavistock Abbey manor of Hurdwick, since much of Hurdwick's land, like much of the cultivated land in the combes and valleys of Devonshire, was made up of fields and closes relatively recently reclaimed. It may also account for the higher rating, in terms of rent and prices, of arable fields in the estates of the Earl of Lacy in the peripheral regions, such as the Honour of Knaresborough and Pontefract, compared with the Earl's lands in the older part of England, such as those administered from Higham Ferrers in Northamptonshire or from Kingston Lacy in the southern counties.

Equally tentative and equally tempting is the possibility of explaining the suspected existence of ancient, partly abandoned and largely decayed common fields within some anciently established manors. There were innumerable pieces of land and entire fields on most manors which the surveys and accounts describe as old, exhausted or impoverished—*terra debilis, frisca quia debilis.*

Indeed the decay and withdrawal of lands exhausted by long periods of improvident cultivation may have been more widespread than the crude totals of demesne acreages could reveal. The progress of reclamations may have helped to replace and renew the total acreage under plough, thus masking from view the lapse of decayed and decaying acres. In dealing with the penalties of marginal reclamation I suggested that the poorer lands broken up for the plough in the later stages of England's internal colonization could not always be relied upon to stay in arable use indefinitely, and frequently returned to waste after their stored fertility had been mined out. But a similar relapse into waste or to other inferior uses could also afflict some of the older and originally better lands, with the result that many more villages than we know of may have gone through a process of decay and renewal which can best be described as metabolic.

The term metabolic, as used by biologists, describes the way in which organic systems maintain themselves by replacing decayed cells with new ones. The term could without much violence be applied also to the complex of plots, closes and furlongs making up the arable areas of medieval demesnes and villages. Measured by the total acreages these areas may often appear to have remained remarkably stable over long periods of time, but the stability frequently masked constant changes in the composition of the total. Some pieces of land, even entire fields, could go out of cultivation while others were brought in to replace them.

So widespread were the metabolic changes in the composition and the use of medieval fields, so closely were they bound up with the main trends of agrarian development, and so well are they served by evidence, that it is surprising to find how little they have been studied and how consistently they have been neglected in textbooks. Yet examples abound in the documents of all the manors which happen to record their annual sowing furlong by furlong. Good examples of such manors are provided by Chilbolton, Houghton-with-Drayton, Micklemarsh and Silkstead—all of them estates of the Priory of St Swithun's on the downs of Hampshire which they shared with some of the chalkland manors of the Bishop of Winchester. The unusually detailed cropping returns of these estates enable us to follow the fortunes of a number of large furlongs, which contract after a number of years in regular cultivation, presumably because some parts are no longer worth sowing. Similar life histories of individual fields and furlongs can be glimpsed through the grange accounts of numerous other manors, especially those of Glastonbury where the cropping returns also happen to be unusually full. On all these estates the acres lost in older fields are as a rule replaced by other lands, which judging by their names, had usually been taken in from the waste.

Most of the instances of field metabolism available to historians date to the thirteenth and the early fourteenth centuries, and help to account for some of the most significant developments of the time. In the absence of detailed manorial evidence we are unable to observe the process equally closely in the late fourteenth and fifteenth centuries. Yet it can be argued on general grounds as well as from some medieval evidence that obsolescence continued to play some part in later centuries as well, and may help to explain the apparent contraction of agricultural output, which I propose to discuss in describing the winding up of the demesne economy in the fifteenth century.

The general argument is simple enough. As long as the metabolism of the field system functioned properly it could be relied upon to maintain the areas under cultivation and even their aggregate output. At times and in places in which reclamation was buoyant, men were able not only to maintain but also to expand the acreage and the output of arable land; this they could not do where reclamation began to peter out. The apparent turndown in the aggregate acreage of arable land in the later middle ages, or what I referred to as the onset of 'decolonization', was thus a composite movement. The proper way of accounting for it is to present it as the growing inability of the new lands to redress the balance of the old.

However, presented in this form, as a brief and schematic model shorn of all the complexities of the actual historical experience, the decline in the area and in the output of agriculture in the later middle ages may appear more uniform, more continuous and above all more inexorable than it could possibly have been. Even in the earlier centuries it could not have been so ubiquitous as not to leave room for local exceptions. To repeat what has already been stressed repeatedly elsewhere, there were always parts of England, however few and remote, where reclamation never ceased. We must also bear in mind that in most villages and manorial demesnes there could be found fields which were either so intrinsically fertile or so well manured as to stay in full productive vigour throughout the middle ages. But even though not universal the break-down of the metabolic system became more general as time went on, and English agriculture as a whole appears to have entered the phase of contraction in both the area under plough and in the aggregate output of grain.

VII

Certain fundamental objections could be advanced, and have in fact been advanced, against viewing the history of agriculture in the closing centuries of the middle ages as one of continuous and inexorable decline of average yields and productivities. On purely theoretical, indeed dialectical, grounds it could be argued that the decline of agricultural production through the break-down of field metabolism was bound, sooner or later, to generate its own cure. On more practical grounds, from evidence which in some people's minds may rank as experimental, it has also been argued that the penalties of manureless cultivation were not cumulative and were sooner or later bound to lose their effect. Both objections deserve to be considered in greater detail.

The argument of self-cure is very plausible and, in some measure, probably true. The petering out of reclamations would in itself have put an end to further inroads into grasslands; but above all, pasture could be expected to increase *pari passu* with lapsing arable. The time would therefore come when the proper balance between straw and grass would be re-established. The supply of manure would in that case increase sufficiently to enable men to maintain and even to improve their arable fields. The average quality of the land still under plough could in any case be expected to improve as its worst and poorest parts were withdrawn from arable cultivation.

This set of expectations can be fitted to the actual experience of the fourteenth and fifteenth centuries. There apparently was some increase in the pastoral use of land, more particularly at the end of the fifteenth century when some lands began to be enclosed for sheep. Such evidence as we have also suggests that on a number of demesnes which were contracting during the period the intrinsic quality of the acres still cultivated (though not necessarily their output) may, on the average, have improved. We certainly know this to have been the case on the Bishop of Winchester's demesnes in the fourteenth century. There is thus no reason why, in presenting the history of agriculture in the late fourteenth and fifteenth centuries, historians should not accept the hypothesis of self-cure as being to some extent true.

Unfortunately the extent of its truth is difficult, perhaps impossible, to gauge. The difficulty is one of evidence. What makes the economic study of agrarian history in the thirteenth and early fourteenth centuries a feasible enterprise is the plethora of the purely economic evidence generated by manorial estates. But as the landlords were winding up the direct management of their demesnes they accordingly ceased to generate the most important agrarian evidence, that of the accounts with their returns of crops, the expenses of cultivation, and that of entries in court rolls directly concerned with the management of cultivation. In their absence we are left in ignorance about yields, about the frequency of manuring or weeding or aftermath ploughing. Here and there we are able to form some judgment of what happened to the relative areas of demesne arable and pasture, but are unable to discover how much of the land withdrawn from the demesne actually went out of arable use. Above all we have no means of knowing to what extent the earlier process of aging and lapse ceased altogether. In the absence of evidence on any of these points we are compelled to base our diagnosis of fifteenth-century productivity on a mere balance of rational alternatives; and with pure reason as their only weight, the balances appear to be very delicately poised.

Let us take the yields first. The average yields per acre on those late fourteenth-century demesnes which had begun to contract before they were given up altogether, e.g. those of the Bishops of Winchester, of Glastonbury Abbey, or the Priors of Christ Church, Canterbury, did not appear to have risen very appreciably. In the years in which the landlords experimented with thinner sowing in order to improve returns to seed, outputs per acre may actually have declined. The fact that the yields per acre did not appreciably decline and those per seed may have risen was in itself something of an achievement, for they might have gone on declining had the demesnes continued to be cultivated on their thirteenth-century scale and by their thirteenth-century methods. But the resulting cure could not have been but partial, since it merely arrested, and did not reverse, the downward trend of the preceding century or century and a half.

Equally uncertain must be our verdict about the other possible aid to self-cure, i.e. the increase in pasture. Were the additions to pasture commensurate with the areas which went out of arable cultivation? We know that the land which the landlords had ceased to cultivate could be put to alternative use, but some of it undoubtedly went out of cultivation altogether. Manorial accounts described it as 'waste', and presumably all waste lands could be used as pasture. But we also know that some of the land withdrawn from the demesne, even land described as poor, was let out to tenants. In the later years, especially in the fifteenth century, when the demesnes were finally dissolved, the entire arable was as a rule let out. Unfortunately we do not know and have no means of knowing what were the uses to which the tenants put the lands they acquired from the landlords. Some of it may have been turned into pasture, but there is some evidence to show that much of it, even the poor oatlands, continued to be exploited for corn-growing. We must therefore conclude that in all probability not all the land lost to arable went to augment the village pastures. Our judgment of the curative effects of this particular medicine must depend on the guess we are prepared to hazard about the proportion of the new lettings remaining in arable cultivation.

Where the balance of probabilities may have tipped in favour of improved productivity is in places and times in which the changes in landholding in the later middle ages made it possible for men to enclose their lands and to cultivate them in severalty. We have seen that there is some evidence of a slow and gradual increase of small-scale enclosures in the later middle ages: at any rate references to pieces of land held as closes occur regularly in such records as we possess. The scale and importance of this movement must not of course be exaggerated. We have already seen that a great deal of land was held and cultivated in closes in the thirteenth century and even earlier; some of the demesnes certainly were to all intents and purposes enclosed units of cultivation. Unfortunately the records are not sufficient to enable us to decide whether the piecemeal enclosures of the fourteenth and fifteenth centuries were great enough in the aggregate to make much difference to the average standards of output and productivity in England taken as a whole. On general grounds the probability of a major transformation by enclosure cannot be rated high. In the eighteenth and the early nineteenth centuries when enclosures became general, and the open-field system was finally wound up, the areas on which the latter had prevailed and on which it was now finally liquidated were very extensive indeed and covered the greater part of mixed-farming areas. At any rate nearly all the places on which we find open-fields in the thirteenth century, and in which holdings held in severalty were few, still appear on the eve of the agricultural revolution in the eighteenth century to have been relatively untouched by enclosures.

Even more tentative, and more negative on the balance, must be our verdict on the second, the practical, argument against the hypothesis of over-exploitation of land. The argument is based on what is known as the Rothampstead experiment in manureless cultivation. From 1843 onward the agricultural scientists at Rothampstead have been regularly cultivating without manuring a plot —the Broadbalk field—which had previously borne a regular succession of crops. Some 120 crops have been taken from that field since the experiment started, and the results, as commonly presented, have turned out to be a mixture of the unexceptional with the unexpected. What is unexceptional is that the denial of manure should have greatly reduced the average yields over the 125 years: the average on manured land of comparable quality has been between 40 and 50 bushels of wheat per acre, but on the unmanured field the average yield was 12 bushels. Where the figures run counter to common expectation is that the decline in yields has not been constant, but has gradually slackened off through the years. Whereas in the first twenty years the yield dropped from about 30 bushels to about 16 bushels, in the subsequent twenty years it dropped, in spite of some bad harvest years in the interval, to about 10–12 bushels, and in the subsequent years the decline has been so light as to justify the Rothampstead experimentalists in concluding that the yields of Broadbalk field have levelled out at about 12 bushels per acre.

On further consideration, however, the argument will appear to be less convincing than the first look at the Rothampstead figures might suggest. Before accepting these figures as applicable to the medieval experience, it is important to make sure that the Broadbalk field and its cultivation were comparable with the fields and the methods of cultivation which historians have in mind when discussing the penalties of manureless cultivation in the middle ages. I have already suggested that the intrinsic quality of some medieval soils was probably high enough to safeguard them from the worst consequences of insufficient manuring. The lands which would be expected to suffer were the marginal ones—either the light, hungry and leachable sands and thin overlays, or else heavy, undrained or undrainable clays. Broadbalk is neither. Its soil is rather light clay well mixed with flint over porous chalk. Unlike medieval fields, it has been under-drained, even though in the opinion of one of the Rothampstead experts this was not strictly necessary since the subsoil was sufficiently porous to prevent waterlogging. The cultivation of the field may also have been different from the medieval. Care was taken not to prejudice the results by deep ploughing, but the implements used were not medieval ploughs but modern ones, and these probably cut a deeper furrow than the medieval *carruca*. Nor was the seed the same, since the Rothampstead experimenters used modern strains of seed, such as Red Rostock in 1878, Club or Square Head in 1899.

Finally there are the more uncertain yet not wholly negligible possibilities of differences in stored up fertility. One of the most interesting and relevant findings of the experts has been the remarkable endurance of nutrients in retentive soils. We know that before being turned over to the manureless experiment Broadbalk had been regularly manured. Good clays and loams such as those of Broadbalk would, if manured for a period, retain the benefits of the manure for many decades to come. In this respect, Broadbalk, even after 125 years of cropping, may have had some advantage over some thirteenth-century fields which had been cultivated without or with very little manure for centuries.

For all these reasons the lessons of Rothampstead may not be easy to apply to the middle ages. Their lack of relevance is betrayed by the very figures of their yields. The level from which the experiments started was by medieval standards unattainably high: about five times that of the Winchester averages. The levels to which they eventually sank were at least twice and perhaps three times as high as the statistical mode of yields in the thirteenth century and were much higher than those gladly accepted by the most efficient and progressive of medieval husbandmen. They were in fact higher than those which the thirteenth-century expert, Walter of Henley, presented as a counsel of perfection. On the other hand if the thirteenth-century yields on the Winchester manors had been halved or reduced by two thirds, as the Broadbalk ones eventually were, they would have sunk to the level of 3–4 bushels per acre or $1\frac{1}{4}$ to $1\frac{3}{4}$ times the seed sown. At this level of yields the land would not have been worth cultivating even by medieval standards.

VIII

The hypothesis of declining yields thus stands. Our sources being what they are it must remain no more than a hypothesis. But it is sufficiently well-rooted in evidence to be accepted as a near approximation to an established fact. Above all it is a working hypothesis, in that it agrees with—indeed connects—the various trends in medieval land use we have observed: the decline in pasture, the extension of arable, the changing values of pasture, the shortage of animals, and above all the low and declining standards of life of the poorer sections of the rural population in the thirteenth century. These standards will form the subject of a later chapter.

References

1. For *rebinatio* as a pre-1348 practice see Dorothea Oschinsky, *Walter of Henley* (1971), pp. 78, 157, 314, 315. For still more frequent (threefold) ploughing in *rebinatio* in later centuries see P. F. Brandon, 'Demesne Arable Farming in Coastal Sussex in the later Middle Ages', *Agric. Hist. Rev.*, Vol. 19, part II (1971), p. 129.

2. Charles Parain, 'The Evolution of Agricultural Technique', *The Cambridge Economic History*, Vol. I, 2nd ed., pp. 148–52.

3. F. G. Payne, 'The British Plough and some stages in its Development', *Agric. Hist. Rev.* (1957); Frere, *Britannia*, p. 24. H. C. Bowen, 'The Celtic Background', in Rivet (ed.), *The Roman Villa*, p. 41; I. B. Passmore, *The English Plough* (1930).

4. For typical examples of the complex and flexible organisation of open-fields see David Roden, 'Demesne Farming in the Chiltern Hills', *Agric. Hist. Rev.*, Vol. 17 (1969); and P. F. Brandon, 'Demesne Arable Farming'.

5. H. L. Gray, *The English Field Systems* (1965); J. Thirsk, 'The Common Fields', *Past and Present*, 29 (1964); J. Z. Titow, 'Medieval England and the Open Field System', *Past and Present*, 32 (1965); Alan R. H. Baker, 'Some Terminological Problems in Studies of British Field Systems', *Agric. Hist. Rev.*, Vol. 17, part II (1969).

6. M. M. Postan, 'Village Livestock in the Thirteenth Century', *Econ. Hist. Rev.*, 2nd ser., xv (1962).

7. Postan, 'Village Livestock'; R. H. Hilton, *A Medieval Society* (1967).

8. These figures are taken from a detailed study of yields in J. Z. Titow, *Winchester Yields*, Cambridge, 1972.

5 The Manor: Origins

I

Material conditions in the narrowest sense of the term—local topography, soil or climate—powerful as they may have been, were not alone in determining the shape and the direction of economic development in the middle ages. We have seen that certain influences, more social and 'man-made', such as demographic change or the social heritage from past generations or the material culture left behind by the previous occupiers of the land, imposed themselves equally strongly on the activities of men. These activities also had to fit into a setting which is commonly described as 'institutional', i.e. that of bodies or of centres of power which created rules, generated customs, defined rights and duties, established hierarchies of authority, and in general ordered the relations of man to man. Of these institutions two, the manor and the village community, are generally and rightly presented as the most powerful, the most ubiquitous and at the same time the most characteristic of medieval economy and society. I propose to deal with their history in this and later chapters, and to begin my history with the rise and evolution of the manor.

We shall see presently that manors varied greatly from place to place and from time to time. In its characteristic and full-fledged form the manor combined a number of functions. Considered in its economic function the manor was first and foremost the landlord's landed estate. Even at its smallest, e.g. when it was hardly large enough to provide a livelihood for a petty knight, it was still larger than the holdings of wealthier peasants. Its land however provided not only a site for the lord's hall and his home-farm but also room for holdings let out to peasant tenants. This twofold division of manorial territory underlay and accounted for the twofold source of the lord's income. Some of this income came from the produce grown on the lord's home-farm or, to use its technical name, his 'demesne'; while some took the form of rent paid by tenants. The most characteristic feature of the manorial economy however was that the two halves of its land and the two sources of its income were intimately linked. The demesne depended on the tenants for its labour. The tenants' rent was therefore payable, in part at least, in labour services; and the tenants' position, both personal and economic, was determined by the lord's need to secure and to safeguard his claim on their labour.

Hence the main social characteristic of the typical manor—the dependent status of its tenants. The latter were unfree or semi-free. They were compelled to stay on their manorial holdings so that the lord's land should be always occupied and able to render its rent and services. Their service dues were accordingly defined not by a free wage contract but by manorial rules and customs, and were safeguarded by the powers which the landlord claimed over his unfree tenants. The latter's dependent status also yielded other ancillary profits to the lord. The miscellaneous rights or 'freedoms' which a free man could claim as his own—the right to move away, to marry or to give away his daughter, to leave his possessions to his heirs by testament, to buy and sell land or cattle, to sue or to be sued in national courts—could not be exercised by the lord's dependent tenants except with his permission, which was as a rule purchasable by a 'fine'.

The dependent condition of the tenant, and the 'finable' exercise of their 'freedoms' would by itself have conferred on the manor a variety of administrative and jurisdictional powers over its tenants. But in addition, a typical manor could also exercise some of these powers by virtue of privileges acquired by the suzerain's grant, or by purchase, or even by an arbitrary decision of the lord himself. The manor thus functioned as a local police authority and as a local agency for the enforcement of criminal law. All these peace-keeping and jurisdictional functions necessitated regular court-sessions and convocations of juries. The attendance at court and the service on juries was therefore an additional obligation on the tenant; and the income from courts and inquests was an additional source of manorial income.

In this form the manor was a characteristically medieval institution, in that it was intimately related to the elements of culture and society regarded as typical of the age. Nevertheless, in considering the manor's origin and development, it is important to bear in mind that its medieval features were grafted on to an economic root-stock which was not specifically medieval, since it was also to be found in other periods of human history and in other parts of the world. This root-stock was that of the great estate. In its essentials the history of the manor is thus twofold: in the first place it is the story of how large estates originated and developed; and in the second place it is the story of the way in which the estate acquired, or lost, those typically medieval features that turned it into a manor—its dependent cultivation, its legal powers, its administrative functions and authority.

In England this history as a rule has been told in conjunction or at least in conformity with the history of the estate in Europe as a whole. We must accordingly begin our story with an account of the large estates in Europe as a whole. This account need not have raised any difficult problems; it could have been taken for granted had it not been complicated by ancient controversies and overlaid by ideological implications. Large estates were the most obvious way in which marked inequalities of wealth could express themselves at a time when land was the chief form of wealth and the main base of power. Historians would therefore have been quite justified in assuming that as long and as early as inequalities existed, large estates went with them, and must have been there at the very dawn of the middle ages. Unfortunately assumptions as simple and as obvious as this were made impossible by the climate of historical opinion at the time and in the place in which the foundations of modern historiography were laid. The time and the place were Germany in the first half of the nineteenth century; and in that particular phase of its development German historiography was dominated by the sociological theories of primitive communism and the political ideologies of Teutonic democracy. According to the anthropological theories then in fashion the peoples of Europe in the early stages of their tribal history knew no private titles to real property and owned their land in tribal communes. Individually-owned properties, and with them the inequalities in the distribution of land, were later distortions of the original order of things. This notion of primitive communism as a rule went together with the politically inspired notion of tribal democracy. The young intellectuals striving to emancipate the German serfs of their own time based their case for emancipation on the belief in the primordial equality of the German folk. According to this belief, the Germanic society in the first, i.e. tribal and Teutonic, beginnings of its history was made up of independent freemen differing little in status, authority and presumably wealth.

In so far as property was not communally owned—and on this point political democrats could differ—it was distributed more or less equally, and in amounts or in a form incapable of conferring on its owners positions of overriding power and authority.[1]

The hold which these ideas had over historical thought was bound to weaken as their underlying political inspiration waned. In any case such argument as could be presented in their support—and the support came wholly from argument, not from evidence—might perhaps hold good of the earliest, the prehistoric, beginnings of European culture; but it would not hold of the Germanic peoples at the time when they irrupted into the Roman territories. By the third or the fourth centuries of our era, the Goths, the Langobards and above all the Franks had moved a long distance away from the stage of original simplicity depicted by Caesar and fondly imagined by the early nineteenth-century historians. By that time the Germans had formed veritable, albeit tribal, principalities and evolved complex political systems marked by hierarchical gradations of power and possession. In these gradations the lowest position was occupied by slaves, the topmost by a tribal aristocracy; and, judging from archaeological evidence, men in the top rank disposed of large accumulations of material wealth. There is consequently every reason to suppose and abundant evidence to show that, having invaded the erstwhile Roman provinces and occupied their lands, the German conquerors knew how to fit into the pre-existing inequalities of rural life and, in doing so, to take over the large estates in the Roman countryside, or even to carve out such estates anew.[2]

Numerous large estates, some perpetuating the Roman villas and others newly formed, must therefore have existed at the very outset of the Dark Ages. There is no need for us to invoke dramatic and rapid transformations in a later period in order to account for the presence of such estates in the eighth or ninth centuries when documentary evidence of their functioning becomes available. This does not, of course, mean that developments favourable to the further spread of great estates had not taken place in the early middle ages, between the fifth century and the tenth. As we shall see presently, the rulers of the new Germanic kingdoms, more particularly those of the Merovingian and the Carolingian dynasties, carved out of the royal fiscs new estates or 'fiefs' with which to remunerate their functionaries or chief followers. Large landed estates were also created by kings and their notables to endow the religious foundations which were springing up all over the continent, and above all the Benedictine abbeys and cathedral chapters.

Throughout the period large property complexes could also be formed or augmented by purchase and seizure. The latter was quite widespread in times and at places favourable to the exercise of arbitrary power by locally based strong men. The time of the greatest opportunity for the strong men came in the ultimate and penultimate centuries of the millennium, when the Norse and Magyar invasions and the break-down of royal authority created a near-anarchy in most parts of the continent. It was during this period that a number of the large feudal estates familiar to historians of later centuries first came into prominence.

In this way several factors converged to create the network of large estates which had come to cover the continent of Europe by the end of the Dark Ages and the commencement of the middle ages proper.

So much for the continental estates. There is no reason why a similar network of estates should not, in the same way, have come into existence in Anglo-Saxon England. At the time of their invasion into Roman Britain the Anglo-Saxons were no more innocent of differences of status and wealth than their contemporaries across the narrow seas. They should have found it no more difficult to fit into the inequalities of the Romano-British countryside and, in doing so, to take over the villas and the villa-like estates they found there.

The societies and principalities they established on the morrow of the conquest, those of the Anglo-Saxon heptarchy, may still have borne the marks of their tribal origins, but principalities they nevertheless were. They provided themselves from the very outset with means of organized government, however rudimentary. Similarly, their economic structure was both complex and differentiated. Archaeological remains and the few literary and documentary sources available to historians bear witness to marked differences of wealth.

In Anglo-Saxon England, as on the continent, large estates were therefore an inescapable feature of the political and the social system at its very inception; and became more prominent as time went on. Throughout their history, but more particularly in the later centuries, the Anglo-Saxon kingdoms depended on their thegns and bishops for the discharge of administrative and judicial functions of the State and for military leadership; and both thegns and bishops were maintained by the revenues of large estates. In addition, all through the Anglo-Saxon era the kings and the great thegns carved out of their landed estates endowments for the religious foundations. So large and continuous were the endowments that by the end of the Anglo-Saxon era the Church had acquired a large part, perhaps as much as one third, of all England's occupied surface. These possessions were, as a rule, also held in large units.[3]

The process whereby England's surface was parcelled out into large estates culminated in the opening decades of Norman rule. We know that in the years immediately following the Conquest the Normans took over the properties of the Anglo-Saxon kings and of their thegns. When not assigned to the Conqueror himself to form part of his own domain, the properties went to the men who had come over with him. The entire system of landholding was thereby reorganized. The superior ownership of all land was vested in the Crown from whom all other land titles now derived. Those of the King's immediate vassals were defined as 'tenancies-in-chief', held directly of the king; all other titles were sub-tenancies of the King's tenants or of their sub-tenants. A uniform and universal grid of large estates and of holdings embraced by them was thus imposed upon the face of the country. The imposition was however that of form and definition rather than of economic fact; for, as we have seen, England's land had already been mainly parcelled out in large units in the course of the preceding centuries. What the Normans did was to tidy up and make uniform the tenurial principles on which this grid was constructed, and to change the personnel of the estate-owning class by replacing most of the Anglo-Saxon landowners by their own followers and agents.

II

Yet even after it had been completed and systematized by Charlemagne and various princes in the eleventh century on the continent, or by the Normans in England, the network of estates would not by itself have established what historians have agreed to consider as the manorial order. In order to function as a manor and to be classified as such, medieval estates had to possess certain political and social features which large estates of other periods did not necessarily possess. Most historians believe that the medieval estate acquired these features by virtue of its role in government and of its owner's position in society. Its special role in medieval government derived from its being held in fief: as a tenancy conditional on the discharge of certain functions in war and administration. In so far as its owner exercised these functions, and as long as he exercised them, the estate was an essential part of the medieval state, its component cell. In Maitland's definition the estate became the state.

The role of the manor in government to some extent accounted for its owner's exalted position in society, but was not wholly identical with it. What gave the owner of the medieval estate his special position in society was the social and economic weight of the land-lordship itself. Manorial estate-owners were landlords to all the men who were not tenants-in-chief of the King. This conferred on them some authority over the land titles and the succession to land of the overwhelming mass of other men. Their authority over men and holdings of higher degree may not have been overwhelming, but their sway over men of the lowest standing, the humble peasants and agricultural labourers, frequently extended not only to the latter's land but to their persons, their ability to dispose of their time, labour, possessions and offspring. A theoretical *raison d'être* for the subjection of peasant cultivators and its justification could be seen in the need to secure for the landlord an income from land. Rents in money or in kind from peasant tenancies were an important ingredient of the lord's revenues. In addition, the lord could claim from many of his tenants, especially from the humblest or the most servile among them, their labour for a number of days per week or per season. These labour dues secured for the manor its supplies of labour at times and in places in which these supplies might not otherwise have been forthcoming. To this extent they were an essential prerequisite of manorial husbandry.

In practice this particular link between the manor and its dependent cultivators may not have been as universal or permanent as it is sometimes represented. We shall see later that the peasant's obligations to his lord, and his degree of dependence in general, could differ from region to region, from village to village and even from household to household in the same village. It also changed from time to time and eventually came very near to disappearing altogether. Nevertheless, dependent cultivation, and the lords' power behind it, were so characteristic of the prevailing system and were so seldom to be found in other, non-medieval, types of rural society, that they must be accepted as the distinguishing economic and social features, the true *differentia*, of the manorial order.

The manorial *differentia* of the large European estate were not of course as precocious as some of the estates themselves, but their roots went back very far, indeed to the very dawn of the middle ages. Nevertheless the precocity of the manorial order or indeed of the feudal system of which it was part has not been universally accepted by historians. On the continent the chronology of the feudal order and of the manorial characteristics has provoked controversies almost as stubborn as those provoked by the rise of the large estate.

The continental controversists have, as in the case of the large estate, been deeply involved with the views of the Teutonic tribal society. The historians who believed in the original equality of the Teutons also believed in their primordial freedom and independence. They were therefore bound to post-date the beginnings of feudalism. In their view the large estate in its feudalized form could not have become widespread until the closing phase of the Dark Ages, or even later.[4]

The post-dating of the manorial beginnings went well with the restricted conception of feudalism current among historians of the old school and still re-echoed in some modern writings on the legal and constitutional history of the middle ages. Some medieval historians have been inclined to confine the meaning of feudalism to the fief, and also to reduce the essence of the fief to its military functions. The rise of feudalism has accordingly been told as a story of the knighthood: the new class of professional soldiers replacing the popular levy of the tribal freemen. The latter were proving increasingly incapable of meeting the mounting military challenges of the time and, above all, the challenge of the new armament characteristic of the age, that of well-mounted and heavily armoured cavalry. This armament only professional soldiers could use; but in order to do so, they had to possess incomes large enough to pay for their expensive mounts, their costly armour and the assistants which the horses and the armament required. Above all they needed income sufficient to support them in their duties as soldiers. Hence the link between military service and the ownership of large blocks of landed property; hence also the impetus which the incessant warfare of the ninth and the tenth centuries is supposed to have given to the spread of the military fiefs and to the conversion of landed estates into military holdings.

Abroad, this delayed chronology of feudalism and its exclusive links with military functions are no longer taken for granted. In recent times historians, such as Marc Bloch, have refused to identify feudalism with the military fief and warfare as completely as most legal and constitutional historians had previously done.[5] It has always been realized that estates were granted and held in return for services, which were often administrative and legal as well as military, and that the estate burdened with services was a very old institution. The practice of temporary land grants conditional on the discharge of office, be it as exalted as that of the Merovingian or Carolingian counts, went back to the earliest centuries of German rule in the west. In the five centuries of the Dark Ages these grants and the estates they established underwent a two-fold change. On the one hand they multiplied and spread and were thus becoming the prevalent and characteristic form of landownership. On the other hand they were gradually ceasing to be conditional and temporary and were transformed into permanent and fully heritable property. The transformation was doubtless fostered by the break up of the Carolingian state and the waning of royal powers in the closing century or two of the period; but it was Charlemagne himself, at the height of his authority, who formally universalized the system. He did so in a famous edict (*Capitulare*) designed to systematize and tighten up the administration of the Empire.[5]

We must therefore conclude that in Europe as a whole the beginnings of the feudal order, considered as a system of government and a pattern of political power, went further back, and that its base was broader, than the older and more purely military versions of the story allowed for. The same conclusion must apply to the social features of feudalism that concerns us here most: the rise and spread of dependent cultivation. On the eve of the Germanic invasion the Roman rural society, more particularly in Gaul, contained a number of elements which bore a clear affinity to medieval serfs. As I have repeatedly stressed, there were slaves, many of whom had in the closing centuries of the Roman era been settled on separate holdings, and who thereby resembled and anticipated the servile villagers of the middle ages. In addition large numbers, perhaps most, of the nominally free cultivators had come to hold and to cultivate their lands as *coloni*, or tenants of substantial landowners to whom they were bounden by various dues and obligations. Other men, nominally free Roman citizens, frequently 'commended' themselves to 'patrons', or in other words placed themselves under the authority of other men, mostly patrician landowners whose 'clients' they thereby became. The Roman practice of commendation was very old, but it spread under the late Empire and in this way extended the pattern of social superiorities and inferiorities inherent in the relations of patron and clients.

We have also seen that on their part the German invaders brought with them into erstwhile Roman provinces customs and institutions which were by no means incompatible with dependent cultivation. Slavery had been anciently established in Germanic societies; and both before and after the invasions slaves could be found occupying separate holdings in the manner of the *servi casati* of Rome or servile villagers in the middle ages. 'Dependent' freemen were also to be found. Even before the Barbarian conquest was completed informal relations of dependence and subordination could arise between leaders and followers; in the course of the Dark Ages more formal contracts placed large numbers of freemen under the authority of great men. The authority often extended over persons and lands, since under the terms of most contracts men not only bound themselves personally to their lords or patrons but also transferred to the latter the superior title to their holdings. This in fact became the prevailing form and purpose of the numerous contracts of 'commendation' preserved in the monastic documents of the time.

No doubt the insecurity of the closing phase of the Dark Ages must have fostered the process of commendation and may moreover have enabled powerful men to reduce free men into dependent condition by sheer force. Both voluntary and enforced subordination were also easier to establish at a time when the ruling classes were acquiring the monopoly of military service while ordinary freemen were losing access to it. Yet there is every evidence to show that much earlier, by the eighth century at the latest, the development had already gone a long way. Charlemagne himself legitimised the subordination of ordinary freemen to feudal lords in his various *Capitulare* dealing with dues and obligations of tenants.

The other features of the system had also developed sufficiently early to establish in many parts of northern Europe, long before the end of the period, complexes of estates as fully manorialized as any manorial estate of later times, e.g. the eleventh or the twelfth centuries. In fact the medieval estate in erstwhile Gaul best known to historians is that of St Germain des Prés, described in remarkable detail and shown fully provided with all the manorial attributes in a survey (*Polyptyque*) of the eighth century.[6]

III

On this view of the feudal and manorial beginnings in western Europe as a whole it is difficult to see why the Anglo-Saxon estates should not have acquired their manorial characteristics in the same way or at about the same time as their counterparts on the continent. Such early evidence as there is certainly supports the presumption that they possessed many of the attributes which historians commonly recognize as manorial or feudal and similarly dominated the lives of their dependent tenants. Their powers over men may not have been quite as extensive as they were to be later, or more exactly, did not embrace areas or ranks of men as wide as those dominated by feudal estates in the manorialized regions of thirteenth-century England. These however were differences of degree. Scanty as is the evidence of the early Anglo-Saxon era it reveals a social order which historians of other periods would recognize as feudal.

The evidence of the order of society, although scarce and often indirect, is unmistakeable. The earliest collections of Anglo-Saxon laws, such as the Kentish Laws of the sixth century and the Laws of Ine of the seventh century, reveal the gradations of social rank comprising the very lowest whose economic condition and status were well below those which historians frequently assume to have been characteristic of ordinary free Saxon tribesmen. To begin with there were slaves and near-slaves. And if we accept the commonly held and highly plausible view that the ranks of medieval villeins were in part recruited from among erstwhile slaves settled as bondmen on villein holdings, we shall have no difficulty in finding in Anglo-Saxon documents all the precursory signs of the process. The Laws as well as such literary sources as Bede's *Historia Ecclesiastica* tell us not only of the existence of large bodies of slaves, but also of their 'freeing' and their settlement on land. Archaeological and topographical evidence including that of place names makes it possible to locate what must have been villages of erstwhile slaves. It does not therefore require too great a stretch of imagination or too free a use of evidence to link up these humblest—slave and ex-slave—layers of Anglo-Saxon England with the most inferior grades of villeins of a later age: the *bondi, nativi, servi* of the thirteenth-century villages.

Historians however commonly assume that medieval villeins descended not only from erstwhile slaves but also from freemen reduced by the pressure of circumstances into dependence on powerful men. In so far as this process took the form of voluntary or quasi-voluntary submission to the authority of powerful men ('commendations') it can also be traced to the earliest phases of Anglo-Saxon rule. The English documents of land leases and land grants involving commendation are much less numerous than the similar documents abroad. The practice however left its traces in the charter evidence; and, relative to the distribution of the charter evidence through the six centuries of Anglo-Saxon history, the traces are no fewer in the earlier centuries than in the later ones. We must therefore assume that the process of social differentiation, and the resulting growth of a large class of dependent cultivators —villeins, serfs and semi-free 'sokemen'—proceeded all through the Anglo-Saxon era, and that from this point of view society was always manorialized to some extent.

How far it had gone by the end of the Anglo-Saxon era is strikingly demonstrated by the *Rectitudines Singularum Personarum*, a unique document of the eleventh century setting out the rights and dues pertaining to different ranks of society. The order of ranks, their numbers and conditions, are those of a fully manorialized society, as described in the pre-tenth-century surveys on the continent and in the twelfth and thirteenth-century surveys in England. With the feudal lords (*gesiths*) at the top, the knights (*geneats*) and ordinary freemen (*ceorls*) in the middle and the semi-servile hands (*geburs*) at the bottom, the resulting image of society appears to be as fully manorialized and feudalized as it was ever to be.[7]

The emergence and the development of a social order appropriate to the manorialized estate does not of course prove that the estate itself was in fact manorialized, i.e had acquired the various attributes of feudal authority. We possess however a certain amount of direct evidence of the 'manorialization' of landownership which, though sparse, is very suggestive: suggestive because it happens to be unanimous. Most students of the period assume that the power and authority of the estate over its dependents stemmed from the functions and powers which attached to landownership. These functions and powers in their turn are supposed to stem from the 'service' character of early land-grants, i.e. from their being linked with the exercise of some administrative or military function. If these assumptions are right they will justify the early dating of the manorialized estate in Anglo-Saxon England, since 'service' estates with juridical and administrative rights attaching to them will be found reflected in Anglo-Saxon land charters however early. The land charter relating to grants of land to religious houses and to or by the greater men frequently mention or imply service obligations or else impose such obligations by virtue of the grants. In spite of its scarcity the cumulative effect of the evidence is to establish a strong presumption of a feudal order taking shape in the earliest phases of the Anglo-Saxon era, and developing gradually in the subsequent four or five centuries.

So early and so continuous are the instances of feudal and manorial incidents attached to land that it is difficult to see why some historians should have found it necessary and possible to telescope the development of feudal landholding into the century or two of Danish invasion. The only plausible reason for doing so is one of military necessity. The wars, we are told, imposed heavy military obligations which only armed professional knights could discharge, who had to be remunerated by land carrying the obligation of service. By the same token ordinary freemen lost their military function and thereby also their status in society and eventually also their independence and freedom.

Plausible as this argument may seem, it is no more than an argument, since evidence of the wholesale creation of armed knights during the Danish wars or of a wholesale reduction in the status of freemen is as scarce or even scarcer than the evidence of the early appearance of feudal incidents. Yet even on general grounds the argument is by no means incontestable and has in fact been contested. Some historians refuse to restrict the essence of feudalism to its military aspects and to account for its evolution solely by changes in the conduct of wars. They do not therefore consider the men who defended the country against the Danish invaders as the main, still less the sole, begetters of the feudal order. Similarly other historians have found bishops and great abbots at the turn of the eleventh and twelfth century maintaining military establishments composed not of knights holding military fees but of whole-time soldiers forming part of the episcopal or abbatial households. Similarly historians of a still later period—the late twelfth and the early thirteenth centuries—have pointed out that at that time garrison duties and other regular military functions were frequently performed by soldiers serving whole-time for wages. This evidence is all much later than the Anglo-Saxon period, but it demonstrates that knights' fees, though part of the established military system, need not always have provided the sole means of meeting the military demands of society. The use of full-time professional soldiers, remunerated in ways other than grants of service lands, was not necessarily a sign of the decay of the fief but evidence of a military system more varied and more flexible than the conventional theory of feudal hosts. No doubt the military demands of the ninth century and the economic and social stresses caused by the invasion were bound to have some effect, above all on the condition of men of somewhat lower rank: the freemen and freeholders of humbler status. The general insecurity at the times and in the places at which the effects of the invasion were worst, and the burdens of the Danegeld, may have stimulated the process of commendation and thereby helped to swell the ranks of the semi-free and not-quite-free. But the ranks were already there and may have been there since time immemorial. Similarly the possessors or the recipients of larger estates may also have found their position strengthened and their status heightened, but their greater strength and importance need not have created wholly new situations. It certainly was not a wholly new departure in English economic and social development. The manorialization of the large estate was completed by the end of the Anglo-Saxon era, but by all appearances it had begun at the very earliest of the era and was far advanced by the time the Danish wars gave it its final spurt.

References

1. Alfons Dopsch, *The Economic and Social Foundations of European Civilization*, English trans. (1937), Ch. 1, 'Influence of Contemporary Movements on Historical Research'.

2. Alfons Dopsch, *Economic and Social Foundations*, Chs. II, IV. S. Dill, *Roman Society in Gaul in the Merovingian Age* (1926), pp. 60–63, 75, 218–23, 226–8. James Westfall Thompson, *The Economic and Social History of Medieval Europe* (1928), pp. 203–208.

3. In England the conventional version is presented at its fullest by Paul Vinogradoff, *English Society in the Eleventh Century* (1908); and *The Growth of the Manor* (1905); and more recently in F. M. Stenton, *Anglo-Saxon England* (1943). For a more recent and wholly different view see T. H. Aston, 'The Origin of the Manor in England', *Trans. Roy. Hist. Soc.*, 5th Ser., VIII (1966).

4. The alternative version of the continental development in its most radical formulation will be found in A. Dopsch, *Wirtschaftsgeschichte der Karolingerzeit*, 2nd ed. (1921), pp. 202–322.

5. Marc Bloch, *Feudal Society*, English trans. (1961), Chs. XI, XII, XXI, XXIV, XXV and the Introduction by M. M. Postan.

6. Auguste Lognon (ed.), *Polyptyque de l'Abbaye de Saint-Germain des Prés* (1895).

7. 'Rectitudines Singularum Personarum', in David C. Douglas and George W. Greenway, *English Historical Documents*, Vol. II, pp. 813–816.

6 The Manor: Variations and Changes

I

In recent writings on agricultural history the prevailing tendency has been to consider the ancient notions of the ever-present and all-important manor as an out-of-date generalization. The first breach in the ancient manorial generalization was made by Stenton's study of North Danelaw. Stenton's lead was followed by other regional historians, who drew our attention to parts of England where manors were few, or where manorial lordships did not imprint themselves strongly upon the economy and the society. In successive local studies, East Anglia, Kent, parts of the west midlands, the northern counties of England immediately south and north of the Pennines, as well as counties on the Scottish borders and the Welsh marshes, have all been revealed to us as wholly or largely non-manorial. Still more recently the historians of south-west England, above all of central and northern Devonshire and of Cornwall, have depicted an economy in which the powers of the manor and its function were not the same as in other parts of England.[1]

The immediate result of these studies was to create the impression that all the peripheries of medieval England were innocent of manors, and that only the core of the country, the anciently and densely settled places of the south and the midlands, conformed to the traditional image of a manorialized countryside. But even this residual area of manorialized England has not wholly escaped the destructive effects of recent researchers. A Russian scholar, Professor Kosminsky, in his study of the Hundred Rolls of 1279, has demonstrated that even within the inner core of manorial England there were to be found areas, such as entire hundreds in Oxfordshire and Warwickshire, in which the hold of the manor and its lord over the village lands and tenants was rudimentary.[2] In this way the famous dictum of 'manors, manors everywhere' has been, or appears to have been, wholly demolished.

Fortunately we are now sufficiently far removed from both the creators of the conventional image of classical manors and from its earliest detractors to see more clearly the extent to which the manorial generalization has or has not survived the effect of later studies. What emerges from this latter-day view is a pattern of villages and estates in which manors conforming to the classical type were few and far between, but in which manors of a kind were invariably to be found. Many of the manors did not dominate the countryside as much as the typical manor was supposed to have done, and had fewer functions or a looser organization; but manors they nevertheless were. The result of recent researches has been not to banish the manor but merely to bring out the variety of manorial types, and the ways in which most manors diverged from their classical image.

The most important variations were linked with the divergences in the respective functions of demesne and dependent tenants. We have seen that the 'ideal' manor was essentially bilateral: the lands composing it and the income it yielded were made up of two distinct parts. One part of the land would be cultivated by the lord himself as his 'home farm' and commonly described as his 'demesne', while the other would be held by his tenants for rent and be cultivated by them. The revenue which the landlords derived from their estates was also bilateral, since it came from two sources: the direct yield of the demesne and the rents which he received from his tenants. This bilateral composition of the manor and of its revenues was the true hallmark of the typical manor. In an 'ideal' manor the demesne would be of a size capable of being served by its tenants, while the land in tenancy would be large enough and the tenants numerous enough to provide the demesne with the labour it required. This essential link between the demesne and the tenancy was not much weaker in the many manors whose demands on the tenants were no more than seasonal—harvesting, sheep-shearing, winter cartage.

It is in this respect however—the strength of the link binding the demesne with the tenants—that manors differed from each other most significantly. The relative importance of the demesne as a source of revenue, the extent to which it was cultivated by the labour of tenants and the degree to which the services of the tenants were geared to the demesne, varied from manor to manor. It would in fact be possible to arrange the medieval manors in a series according to the respective roles of their demesnes and rents. The series would begin with manors wholly composed of lands in tenancy and yielding nothing but rents; it would end with manors all made up of demesne land and yielding all their revenue in the form of the direct profits of cultivation. Most villages and estates however will be found in the intermediate ranges of the series, since they possessed some demesne and some land in tenancy, and derived their incomes from both rents and the produce of the 'home farm'. Where they differed is in the proportion and the manner in which these two elements were combined.

II

In considering the varying combinations of the two elements, the regional differences would be the ones to strike the attention of a student most forcibly. Some of these differences were embedded in the entire history of England's regions and, like most other regional characteristics, reached back to the hoary pre-English past of the tribes which composed the invading Germanic hosts. Professor Stenton has taught us to derive the social and economic peculiarities of the 'Danelaw' areas of eastern England from the social structure and customs of the Danish settlers; Mr Jolliffe has similarly traced the social peculiarities of Kent and Northumbria to the social pattern imported into these regions by the Jutes and the Northumbrian Saxons. More recently Professor Homans has argued that a similar connection existed between the management of medieval fields and the social and legal systems in Suffolk and Norfolk on the one hand and the tribal customs of the Frisians who settled there on the other.[3]

However, these regional differences with their tribal implications, even if they were accepted as established, would provide us with only one of the designs composing the manorial pattern of rural England. Even before Stenton and his followers drew our attention to the different social and economic systems brought into medieval England by the invading tribes and races, the geographers had isolated certain regional differences in the shape of villages and types of manor and their relation to the purely physical features of local landscape and climate. In their view a typical manor with its large demesne and numerous tenantry was most appropriate to the predominantly arable plains of central and southern England. By the same reasoning the hilly uplands were unfavourable to the formation of typical manors with large arable demesnes and a numerous servile tenantry, and were characterized by small hamlets and pastoral husbandry and a relatively free peasantry.

Many, perhaps most, of the local differences in manorial types could be related to the differences in landownership itself. For landlords differed very greatly in their needs and their function in society. Some of the differences were purely personal and accidental. Some lords were more efficient than others and anxious to build up and to conserve their possessions, others were profligate; some were resident, others were often absent; some were compelled to maintain large households, others were not. These differences were of course highly individual and often accidental. It is nevertheless possible to discern a certain regularity in the manner in which these differences occurred, and to group them into types or categories of landownership, each distinguished by a characteristic mode of exploiting land.

One such group most frequently singled out by historians is that of ecclesiastical landlords, but on close inspection it will be found that ecclesiastical landlords did not form a single category. True enough, manors closest to the ideal type were most frequently to be found on Benedictine estates. The predominance of typical manors on these estates is partly a matter of age and location. The Benedictine houses were among the most ancient monastic foundations, and were therefore apt to be sited in the most anciently settled areas of medieval England. But the main reasons for the conventional structure of their manors will be found in their material needs. The Benedictine monasteries housed resident communities of monks which were frequently large and as a rule grew in size and numbers in the course of the late twelfth and thirteenth centuries. The numbers of monks in the greater Benedictine Abbeys, like those of Peterborough, Glastonbury and Bury St Edmunds, could be very large; but the monks formed only a part of the monastic households. The latter also contained servants and attendants whose numbers exceeded those of the monks themselves. Moreover the Benedictine monks enjoyed what by medieval standards were high and rising levels of sustenance. Their direct requirements of food for themselves and their servants and of fodder for their horses were great and growing and could best be safeguarded by direct liveries from their manors. Hence their tendency to maintain functioning demesnes on as many estates as were necessary *ad victum monachorum*. On the other hand they also needed ready money and could not restrict their revenues to the direct produce of their home farms. They and their abbots were regular buyers of cloth, vestments, condiments, books and other merchandise; they also bore a heavy burden of taxes to the pope and the king. Above all ready money was also required for their building operations.

These requirements of ready money could be met in two ways. One was the sale of agricultural surpluses, but the other was rents and other rent-like payments of tenants. Hence the emphasis most Benedictine houses in the late twelfth and thirteenth centuries laid both on their demesnes and on their rent revenues. They seldom provided themselves with manors wholly or mainly made up of demesne, but they also maintained their demesne cultivation more continually and for a longer period than most other landlords. Moreover, like other institutional owners, they were conservative and traditional in their administrative methods, and were for this reason alone more determined and better able to maintain on their demesnes the traditional system of villeinage.

However, not all ecclesiastical landlords ran their estates on the Benedictine model. The typical Cistercian estate was a 'grange', a property wholly made up and run as a demesne and cultivated by *conversi*, i.e lay brethren of the order. The Cistercian rule enjoined the monks to settle in places undefiled by daily contact with the mundane world. They accordingly tried to establish their houses either on empty lands beyond the anciently settled areas of medieval England, such as the underpopulated dales of Yorkshire or the Welsh marches, or else to create empty sites for themselves by forcing out the lay population in their neighbourhood. In these conditions they could not derive their income from rents of tenants on their estates, or depend on the labour of their tenants for the cultivation of their demesnes.

At the other extreme of ecclesiastical land ownership were the estates of the military orders: the Templars and the Hospitallers. These orders were not as large in England as they were in some other countries, but they were wealthy, and what is more, they were run mostly for money incomes and were composed very largely of tenancies, as a rule widely dispersed, held wholly for rent. In the course of the thirteenth century the Templars reclaimed and colonized vast areas of land round Temple Brewer and Temple Newsam, in Lincolnshire and Yorkshire and elsewhere. But even the large and compact estates thus created were also conducted mainly as sources of money incomes. It is therefore not surprising that, when in 1185 the Templars estates were surveyed all over England, the survey should have revealed a vast complex of properties, some of which were grouped and managed as manors, but nearly all of which appeared to yield their income mainly in the form of rents.[4]

Finally there were the episcopal estates which as a rule resembled the great lay estates. The episcopal households had to be supplied with food and fodder; but they also required large money incomes to maintain the Bishops and their retinue on the 'baronial' scale which befitted them. Hence the inclination to maintain the income from rents and also to run the demesnes both for the sake of provisions and as sources of money income.[5]

The differences in manorial types on ecclesiastical estates were matched by those on the lay estates. The differences between types of lay manors could be more profound than those which marked them off, taken together, from ecclesiastical estates. At one extreme were the possessions of smaller lay landowners and wealthier freeholders of non-military rank; most of them men whom the chronicles might describe as *agrarii milites*, or husbandmen-knights who worked their demesnes themselves and lived off the produce of their land. A Petition to Parliament of 1368, the time of the great debate over agricultural wages, purports to speak on behalf of the smaller proprietors, whom it defines as men who subsist on the produce of their lands and have no villeins to serve them (*vivent par geynerie de leur terres .... et que nont ... villeins par eix servir*). Our sources can tell us very little about the daily routine on diminutive estates of this type, since most of them were too humble and were run, so to speak, too informally to have kept and left behind them any elaborate documentary records. But the *Inquisitiones Post Mortem*, i.e. official surveys of properties of deceased tenants-in-chief, or the great national surveys like the Domesday Book or the Hundred Rolls of 1279, record them by the score.

Needless to say the smaller estates themselves varied according to their size, their needs, the predilections of their owners and their geographical location. Larger knightly estates, like those of the Pelham family in Sussex, the Fitz Hammes in Buckinghamshire, or the Beauchamps in the South Midlands, would also be greatly dependent on their demesne, but being fairly large also possessed some rent-yielding properties.

Manorial properties in which rents played a very important part will be found among the great honorial complexes which in some cases, such as that of the de Lacys and the dukes of Lancaster, contained hundreds of manors in all parts of the country. Although on all these estates functioning demesnes could be found until quite late in the middle ages, a very considerable share (on the earl of Cornwall's estates, the bulk) of the revenues, even in the thirteenth century, came from rents and feudal rights.

What distinguished these estates from those of humbler laymen and resembled the estates of bishops and abbots was the managerial continuity conferred upon them by their 'conciliar' administration. By the middle of the thirteenth century, and possibly earlier, most of the great 'honorial' estates had come to be administered by officials of baronial councils, and thereby acquired most of the features of institutionalized landownership commonly associated with ecclesiastical properties.[6] This insulated them from some of the vagaries of absentee ownership. This they were able to do not only because conciliar administration was more efficient, but also because in the lord's scale of requirements money figured more prominently than his needs for food and fodder.

So much for the differences in manorial types related to the variations in the character of landownership itself. These differences were sometimes overlaid and conceded to differences related to the antiquity of the estates. The typical manors were as a rule the old ones: anciently established and therefore bearing the marks of the early medieval past. The endowment of the Benedictine abbeys and of the great episcopal estates was largely made up of old vills in anciently settled parts of the country, and this is one of the reasons why typical manors are so often found among them. On the other hand estates more recently carved out from the waste were less likely to conform to the 'ideal' proportion of demesne and villeinage. Thus the abbots of Peterborough's manors of Belasize or Novum Locum, established in the thirteenth and the early fourteenth centuries in the previously unsettled Rockingham Forest, could not be sufficiently provided with dependent tenants and were not thereafter run as conventional manors. They were either managed as 'granges', i.e. all-demesnes cultivated by labourers hired or drafted from outside, or else let out in rent-paying tenements.

In general the dates of settlement and the chronology of the local agrarian origin were bound to imprint themselves on the social structure of a region and on the types of manors to be found within it.

III

The effects of age on the composition and management of individual manors revealed itself most clearly in those differences of manorial type which were not so much local as historical, i.e. evolved through time. They were differences in the organization of estates from period to period irrespective of their location or ownership; and they could best be observed not by comparing estate with estate at the same period of time, as we have so far done, but by comparing the conditions of the same estates at different dates.

Generally speaking the changes through time proceeded everywhere in more or less the same direction: that from demesne to rent. A number of causes combined to set up a general drift in this direction. The most potent factor behind it could best be described as 'managerial'. The purely administrative difficulty of running a demesne economy efficiently were those of supervision and control. Where the demesne happened to be close to the Lord's administrative headquarters, he or his chief officials (stewards) could supervise it regularly without much difficulty. He could also in this case draw his supplies without the expense and risk of transport over long distances. But a large number of manorial estates were too far removed from the lord's physical presence and had to be left in the charge of local agents occasionally controlled by intermittent audits or visitations. Control as remote and intermittent as this offered great opportunities to dishonest bailiffs and reeves. Landlords therefore tried from time to time to relieve themselves of their managerial risks by letting out the demesnes as going concerns, or else by dissolving them altogether into peasant tenancies.

A drift towards rents and away from the direct management of demesnes could also result from the cumulative action of piecemeal concessions. From time to time on most manors individual villeins were freed or their holdings might be enfranchized by purchase or an act of grace; from time to time small portions of demesne might be let out for rent or even sold. But once villein services were foregone or the demesne acres were alienated, they could not easily be regained. In this way the manorial structures on many estates could wither away by the slow accumulation of small changes.

More purely historical, less dependent on the accidental and piecemeal attrition of the lord's mastership, were the changes brought about by more general shifts in the historical scene. In some periods the historical circumstances helped to accelerate the movement towards rents; in others they could slow it down and, for a time, even arrest it altogether. Direct management of demesnes was easiest in periods when the legal and political regime was so stable and so well ordered that lords could easily exercise their control over their local officials. If and when these orderly conditions coincided with high prices for agricultural produce, or low wages, or both, or when transport and trade in agricultural produce proceeded smoothly and safely, there was every additional inducement for the more efficient landlords not only to maintain the output of their demesnes but also to try and expand it. Such appear to have been the conditions in certain periods during the thirteenth century. On the other hand direct management became more difficult and less profitable at times when the general conditions worsened: when prices and costs moved so as to reduce the profits of exploitation, or when law and order so deteriorated as to impede the exercise of the lord's authority over his agents and tenants. Such was the general situation in the mid-decades of the twelfth century and again in the second half of the fourteenth and the greater part of the fifteenth centuries.

It is therefore possible to distinguish at least three phases in the development of the manorial economy. The earlier period, covering the greater part of the twelfth century, when the movement away from the demesne proceeded fast; the thirteenth century when for several decades the movement was slowed down, or arrested or even reversed; and the period after the middle of the fourteenth century when it was resumed again and eventually brought about the complete dissolution of the manorial economy.

Let us begin with the twelfth-century retrenchments of the demesne. Most manorial surveys of the late twelfth and early thirteenth centuries (some eleven out of fourteen or fifteen such surveys known to historians) record numbers of peasant holdings recently carved out of the demesne. On most of these estates, perhaps on as many as nine out of the fifteen known to us, the inroads into the demesne were too widespread or were on a scale too large to be wholly explained as by-products of the slow and piecemeal movement towards rents. Something must have happened in the general setting in the middle decades of the twelfth century to accelerate the movement away from the demesne.

In the period between, say, 1130 and 1175 the conditions unfavourable to the direct management of the demesne can easily be identified. These were years of civil war between Stephen and the Empress Matilda, of the disruption of central government and near-anarchy in the countryside. Both sides recruited their parties by subinfeudating local followers and by setting them up on newly carved out estates. But the worst effects of party war and of weakened government were to let loose upon the country a swarm of strong men capable of preying upon their neighbours. The more purely economic conditions were to match. We have seen that such evidence of prices as we have suggests that differences in prices from region to region were greater than in the late twelfth or thirteenth centuries. This in its turn may have reflected the imperfections of inter-regional traffic—imperfections which must have grown because the king's highways were insecure and the peace of the market cross was in constant jeopardy.[7]

In these conditions, the lords could have been expected to do all they could to rid themselves of direct managerial responsibility. The middle of the twelfth century was consequently the period of wholesale 'farming' of manors—an arrangement whereby lords let their demesnes and sometimes their entire manors to middlemen for a fixed rental of money and food, or money alone.

The farming of demesnes was not of course a wholly new device. It does not require a great degree of economic sophistication or an advanced stage of economic development to demonstrate to recipients of uncertain and fluctuating revenues the advantages they might in certain circumstances derive from letting out the revenues for fixed payments. It is therefore not surprising that 'farms' for 'payments certain' in substitution of fluctuating incomes should have been found in all periods of history for which documentary evidence is available. The type of farming commonest in pre-medieval records is that of taxes (the practice was widespread in the Roman Empire and was probably known in even earlier times). But the farming of estate revenues was also prevalent in pre-medieval times in almost every country. In medieval England the evidence of 'farms' similarly reaches to the earliest centuries. It could be detected in the various tenurial contracts of the late Anglo-Saxon era, and must have always existed on royal estates. Vinogradoff and Lennard have argued convincingly that manorial 'values' recorded in the Domesday Book were those of manorial incomes when at farm. It is also probable that since the very earliest times manors, especially monastic ones, which appeared to be directly managed by local agents, were in fact required to deliver fixed amounts of food and money, and were thus to all intents and purposes 'farmed'.

There is little doubt, however, that farming contracts became more general in the twelfth century. The twelfth-century farms which first drew the attention of medieval historians were those of the shires and their boroughs (*firma burghi*): the latter representing an arrangement whereby the burgesses collectively rendered to the king fixed annual sums in lieu of the fluctuating yield of earlier imposts. Farms were now to be found on most manors on nearly all the estates for which mid-twelfth-century evidence is available. Moreover our documents frequently refer to them in a manner which clearly suggests that they had been instituted at some twelfth-century date or somewhat earlier. But even where the records happen to be silent on this point the early history of the manors, their creation and stocking, as far as it can be reconstructed, would be unintelligible except on the assumption that some of the landlords who farmed out their demesnes in the twelfth century had at one time managed them directly. Thus the farming contracts preserved in the records of the Canons of St Paul's, or the early twelfth-century surveys of the manors of the abbeys of Glastonbury and Ramsey, bear clear reflections of somewhat earlier times when the estates had not yet been at farm.

The uncertainties and risks of direct management in the twelfth century were obviously the circumstances most conducive to the practice of farming, though other conditions of the time may also have favoured it. Some historians have linked the practice with the desire of monastic administrators to secure for themselves a regular render of provisions. The possible etymological link between the terms 'farm' and 'feorm', the latter being an Anglo-Saxon term for food, lends additional strength to this hypothesis. Yet however strong this additional inducement was, it does not account for the great movement towards 'farms' and does not do full justice to the main function of a 'farm'. The most likely etymological link of the term is with 'firma' in the sense of 'fixed' or 'settled'. The fact that it was also used to describe fixed renders of king's taxes shows that the connection between farm and food was largely accidental. What makes the connection even less close is that, whereas the monastic needs of food were no greater in the middle of the twelfth century than in the preceding and the following centuries, the farming of monastic demesnes had apparently been less general before

1125 and, as we shall see presently, was to be given up by most houses in the thirteenth century.

We must therefore assume that the main reason why 'farming' spread in the mid-twelfth century is that the conditions of the time were unfavourable to the direct management of demesnes. We must not, of course, exclude altogether the possibility that some landlords were led to adopt farms by desires more positive, less so to speak defensive, than the mere wish to safeguard themselves from the risk of uncertain and fluctuating revenues.[8] What these desires were and how realizable they were is difficult to say. Indeed in some places the pursuit of certain and stable revenues may also have proved vain, or at any rate very costly. Many of the 'farmers' who took over the running of the manors proved incapable and unwilling to protect the lands and the equipment they took over. Some were obviously predatory. The depredations of farmers like Simon of Felstead, who farmed the Suffolk manors of the Trinity of Caen, or of Richard Ruffus, who farmed wards' manors in Soham and Kimbolton, do not stand out as exceptional.[9] Is there any wonder that on estates like those of Glastonbury or Ramsey, for which we possess surveys for both the first and the second halves of the century, the documents should record the impoverishment of the farmed demesnes and recall 'the time of Henry I', when most of the manors were still directly managed, as the golden age of the estates' prosperity?

Farming was often the choice of a lesser evil: the substitution of waste by farmers for the peculations of lords' bailiffs. In other words some twelfth-century demesnes suffered losses or lower profits whether farmed or not. The losses, however, were the lord's, not necessarily his tenants', since the difficulties of running the demesnes could redound to the advantage of the villagers. On the twelfth-century estates which were not farmed as a whole, some of the demesne lands, or even entire demesnes, passed into the hands of the villagers. Numerous servile holdings were commuted to money rent, and labour services were released either because the demesne was contracting or because the prevailing unrest and lawlessness were making it impossible to enforce the obligations of villeins.

IV

The fortunes of the demesne showed signs of revival in the last two decades of the twelfth century. This they may have done because the historical circumstances were more propitious. In spite of recurrent political upheavals, such as the Baronial Wars in Henry III's reign or the interlude of weak and unsettled government in Edward II's time, the period between, say, 1175 and 1325 was one of relative peace and order. The organization of government and justice appeared to continue the progress begun under Henry II. It may well be that even in this period border raids and the passage of armies in the northern counties and on the Welsh marches were ruinous to both landlords and peasants, but elsewhere life was relatively secure, traffic on the roads unmolested and the king's law enforced. The politics and governance of the time were thus propitious to the lord's control over his estates and to his disposal of his produce.

The economic conditions were also auspicious. As the population continued to increase supplies of labour were getting more abundant, money wages remained stable and real wages were falling. They were falling because prices of agricultural produce were rising—rapidly until the second and third decades of the century and gently thereafter.

There was thus every reason why landlords should have found direct exploitation of their demesnes easier and more profitable, and why those landlords who could terminate their farming agreement or regain the demesnes they had lost should have tried to do so. In the period between 1185 and 1225 most monastic landlords, such as the abbots of Ramsey and Glastonbury, were able to re-establish their authority over some of the estates seized from them by military gangsters, even though they may not always have succeeded in regaining possession of all the lands they had lost at the time of the disorders.

The revival of the demesne went further than the mere resumption of direct management by landlords. It manifested itself in a variety of ways: in the higher efficiency of its management, in a more rational use of its land, and sometimes also in accretions to its area. Many manors and demesnes within them began to expand again. Here and there parcels of demesne land continued to be let out to tenants, but on most estates the acreages lost to the demesne by letting were more than compensated for by new conquests of the waste and sometimes by acquisitions through purchase. This should not, however, be taken to mean that the shedding of demesne acres and the sub-letting of demesne fields ceased altogether. As I shall stress again presently the demesnes, especially on the larger and more progressive estates, were now run with greater efficiency than ever; and it was a sign of greater efficiency that here and there some lands should have been let out to rent. Poorer lands (e.g. those permanently given over to oats) could now be let out or abandoned altogether merely because their yields descended below the level at which the lords considered them worth cultivating; others were let out not because yields were falling but because rents were rising. A rational and profit-conscious manager of a manor would repeatedly be confronted with the choice of bounty: to let or to plough. Both the ploughing and letting might promise higher profits; but when with the growing shortage of land and with higher rents the letting alternative appeared more promising, the manorial lord could decide to let, even though his demesne was more profitable than ever.

Of the other manifestations of manorial revival, none were more obvious or effective than the administrative innovation of management, the most important element in which was the introduction of accounts. The manorial account in the form historians know it is a late twelfth- or thirteenth-century innovation: the earliest full-fledged account known to us being that of the bishops of Winchester of 1208–9. In the course of the subsequent thirty or forty years the formalized bailiffs' accounts came to be adopted on most estates of any size. In spite of many local variations, the surviving accounts follow the same largely uniform pattern, and this uniformity of accounting procedure shows how anxious the manorial administrators were to learn from one another, and how speedily administrative lessons spread fom lordship to lordship.

The lessons came from certain much-used sources. One such source was the formularies designed to teach the manorial administrators the art of manorial accounting. But historians have always known that accounting was not the only art which improving landlords could now learn from books. Treatises on estate management, such as those of Walter of Henley, the *Rules* of Robert de Grosseteste, the *Senechaucy* and the *Fleta* were all composed during this period. In addition manorial documents of some abbots, e.g. those of St Peter's Gloucester or Christ Church Priory, Canterbury, contain local sets of rules for efficient management, or excerpts from well-known treatises on farm management. The age was one of 'improving landlords' obviously interested in the rational exploitation of their demesnes.[10]

On the other hand the signs of economic buoyancy which the student of modern enterprises would look for—higher investment and technological innovation—are not exhibited equally clearly though they are not altogether absent.

Generally speaking new investment in the form prevailing in modern enterprises—that of higher outlay on equipment—was not and could not have been very high. This failure of investment was to some extent the fault of the manor and its lord. Considering the resources at its disposal the average manorial estate invested relatively little. Their rate of investment was low and irregular. Most of the investments revealed in our documents went into livestock. But even though these investments could sometimes be quite high they were not cumulative; they did not grow much in the course of the thirteenth century and were not apparently designed to compensate for the slowing down of reclamations.

On most estates these investments came in fits and starts, and spurts of investment into stock often succeeded years or sequences of years when livestock was depleted by sheep murrains or marauding raids by troops and bands. On episcopal estates from which much of our evidence comes the numbers of livestock fluctuated in accordance with the rules which governed the takeover of estates by incumbents. It was an established rule of succession to episcopal estates that the executors of an outgoing bishop were accountable for no more than the stock he had received on his accession. It was therefore the established policy of the executors to liquidate all the increments to the stock made during the deceased bishop's tenure. Starting from these low levels each incoming bishop proceeded to build up his stocks until they reached the point approximately as high as the previous highest, but no higher than that.

Monastic estates were perhaps afflicted by even worse bouts of disinvestment during the vacancies which intervened between the death or translation of one abbot and the succession of another. The royal commissioners who often administered monastic estates during the vacancies were 'out for quick profits' and were apt to make their profit by running down the capital equipment, including the flocks and herds.

So much for the trends or rather the absence of trends in the history of ecclesiastical livestock. The probabilities are that on the lay estates continuous capital accumulation was also impeded by forfeitures, by the administration of escheators and by frequent transfers resulting from grants, inheritance, jointure and dowry. We now know that by the end of the thirteenth century the largest honorial estates came to be administered by baronial councils able to ensure them from the worst penalties of discontinuous ownership and from predatory administration by royal officials. But not all the lay estates acquired the blessing of conciliar administration, and even those which acquired them were seldom able or willing to increase their investments in agricultural improvements.

The probability is that, even in periods when estates were well administered, the prevailing values and conventions of upper class life would have prevented their administrators from dedicating a large proportion of revenues to progressive improvements. We shall have occasion to emphasize again that the building of castles, expenditure on retinues and on various attributes of status, must throughout the middle ages have absorbed the lion's share of estate profits. Now and again there appeared among the landlords provident estate builders, and there were more of them in the thirteenth century than in any other period. But for most of the land-owners, be they never so provident, the preferred road to economic aggrandizement lay through the purchase of land.

Needless to say, some productive investments were undertaken. Documents tell us of investments into estate buildings such as barns and byres, and into permanent dykes and fences. At the turn of the thirteenth and fourteenth centuries, when holdings began to fall vacant in large numbers, and stayed vacant for long periods of time, we can find some landlords—the Earls of Lancaster on their Staffordshire and Derbyshire estates or the Earls of Stafford on their Gloucestershire estates—investing continually in enclosures and conversions of vacant arable holdings into pasture. But in the thirteenth century, instances of large scale enclosures were very few and far between and the largest single enterprises requiring massive investment were, as a rule, connected with reclamations. The Bishop of Winchester's outlay on the assarting and the building of the new village of Losanger, the Abbots of Peterborough's expenditure on the new 'granges' at Belasize and Novum Locum, the Abbot of Eynsham's investment into a new borough and the colonizing enterprises of the Abbots of Evesham are the most obvious examples to spring to mind.

Though not concerned with improvements of older land, these enterprises may be cited to show that medieval landlords were able and sometimes willing to undertake projects requiring the application of capital. Yet even at their costliest these enterprises did not make great inroads into the landlord's wealth. More significant still is that investments did not rise towards the end of our period and were not so timed as to make up for the dwindling opportunities of reclamation. More particularly the account of the manors which expanded most by reclamations in the earlier part of the thirteenth century, such as Witney, Brent or Zoy, contain no evidence of large-scale improvements in occupied lands at the end of that or the beginning of the following century when reclamations were petering out.

In general, on most medieval estates the volume and the cost of agricultural investment varied from epoch to epoch, and the variations as a rule could be put down, as the monastic chronicles invariably do, to the personalities and circumstances of individual landlords. A spendthrift or negligent landlord will be found spending less on manorial buildings, on enclosures or bridges, than a provident one. So also would a bishop or an abbot operating at a time of high taxation, such as the period of heavy papal impositions in the early thirteenth century or the still heavier royal impositions in the opening phases of the Hundred Years War. It is thus very difficult to discern a consecutive trend in the records of agricultural investments of landlords. Greater use of capital was obviously not the landlords' most effective response to the thirteenth-century opportunities for greater economic activity.

Some response there nevertheless was; and where it occurred it could not fail to improve the fortunes of manorial landownership. The effects of new investment, such as there was, of additional acreage and of improved management could best be judged by the evidence of manorial profits. On some estates profits remained fairly stable, but historians have so far found hardly any estates on which profits consistently declined during the period, and can cite many estates on which profits were rising all through or during the greater part of the century. The rising trend of profits on estates of the Bishop of Winchester between 1209 and 1340 lifted them by at least 30 per cent. The corresponding returns of the Abbey of Glastonbury are less continuous, but they indicate a rise of the same magnitude. Some of the rise was made possible by the buoyancy of rents and miscellaneous manorial imposts. Some of it however came from the higher profits of cultivation; and this, in its turn, was due partly to the rising prices and partly to larger sales and higher sums realized for demesne grain and wool.

V

On most estates the rising trend showed signs of levelling off, or even of turning downwards, at some time before 1348. For as far as we can judge the phase of buoyant demesne cultivation came to an end at some time between the end of the thirteenth century and the outbreak of the Black Death in 1348. On most estates for which evidence is available the general prosperity of manorial land-ownership characteristic of the thirteenth century was beginning to slacken as the century neared its end, more particularly after a sequence of very bad harvests between 1315 and 1317.

The landlords' response to the changed circumstances was the same as in the twelfth century. They resumed the practice of 'farming' so that by the second half of the fourteenth century most of the larger estates began to be affected by it. By the middle of the fifteenth century very few demesnes—mostly home farms or Benedictine abbeys—still functioned under the direct management of their lords.[11]

Some demesnes had by that time ceased to function at all. We have seen that on a number of manors piecemeal and sporadic letting-out of unwanted lands never ceased. In the late fourteenth century the movement gathered speed, even though the inducements behind it were different. Whereas in the earlier period the landlords' dilemma—to let or to cultivate—was how to choose between alternative roads to still higher profits, the same dilemma in the fourteenth and fifteenth centuries was how best to escape from threatening losses. The letting-out of the demesne in parcels had now become one of the ways of arresting the decline of profits.

What we know of the economic conditions of the time suggests several reasons why demesne profits should have been on the decline. Political events may, on the whole, have been unfavourable, though the damage they inflicted on the landlords and their husbandry could not have been very great. Even in the middle of the fifteenth century, in the worst years of the Wars of the Roses, the ruin of government could not have gone as far as in the mid-twelfth century. On the other hand the preceding 120 years of war with France must have hurt the landowners in a variety of ways. Edward III's war taxes and purveyances and his levies on wool harmed the woolgrowers, especially the monastic ones.

But if there may be some doubt about the political factors behind the declining fortunes of the demesne, there can be none about the economic ones. In the first place the costs of demesne cultivation were rising, mainly as a result of higher wages. They began to rise in the first quarter of the fourteenth century, and continued on the ascent until some time in the second quarter of the fifteenth century. They stayed thereafter upon their high plateau until the end of the century. On the other hand we have seen that agricultural prices remained stationary, or perhaps even sagged somewhat. And as the bullion-content of the currency was reduced in 1343 and 1344, and again in 1351, 1412 and 1465, prices expressed in weights of silver were clearly on the decline throughout the period.

It is therefore not surprising that, with profit margins narrowing all the time, the lords should again have tried to stabilize their incomes, as they had done in the twelfth century, by letting out their demesnes to farm. By this means they sometimes succeeded in holding up their profits—at least for a time. On demesnes let out at farm incomes did not move down as long as the original farming contracts were in force. Those landlords who happened to retain in their hands the manorial pastures and flocks were also able to profit from the buoyant demand for wool in the last third of the fourteenth century. The estates of the bishops of Winchester provide a good example of successful resistance to fourteenth-century adversities. At certain times in the second half of the century the bishops were able to build up their flocks to heights as great as their thirteenth-century ceilings. Under William of Wykeham's ruthless management the other sources of manorial revenue also remained remarkably (though also precariously) high.

Few estates, however, were equally able to benefit from the late-fourteenth-century flutter in wool prices, and very few indeed had a William of Wykeham to manage them. Many of the estates which had successfully defended themselves in the closing decades of the fourteenth century saw their defences crumble in the fifteenth. Farming contracts could not insulate them for ever from rising costs of cultivation, and on a number of estates the values of the farms themselves fell. On the very large estates such as those of the Duchy of Lancaster, with possessions in almost every part of England, farms of demesnes stood in the last quarter of the fifteenth century at a level seldom higher and often much lower than two-thirds of that at the beginning of the century.

In the end the farming of entire demesnes for terms of years no longer commended itself to the landowners as a certain defence against falling demesne incomes. For this and other, more purely local, reasons manorial landlords were gradually moved to wind up their demesne in a more radical and permanent manner. Some great landlords, more particularly the chieftains of the two warring feudal parties in the middle of the fifteenth century, transferred some of their demesnes to lessees for entire lives or even a number of lives: their object often was to secure and to remunerate important followers. When this happened the farming contracts resembled the subinfeudations of the eleventh and twelfth centuries. It was one of the features of the informal feudalism—or 'bastard' feudalism as Mr MacFarlane described it—which emerged for a time at the close of the middle ages.

Even more radical and more directly affected by economic factors was the piecemeal letting out of the demesne lands to smaller tenants, mostly to villagers. As a result of these lettings, many demesnes previously cultivated by the landlords, or let out by him as a whole to farmers, came to be completely broken up.

In general it would therefore be too much of a generalization to speak of demesne, more particularly demesne pastures, vanishing altogether. We know of several landowning families in such sheep-farming counties as Northamptonshire or Wiltshire, the Hungerfords or the Brudenels, which in the late fifteenth or even sixteenth centuries still ran their demesne pastures as directly managed enterprises or else let them out as wholes. These particular instances must not however be taken to show that in the closing decades of the middle ages most landlords were always able to compensate fully for the falling fortunes of their arable farming by turning their demesnes over to sheep-farming and increasing their livestock in the process. Here and there increases in demesne flocks and herds may have occurred; where they occurred they may have proved profitable. On the estates which kept their demesne flocks while reducing their acres under plough, such as those of the Bishops of Winchester or the Abbots of Glastonbury, we can find some evidence of increases in the numbers of sheep in the fourteenth or early fifteenth centuries, but almost none later. On some manors, e.g. those in the northern and north-eastern groups of the Duchy of Lancaster estates, vaccaries and studs were greatly reduced and even liquidated altogether in the fifteenth century. The same need not be true of peasant herds and flocks, but in the absence of any reliable evidence about peasant husbandry, our notions about village sheep and cattle in the later middle ages must remain no more than guesses.

Another and perhaps a more effective escape from the prevailing slump were the wholly non-agricultural sources of demesne revenue, where this existed. We have seen that some estates derived their income from industry and mining. The accounts of the Northern estates of the Earls of Lancaster suggest that the revenues from their Yorkshire mines and iron-works held up better than their agricultural revenues. The income which the Earls of Cornwall derived from tin-mines fluctuated in the late fourteenth and fifteenth centuries, and slumped very low in the middle period, but towards the end of the period appeared to recover sooner and more completely than the purely agricultural revenues. The recovery, when it came, affected both the yields of imposts on tin and of rents paid by tin-working householders. Miss Carus-Wilson has also shown that in places in which the cloth industry developed in the course of the late fourteenth and the early fifteenth centuries (her examples were mostly in the south Cotswolds) the landowners benefited from increases in the rent-paying industrial population.

All these non-agricultural opportunities for relieving the economic fortunes of the demesne must not be allowed to obscure from view the continued existence of some, admittedly few, purely or largely arable demesnes operating as 'home farms' in the fifteenth century. In that century, and even later, a few fully-fledged demesnes could still be found on some monastic and collegiate estates, e.g. on the manor of Granchester belonging to King's College, Cambridge, or even on the estates of lay landlords such as the Pelhams in Sussex, or the Hungerfords in Wiltshire. But, as a rule, these demesnes were no longer representative of the agrarian system as a whole and were often restricted to lands directly serving the lords' kitchens. On some estates landlords tried, before giving up, to retrieve the fortunes of their demesnes by economic innovations. In the midst of the late-fourteenth-century depression we find some manorial managers, i.e. those of the bishops of Winchester or the abbots of Ramsey or the earls of Stafford, trying to remodel their field systems, enclosing and emparking disjointed fields, and continuing to introduce new crops, mostly legumes, in the fallow course, and to experiment with different seeding ratios. It is probable that in this way some landlords may have succeeded in arresting or slowing down for a time the decline of demesne profits.

Yet even where and when the landlords succeeded in salvaging a semblance of a functioning demesne, a mere semblance it nevertheless was. For in most of its essential characteristics—in its economic function, in its role in the make up of the landlords' revenue, in its organization and management, in the provenance and uses of its labour, and consequently also in its links with the village and its hold over the land and persons of the villagers—the demesne, where it survived and in the form in which it survived, differed very profoundly from the typical demesne as a constituent of the classical manor.

VI

The general conclusion emerging from our survey of manorial economies is, therefore, one of infinite variety. At any point of time, even in the hey-day of the manorial economy in the late twelfth and the early thirteenth centuries, manors differed very greatly in every respect, and more particularly in the relative weight and management of the lord's demesne. At any given point of time manors and demesnes within them differed in accordance with their geographical location, or the type and size of ownership or their size and antiquity. And irrespective of their differences at the same points of time all manors and demesnes within them were bound to change from period to period. No manor, however 'classical' and 'typical', remained the same in composition or management during the four or five centuries of its medieval history. It is because the variety and flux of manorial types has not always been taken into account that some historians, having failed to find the typical manor in the particular place or the particular period they happened to study, removed the manor from their picture altogether. If full allowance is made for the extent to which in real life manorial estates differed from the idealized type of the manor, some manors will be found in almost every place and at almost every time between the twelfth century and the fifteenth.

References

1. F. M. Stenton, *Types of Manorial Structure in the Northern Danelaw*, Oxford Studies in Social and Legal History, II (1910); D. L. Douglas, *The Social Structure of Medieval East Anglia*, Oxford Studies in Social and Legal History, IX (1927); I. E. A. Jolliffe, *Pre-feudal England: the Jutes* (1933); I. E. A. Jolliffe, 'Northumbrian Institu-

tions', *Eng. Hist. Rev.*, vi (1936); H. R. P. Finberg, *Tavistock Abbey; A Study in the Social and Economic History of Devon* (1951); J. Hatcher, *Rural Economy and Society in the Duchy of Cornwall, 1300–1500* (1970); R. H. Hilton, *The Social Structure of Rural Warwickshire in the Middle Ages* (Dugdale Society Occasional Papers, IX).

2. E. A. Kosminsky, *Studies in the Agrarian History of England in the Thirteenth Century* (1956).

3. G. C. Homans, 'The Frisians in East Anglia', *Econ. Hist. Rev.*, 2nd ser., X (1957).

4. B. Lees (ed.), *Records of the Templars in England in the Twelfth Century* (Brit. Acad. IX) (1935); L. B. Larking (ed.), *The Knights Hospitallers in England* (Camden Soc.) (1857).

5. H. Hall, *Pipe Roll of the Bishopric of Winchester, 1208–9* (1903).

6. N. Denholm-Young, *Seigneurial Administration in England* (1937).

7. J. Raftis, *The Estates of Ramsey Abbey* (1957). A somewhat different explanation of the twelfth-century changes will be found in Edward Miller, 'England in the Twelfth and Thirteenth Centuries: an Economic Contrast?', *Econ. Hist. Rev.*, 2nd ser., XXIV (1971).

8. Miller, 'England in the Twelfth and Thirteenth Centuries'.

9. Titow, *English Rural Society*, pp. 49–61; Oschinsky, *Walter of Henley*.

10. Monographs on the agrarian history of the later middle ages are still very few. A general treatment will be found in M. M. Postan's chapter in *The Cambridge Economic History*, Vol. I, 2nd ed. (1960) and in his 'Some Economic Evidence of Declining Population', *Econ. Hist. Rev.*, 2nd ser., II (1950). For local evidence see note 11 below, and Marjorie Morgan, *The English Lands of the Abbey of Bec*, Oxford 1946.

11. On the farming out of demesnes, see R. A. L. Smith, *The Estates of Christchurch Priory, Canterbury* (1944); Finberg, *Tavistock Abbey*; F. M. Page, *The Estates of Crowland Abbey* (1934). On falling yields of rents and demesne farming see F. G. Davenport, *The Economic Development of a Norfolk Manor 1086–1505* (1906) and the same author's 'The Decay of Villeinage in East Anglia', in E. M. Carus Wilson (ed.), *Essays in Economic History*, Vol. II (1962); Barbara Harvey, 'The Leasing of the Abbots of Westminster's Demesnes in the Middle Ages', *Eng. Hist. Rev.*, xxxii, No. 1 (1964). For an instance of a large estate where incomes in the fifteenth century may not have fallen below their thirteenth-century level, see F. R. H. du Boulay, *The Lordship of Canterbury* (1966), and the same author's 'A Rentier Economy in the Late Middle Ages: the Archbishopric of Canterbury', *Econ. Hist. Rev.*, 2nd ser., xvi, No. 3 (1964).

7 The Village

I

The manorial estate was not the only institution to organize and to regulate the agricultural activities and lives of medieval countryfolk. The village and the community of men inhabiting it provided a collateral or an alternative system of ties, rights and obligations. The village, like the manor, was ubiquitous, since the overwhelming majority of medieval countryfolk lived in group settlements of one kind or another. Like the manor, the medieval village possessed a number of characteristic features which combined into a recognizable pattern of typical or 'ideal' medieval vill. The ideal type of medieval vill is of course an historical abstraction. The villages we actually find at different times and in different places diverged from the ideal type in some respects, and the local and historical deviations from the ideal type could be as wide as those we have observed in the history of the manorial estate.

Some of the features of the typical village were inherent in the essential needs of agriculture and of social life, and may therefore appear too obvious to be worth specifying. The most obvious characteristic of the village was its topography. It was a collective, i.e., grouped, settlement; and the form of grouping most characteristic of the medieval countryside was that of a 'nucleated' village consisting of a cluster of households round a natural centre, topographical or economic—a well, a pond, a village green—which would also include or be contiguous with the site of the village church. Its other characteristic was, so to speak, constitutional or tenurial. A typical village was bound to a manor with an exclusive link, which can best be expressed by the formula of 'one manor, one vill'. The third feature was social and administrative. The inhabitants of a typical village formed a village community collectively administered and possessing formal and informal bodies, courts, assemblies, 'chests' and gilds, which issued and administered the rules of husbandry, watched over local customs of tenure and inheritance, and enforced local peace and order. As many of these functions also belonged to the lord and his manor, they were frequently exercised by the village courts functioning also as organs of manorial administration and in fact presided over by manorial officials.

Villages wholly conforming to type could be found at all times all over England. At any given point of time, however, it would be possible to find villages lacking some of the typical features. Numerous villages all over England also lost or acquired some typical characteristics in the course of their medieval history. These local and historical divergences from type are now well known to historians, though the variations in village types which have drawn most of the historians' attention are those of topography or village layout. This is to a large extent a matter of academic tradition. The continental studies of village topography, especially those of Meitzen, were among the pioneering studies of the medieval countryside, and greatly influenced the earlier writings on medieval economic history. The founding fathers of English agrarian history followed the established tradition and put a heavy emphasis on the topographical differences.[1]

Seebohm, to whom we owe the fullest account of a typical nucleated vill—that of Hitchin—was among the first to exhibit the difference between the nucleated villages on the one hand and the small hamlets and detached farmsteads on the other. Like the other historians of his generation, he rightly traced this difference to the geographical location of settlements and the corresponding differences in the types of husbandry. The underlying assumption was that nucleated settlements, especially the larger ones, were best suited to arable agriculture and to the collective management of common fields. They were therefore to be found mainly in the predominantly arable regions of southern and midland England. On the other hand, the smaller settlements in hamlets and individual farmsteads went naturally with the occupation of upland combes and valleys. In these regions the lay of the land itself did not permit the formation of large and extensive villages, such as most nucleated villages were. Moreover the pastoral husbandry practised in them did not require collective controls or cooperative activities as continuous and on a scale as large as those appropriate to the complexes of open fields in the great plains of England's arable core. Hence the broad distinction between the nucleated villages in the arable lowlands, and detached households or small groups of households in pastoral highlands.

Needless to say the differences between the nucleated villages of the plains and the dispersed abodes in the mountains were not the only topographical variations connected with geographical location and economic function. For one thing, pastoral husbandry was not the only alternative to arable farming. Some, admittedly few, villages were industrial and commercial to an extent sufficient to affect their size and shape. Villages favourably situated for commerce functioned as centres of local traffic without being urbanized. The numerous villages with the prefix of 'Chipping-' especially numerous in the north Cotswolds, or 'Market-' particularly common in the eastern counties and in the east midlands, were part-mercantile villages. They were, as a rule, larger than their purely agricultural activities warranted, but were also laid out accordingly: either huddled round their market place or strung out along the road running through them. The latter was, as a rule, the shape of the villages which derived much of their livelihood from the traffic of important trade routes. Such were some of the villages on the Oxford-Gloucester road, e.g. Northleach. Some of these villages would be described as 'long', e.g. Long Melford in Suffolk; others would in fact be long without being so named, e.g. Barkway on the Cambridge-London road.

Villages with considerable industrial populations would also be characterized by their lay-out as well as by their composition. The cloth-working villages of the south Cotswolds or Suffolk in the fourteenth and the early fifteenth centuries carried large numbers of weavers and fullers and therefore contained more than the average proportion of smallholdings or cottages, frequently huddled together. The coal and iron-mining villages of the Earl of Lancaster in the West Riding of Yorkshire, the colliers' settlements on the northern and eastern fringes of the Epping Forest, the tin-mining villages in west Cornwall do not appear to have been as invariably arranged around the village centre as the nucleated villages. Above all, the fishing and seafaring villages, such as we find on the estate of Battle Abbey on the Sussex coast, or all along the Norfolk coast or on the bays and creeks of the west country, were assemblages of small holdings and cottages, some of which appeared to have been strung out along the sea shore or round sea-bays.

In some villages the layout of fields and the ground-plan of village houses reflected the historical peculiarities of their origin and development. These reflections were at their clearest in villages which happened to have arisen in the course of relatively recent reclamations. Certain large-scale draining enterprises in the eastern Fens between the eleventh and the early thirteenth centuries created new villages set out in a manner orderly to the point of being artificial. One such artificial village with a wholly symmetrical grid of houses and fields was the fenland village of Fleet in Sutton described in Miss Neilson's well-known study. It was a relatively recent intake from the Fen, and as befitted the product of a single and well-planned colonizing enterprise, it was composed of a regular row of homesteads abutting on their portions of the fields each of which stretched ribbon-wise into the heart of the reclaimed fen.[2]

However, the commonest characteristic of many thirteenth-century villages on recently reclaimed terrain was not so much their ground-plan as their size and composition. They were very frequently small villages—small not because they were necessarily pastoral or confined to the uplands, but because, as often as not, they occupied marginal lands incapable of supporting large and close settlements. Such were the hamlets and villages on the Earl of Lancaster's estates sited at the upper reaches of the Pennine valleys; or the 'den' villages in the weald of Kent and Sussex which had begun as wealden outposts of the older villages on the coastal plain; or recently established hamlets on the chalk pastures of Hampshire and Wiltshire, such as St Swithun's Priory of the downland manor of Barton, or some of the 'hafods' in the hills of Wales and the Welsh border. The latter were summer outposts in the hill pastures, some of which had, by the thirteenth century, come to be occupied all the year round.[3]

Yet another variant of the smaller village, which owed its origin and its character to recent changes in the countryside, was the 'filial' vill which had budded off an older and larger village in the course of the demographic and territorial expansion of the late twelfth and thirteenth centuries. In the process of this expansion the population of some of the older vills burst through their confines and settled on new sites in other parts of the village territory. In the thirteenth century satellites of this character will be found within most of the large manors. They were sometimes described as 'berewicks' and, when so described, did not appear to possess any independent status as village communities or as manorial units. But we also find filial villages not referred to as berewicks but equally closely linked to the paternal vill, as well as berewicks which had not wholly detached themselves. Latter-day filial villages of this and other kinds were very numerous: indeed more numerous than their place-names alone would suggest, since many a seemingly independent village will on closer inspection turn out to have been a recent off-spring of an older village. The large and important Glastonbury manor of South Domerham in south Wiltshire was in fact a joint manor of Domerham and Merton. The latter was largely a sheepfarming settlement on the Domerham downlands, and it will not be altogether fanciful to assume that it had grown out of a sheepfarming 'hafod' of Domerham. Many other composite manors abounding in the thirteenth-century documents may have arisen by a similar process of parturition. The eight small villages in the great composite manor of Taunton may all have sprung from the original settlement in Taunton itself; and we know well the stages by which the great composite manors of Brent and Zoy had grown out of their older nuclei in the Sedgemoor of Somerset. In this way large and nucleated villages and smaller hamlets, the latter sometimes no more than assemblages of dispersed homesteads, coexisted side by side in the same localities.

These topographical changes of the twelfth and the thirteenth centuries, more particularly the formation of berewicks and the budding off of satellite villages, were symptomatic of the growing population and expanding settlement. They were to be matched in the later centuries by topographical changes equally symptomatic of an arrested reclamation and of declining population. Of these symptoms the one most discussed nowadays is that of decayed villages. With the introduction of aerial photography in the inter-war period historians and archaeologists have been able to locate a very large number, in fact many hundreds, of sites which had once upon a time in the later middle ages carried agricultural settlements but have at one time or another been abandoned and are now represented by little more than mounds overgrown with grass and scrub, or mere shadows in standing crops. Abroad, more particularly in Germany, historians have for a long time been aware of the full significance of abandoned village sites, and have rightly interpreted them as evidence of retreating cultivation in the later middle ages. In this country their use in medieval research is still very tentative. Their importance as evidence appears to be less obvious than abroad, since many of them appear to date from the enclosures for sheepfarming in the sixteenth century. On further study, however, the relatively late date at which they appear to have been abandoned may turn out to be much less of a disqualification than it at first sight appears. As Professor Beresford has shown, many of the villages abandoned at the turn of the fifteenth and the sixteenth centuries were small and declining ones. Their abandonment in the sixteenth century was often a mere final act of demise brought about by deliberate decisions on the part of the landlords.[4]

Unfortunately the existence of contracting villages is more difficult to uncover by aerial photography or topographical survey than the evidence of their total disappearance. Most difficult of all is to recover the evidence of contracting sites in villages which for various reasons revived again in later periods. Many a clothmaking village grew in the course of the fourteenth and the early fifteenth centuries in those very marginal areas of Yorkshire or the south Cotswolds on which agricultural villages had been contracting at about the same time or some time previously; and here and there the cottages of the cloth workers could be filling out again or adding new areas to villages where the landworking population had been declining, as in the clothworking villages in the south Cotswolds described by Miss Carus-Wilson. Nevertheless, the evidence of contracting village sites and village fields can be found all over England. The scars of erstwhile fields and of abandoned terraces on the hillsides of Wiltshire and Hampshire downs, on the sides of the Yorkshire dales, such as Upper Swaledale, could be matched elsewhere by the superficial marks of decayed crofts and tofts on the outskirts of villages which escaped the total foreclosure in the fifteenth or sixteenth centuries, but had obviously declined in size and changed their shape in the late middle ages.

II

So much for variations in the topography and lay-out of villages. Equally wide were the variations in the links which bound the villages to the manors. We have seen that the typical link was the exclusive one—'one village, one manor'; and students of medieval agriculture will easily find villages which closely conformed to type in this respect. At least every other manor in the Bishop of Winchester's estate comprised the whole of the corresponding village and had no outlyers in any other villages. On the other hand the Bishop's manor of Taunton or that of Downton embraced more than one village. An even more important departure from type was represented by the villages which contained within them possessions of several manors, sometimes several entire manors. These vills, larger than the manor, were specially characteristic of the eastern counties, especially Suffolk and Norfolk and perhaps also Lincolnshire. Sutton-in-Holderness, Imingham and Haylsham in Norfolk, and Witham in Essex are good examples of multi-manorial vills. They were multi-manorial at the time of the Domesday survey and remained multi-manorial throughout their later history.

What makes a village of this kind historically important is that in it the unit of economic administration and social organization was not the manor but the vill. In these villages courts and juries operated over a territory and a population more extensive than that of any one of its constituent manors. It therefore fell to them to regulate the field system and to administer local customs. The social and economic organization of such villages would be more appropriately described as communal rather than manorial. And where the main channel and instruments of control were communal and not manorial, the strength of manorial power and its economic burdens were found to be much lighter than in villages embraced in their entirety by single manors.[5]

Yet, even in villages wholly contained in corresponding manors and subordinated to them, certain functions were in their nature communal and were exercised by village assemblies, or the 'communities of the vill'. Some of these communal gatherings could take place on what were formally sessions of manorial courts, and could be presided over by manorial officials; but even where this was the case the court and its officials frequently occupied themselves with matters with which the lords were not directly concerned, and from which they did not derive any profit. One such function was that of formulating and applying local customs relating to inheritance. Adjudications on issues of this order were frequently dependent on the findings of juries; and the setting up of juries and of jury-like bodies for inquests was frequently treated as strictly communal business. Formally juries might be appointed in manorial courts and their findings be reported and recorded there, but the entries in the manorial courts' rolls and still more their silences suggest that the actual selections of men to serve on juries and the subsequent proceedings of the juries themselves were the concern of the villages and not that of the manor and its courts.

In fact, it is quite common to find among the jurymen named in manorial court rolls the names of men who were not tenants of the lord but were obviously residents of the village.

Local inquests and the selection of juries were so obviously communal in principle and administration that they naturally imposed upon the village a great variety of functions requiring inquests. One of these functions was royal taxation. Royal imposts, especially the fourteenth-century taxes on movables levied by Edward III, or the Poll Taxes of the 1370s, were as a rule assessed by local juries. The surviving documents also make it clear that the units of assessment were as a rule the vills, and the assessing juries were selected from among the respectable members (*probi homines*) of the village communities—as a rule representing the humble as well as the rich. Akin to taxation in their administration and in their dependence on the cooperation of the vill were the military levies. In the active phases of the Hundred Years War in the late fourteenth and early fifteenth centuries, such levies were fairly common, but the very fact that manorial court rolls are remarkably silent about them suggests that the business of imposing military service on villages, and of electing the men to serve, was conducted in and by the village.

To a large extent the same is also true of the administration of public security or police. The keeping of the peace and the associated administration of the local criminal law were the business of the 'hundred' and the 'tithing'. In theory these were groupings of households in units of hundreds and tens. By the time when our records became sufficiently abundant the hundred and the tithing had lost their purely numerical identities, but they still remained what they had been to begin with, i.e. groups of households in the village bearing collective responsibility, or 'frankpledge', for the keeping of order. The responsibility was essentially extramanorial. In places in which manorial lords had appropriated the profits and duties of the hundred, the actual 'views of the frankpledge' often took place in manorial courts and were enrolled on their records. But even in these cases the names of people appearing at court as members of the tithings invariably contained names of men who were not the lords' tenants.

In addition to these, so to speak, official functions, the village community apparently discharged, as any communal organization would have done, various informal duties touching upon matters of common concern and interest. One of these matters must have been as ancient as the community itself and must originally have been one of the main purposes of communal organization, i.e. common action in the reclamation of land and in the defence and protection of common land rights. We have argued earlier that communal land use, and indeed the entire existence of the village community, was largely dictated by the necessities of reclamation in the wooded clay lands of England. These necessities persisted and required communal action throughout the middle ages. When we read, as we frequently do, in the records of royal forests that large pieces of land in this or that royal forest had been assarted and were held collectively by neighbouring villages, we must assume that some organized communal action preceded the assarting, and that there existed a communal organization able to continue the assarting and to negotiate the year-to-year changes in the terms of the old assarts. The same is probably true of other collective transactions in land. When we are told that the Glastonbury demesne of Grittleton was let out to the village in its entirety, we must presume that the village possessed a communal organization capable of negotiating the lease and of administering its operation. In fact, some such collective organization is presumed by the manorial officials themselves, since they will frequently be found imposing tasks or fines on the 'entire village' (*tota villata*), without specifying the man or men charged with the actual execution of the tasks.

These collective actions by the villages could sometimes be taken without official recognition by the manor, and even in opposition to it. Now and again we find a village acting collectively to resist the manorial lords or to press certain collective claims against him. Such acts of collective opposition became particularly common in the thirteenth century, when the lords frequently attempted to exact from their tenants, in particular from their rent-paying tenants, the labour dues which had lapsed in the course of the previous century. Many of these attempts were resisted by the villagers in royal courts, and the resistance was in almost every case collectively organized and conducted. One of the best known and best recorded of these collective suits was the famous litigation between the priors and the villagers of Burton in Staffordshire. In this, as in most similar cases, the lords accused the villagers of conspiracy and alleged the existence of secret bodies led by ringleaders. Ringleaders there may well have been; we hear of 'troublemakers', sometimes clerks, sometimes parish priests, acting as spokesmen for the community. And where there were spokesmen there must also have been communal assemblies. We do not know whether these were *ad hoc* gatherings or permanent organizations, but that some of them were so to speak standing bodies, functioning continually, is suggested by occasional references to the institutions under whose cover the communal organizations functioned. The parish 'gilds', where they existed (and as far as we know they have been much more ubiquitous than our scarce evidence could reveal), acted as *foci* of communal action. Sometimes we also hear of something in the nature of a communal chest. In their allegations of conspiracy the landlords sometimes referred to the unlawful collection of funds raised to finance their lawsuits against the lord.[6]

In general much less is known about the communal bodies, about their functions and activities, than would have been known had they possessed a legal status comparable to that of the manorial courts, or had they been headed by officials as articulate and as literate as the clerks of the manorial courts. That in spite of these disabilities the communal activities of the villagers can so frequently be discerned behind the silences and disguises of manorial documents, goes to show that the village communes could be as active and as effective a vehicle of local authority as the manorial organization itself.

References

1. The topographical variations known to the historians in the early years of this century are summarized in E. Lipson's *An Introduction to the Economic History of England*, Vol. I (1915). The most up-to-date information on changes in village plans will be found in W. M. Beresford's 'An Historian's Appraisal of Archaeological Research' in M. Beresford and J. G. Hurst (eds.), *Deserted Medieval Villages* (1971).

2. N. Neilson, *The Terrier of Fleet.*

3. N. Neilson, *Cartulary and Terrier of the Priory of Bilsington* (Brit. Acad. VII) (1928).

4. Beresford and Hurst, *Deserted Medieval Villages*, particularly Chs. 1, 2, and 4.

5. F. M. Stenton, *Types of Manorial Structure, etc.* pp. 52, 62–70; D. L. Douglas, *Social Structure* pp. 3–5, 160 ff., 209, 217–70.

6. The role of the village communities and assemblies in managing the village field systems is discussed in the works of W. O. Ault, more particularly in his 'Open Field Husbandry', *Trans. Am. Phil. Soc.*, New Series, Vol. 55, part 7 (1965). These and other aspects of social life in a village are discussed in J. Raftis, *Tenure and Mobility: Studies in the Social History of the Medieval English Village* (1964).

8 The Villagers: Economic Conditions

I

The condition of medieval peasants cannot be measured solely by conventional yardsticks. We shall see presently that the yardstick commonly used by the historians of modern peasantry, especially by writers in the Russian sociological tradition, has been the sizes of family landholdings. Yet, even in modern peasant societies, this and the other purely material yardsticks measure very imperfectly the real wellbeing of individual families; they are even more imperfect as measures of the wellbeing of medieval peasants. In general the tendency among historians has been to concentrate on other, not strictly economic, conditions of peasant existence; and this attitude can easily be accounted for by the peculiarities of medieval village society as well as by certain traditional predispositions of medieval historiography.

The medieval peculiarity bearing directly on the condition of medieval peasants was serfdom. The unfree or semi-free status of the majority of medieval villagers was so characteristic of the period that the historians of rural society in the middle ages have been inclined to give more attention to the peasants' freedom and unfreedom than to their wealth and income. This inclination was also favoured by the political preoccupations of historians in the first half of the nineteenth century. I have already mentioned elsewhere that liberal opinion all over Europe, but mainly in Germany, was at that time mobilizing itself for a war against the peasant serfdom which still survived in central and eastern Europe; the history of peasant freedom was therefore bound to rank high in the preoccupation of historians. Moreover the education and the prevailing intellectual tradition in the historical profession was political and legal. Purely economic standards in use nowadays seldom entered into the range of judgments and interests of the academic 'intelligentsia' of the day.

It is therefore no wonder that in the established tradition of medieval studies the problem of status should have dominated both continental and English historical studies of the peasantry. It is only recently that historians have come to realize that, characteristic as servile status was of medieval villagers, it was only one of the patterns in the palimpsest of rural society, and that other patterns, including the purely economic one, entered into the overall design, and could at times over-shadow the imprint of serfdom and freedom.

Unfortunately historical judgments of the material conditions in villages are more difficult to form than are corresponding judgments about legal and personal status. The latter, frequently defined in documentary sources, are as a rule elaborately set out in manorial custumals and surveys and are sometimes illuminated by legal proceedings. No such definition or elucidation by the courts and professional specialists was possible in matters purely economic, with the result that the economic historian must perforce operate with standards and measurements entirely his own.

Most difficult of all is to assess with any precision the general economic position of individual villagers. We have much less evidence of the peasant households than of the organization and evolution of the manor and its demesne. Our ignorance, however, is not a sufficient justification for assuming that all we have learned about the lord's husbandry must also apply to that of his tenants. What little we can gather about the villagers from our records is sufficient to show that they did not always exploit their land in the same manner as the lord, and did not always benefit or suffer in the same way as he did from changing economic conditions.

To begin with, the relative importance of different cereals in villagers' husbandry was frequently different from that on the lords'. Various evidence, such as liveries of food to manorial servants or agreements about payments in kind to retired parents, but especially the evidence of multure (millers' deductions from grain milled by villagers), suggests that barley and oats, or various mixtures of oats and barley, wheat and rye, formed a larger proportion of the villagers' diet and of their crops than of the diet and crops of the manorial lords. On the other hand wheat was undoubtedly grown by villagers in most parts of England capable of growing it, since assessors to royal taxes on movables often found wheat in peasant houses.

This apparent conflict of evidence—the greater importance of inferior grains in peasant multures and the presence of wheat among peasants' taxable goods—is, however, somewhat unreal, since the two classes of evidence relate to two different problems. The evidence of multure is most relevant to the problem of diet, whereas the evidence of taxable goods is relevant to the problem of output; and the two are by no means identical. The villagers did not eat all the grain they grew and did not grow all their grain for food. Allowing again for local differences it appears that wheat was to a large extent a cash crop grown to provide for the money outgoings of villein households, while other grains were grown largely for food and fodder. This division between crops to be eaten and crops to be sold will be found in most peasant communities burdened with payments. The most recent and the best known instance of this is Ireland before the potato famine of the forties where peasants grew grain for rent and potatoes for food.[1]

This earmarking of wheat for special purposes was not a matter of choice but one of necessity. In many parts of the country the villagers had to confine their wheat to special uses, because their ability to grow it was smaller than the lord's. It was smaller mainly because, compared with the lord, the villagers were often under-provided with better land. It can be argued, though not demonstrated, that a division of land between the demesne and the tenants in the earliest days of settlement had favoured the lords. But whatever may have been the division of land between the landlord and his tenants in the dim beginnings of manorial history, it was bound to evolve to the disadvantage of the tenants in later centuries. To begin with, with his rights of fold and with his superior command over pastures, the lord was better able to keep his lands in good heart. Then there is also the effect of demesne leases. We do not know what principle guided the lord in his choice of bits and pieces of demesne to be let out to tenants in the eleventh and twelfth centuries; but when the process is resumed in the later thirteenth century we very frequently find that the lands the lords got rid of first were the poorer ones, often lands described as *terra debilis* or *terra avenae*. And this alone would, in the fullness of time, have raised the villagers' share of inferior lands and compelled them to grow higher proportions of inferior grains.

This however is not what some historians have taken for granted when dealing with medieval yields. In discussing here the evidence for declining productivity we have relied mainly on the evidence of the demesnes of the bishops of Winchester as representing medieval agriculture as a whole. This use of the Winchester yields may be somewhat too sweeping. The bishops' yields may perhaps be a sufficient guide to the yields of the demesne lands of other lords. This would not, however, be a sufficient reason for accepting them as typical of the villagers' yields as well.

In view of what we already know about the shortage of village pastures and livestock, and of what we can guess about the lower quality of their land, we could not expect their output per acre to equal that of a well-managed demesne in the same locality. On the few thirteenth-century manorial demesnes still ploughed and sown by compulsory labour services the work may have been inefficiently organized and grudgingly performed; and the lord's yields may have suffered accordingly. On some manors demesne fields lay interspersed with the tenants' strips and were cultivated by tenants' ploughs and even sown with tenants' seeds: their yield must also have been as low as that of peasant acres. But on many demesnes in the thirteenth century fields were ploughed and sown by permanent manorial servants; and demesne fields frequently lay apart from the villagers' holdings and were cultivated separately from them. On these demesnes the higher quality of the lord's land, his superior command over capital, equipment, pastures and folds, was bound to tell, and his yields were bound to be higher. If on the Bishop of Winchester's demesnes the average return for all his crops was about four times the seed at the beginning of the thirteenth century and three to four times at the end of the century, the output on his tenants' lands may well have been lower than that: lower than three to four times the seed towards the end of our period.

These lower yields and lower overall output had to support fixed outlays much higher than the charges on gentlemen's property. As a rule payments due from customary, i.e. villein, holdings were exceedingly heavy compared to the charges borne by manorial estates, or even to those of substantial peasant freeholders. What they were is well known to historians, though their aggregate weight has seldom been properly appreciated. So at the cost of appearing unduly repetitive I propose to recapitulate the catalogue of payments borne by villeins.

To begin with, nearly all customary holdings in the thirteenth century were burdened with money rent, supplemented by other rent-like charges like church-scot or various 'pennies' representing some very ancient commutations of still more ancient services. Then there were various 'farms' for additional pieces of land, payments of pannage of pigs, the agistment of animals and the use of the lord's pastures. These were from time to time augmented by various 'once-for-all', or 'capital' payments, such as heriots from deceased men's property or entry fines from new tenants. There were also personal payments characteristic of a villein status such as 'chevages' or 'recognitions' levied in various pretexts, as well as marriage fines and, above all, amercements imposed in manorial courts for transgressions of every kind. The latter were punitive in theory, but were in fact so regular and apparently unavoidable as to constitute a regular imposition. On many estates the miscellaneous fines were overshadowed by tallage, which was frequently a heavy annual tax, almost as heavy as the rent itself.

Finally there were money equivalents of labour services. In places and at times in which labour services were commuted this equivalent would be directly paid to the landlord and might be eventually consolidated with the rent. But even where labour services were exacted in kind they still frequently involved the villein in money outlays. There is much evidence to show that the holder of a tenement as large as a virgate or even half a virgate would often be unable to discharge his full quota of labour services without hiring a man to deputize for him at the demesne or to replace him at home.

To all these manorial payments we must also add the tithes to the church and occasional royal taxes. But even without these extra-manorial obligations the money dues of a villein tenant would absorb a very large proportion of his gross output. The proportions varied a great deal, but on holdings of middling size, those of half-virgates comprising ten to fifteen acres, the average was frequently near or above the 50 per cent mark. That this had come to be regarded as the landlord's normal 'rake-off' is shown by the terms of certain free leases. For when land was held freely on crop-sharing terms (*ad campi partem*) the lord's share was frequently one half of the profits, as in the continental *métayage*. Similarly, on thirteenth-century manors on which customary tenants had recently come to hold their land free of most services other than rent, rents could easily rise to the *métayer*'s level: as on Thomas de Havile's Lincolnshire manor of Hacunby, where bovates of sixteen acres carried the rent of £1 each*.[2]

The weight of the various money obligations was thus very great. But what differentiated the servile peasant husbandry from

* *Inquisitions Post Mortem* 30 Edw. I 106 (8).

the economy of the demesne was not only the weight of the payments but their obligatory nature. They were as a rule fixed; they were nearly all inescapable; and they had to be treated as prior charges. They could not be reduced to suit the harvest or the tenant's personal circumstances or to reflect his preferences for higher or lower consumption. The tenant's need of food and fodder had to be covered by what was left after the obligatory charges had been met.

The size and the prior nature of these obligatory charges, and the residuary character of all other claims on his produce, not only determined the peasant's standard of life, the amount of his food, or his ability to invest, but could also affect the way in which he responded to economic changes. His responses would be frequently at variance, and often directly contrary, to those of the manorial landlords. The situations which favoured the manorial estate and boosted its profits might depress and impoverish its tenants, and *vice versa.* Falling yields or sagging prices might induce the landlord to curtail the cultivation of his demesne, but might compel the villein to increase his sowings and his sales; similarly, rising prices or good yields would stimulate the activities of profit-conscious owners of demesnes, but relieve the villein of the pressure to sell and hence also of the pressure to grow more.

These reactions, however, could not be uniform. They were bound to vary not only from place to place—this goes without saying—but also from one group of villagers to another in the same village. Above all they weighed most heavily on the servile villagers, and very lightly on the freeholding ones. Their weight was also more oppressive when borne by small men than when imposed upon the well-to-do peasants. To be properly understood these burdens must be related to the social and economic differences among individuals. To these differences we shall now pass.

II

Historians vary in their methods of measuring the economic conditions of individual householders and of the economic differences between them; and, worse still, are apt to produce divergent measurements varying with the standards of measurement they have chosen.

The measure most frequently used by historians has been that of sizes of holdings. This is still the best standard available to us, and it will be used here. Yet, before this is done, the reader must be warned that in medieval villages, as in modern ones, the poverty or prosperity of families was not entirely or always a matter of acres. Human conditions, or what in everyday speech are sometimes referred to as family circumstances, could at times be equally important. A family consisting of healthy and industrious parents and well-supplied with employable sons and daughters would fare much better than a childless couple, especially if they happened to be old or lazy or otherwise decrepit. Our records contain instances of tenants of large holdings, whole virgates, who had to be forgiven court fines on account of their poverty. When in 1296 Alexander Pope, a tenant of the prior of St Swithun's, Winchester, was forgiven the payment of heriot *quia pauper est*, his poverty was obviously real; yet he held an entire virgate. On the other hand we find men who at one time possessed in customary tenure nothing more than smallholdings but whose diligence, vigour and presumably family labour enabled them to lease and otherwise acquire additional land. A few years before the outbreak of the Black Death, one Robert Stephen, a tenant of the Abbot of Glastonbury, had to be forgiven the tax of two shillings because he had no goods on which it could be levied; yet some time previously he was able to pay a price of over £30 for his holding. On the other hand we possess numerous genealogies of wealthy villagers—such as that of Richard of Paston, in the *Carte Nativorum* of the Abbey of Peterborough—whose wealth was founded by poor but industrious and acquisitive progenitors.

Yet in considering medieval rural society as a whole and its transformation through centuries we need not assign too great a role to accidents of age, health or personal character, since they were wholly random and unstable. Enduring differences in the wealth of individuals and the more permanent demarcations between the different layers of society were in most cases reducible to those of land, i.e. the sizes of family holdings.

III

What, then, was the distribution of land among villagers? This question is easiest to answer for the thirteenth century, for which our evidence is most abundant. Yet in one important respect the evidence may turn out to be misleading. In a typical manorial survey of the thirteenth century most of the customary holdings and some free holdings are as a rule listed in regular and uniform units of virgates, half-virgates and quarter-virgates, or bovates and half-bovates. These units are commonly and rightly regarded by historians as standardized shares in the common field of the village related to the individual's contributions to the collective plough: the bovate or half-virgate corresponding to one ox or horse in the plough team. Not only was land thus apportioned but the payments and obligations due from the land were similarly allotted—per virgate or per bovate. But does this necessarily mean that all actual peasant holdings in fact fitted into this regular grid of virgated units?

Our first impulse might be to answer this question in the affirmative, for we know—or at least we are told—that the lords were interested in preserving the integrity of the virgated unit as a standard for computing and levying manorial dues. But we also know now that the lords were unable to resist the action of the village land market, or to prevent accretions to holdings by piecemeal reclamations, or to prohibit all sub-divisions through inheritance and marriage. As a result, most villagers in most villages either owned irregular portions of virgates or added odd pieces of land to their virgated holdings; or, as we suspect, let out or leased from time to time entire customary holdings or portions of them. So even if in some distant past the majority of the villagers had in fact been holders of virgates or symmetrical portions of virgates, in the twelfth and more especially in the thirteenth centuries they most frequently possessed or cultivated holdings which were both more unequal and more irregular than the virgated lists of tenements might suggest.

Where the sizes of holdings ranged widely and irregularly, all lines of demarcations between them are bound to be arbitrary. In the discussion to follow here, such demarcations are nevertheless made, and the villagers of middling substance are distinguished from the rich and the poor. The middle group is defined here as that composed of men in possession of customary holdings larger than those of substantial cottagers holding quarter-virgates, but smaller than those of fully-fledged villeins with entire virgates and more. The bulk of such holdings—their statistical mode—would as a rule be found somewhere near a bovate or a half-virgate, i.e. the equivalent of say ten to fifteen acres of arable land of average quality situated in one of the mixed farming areas of England.

In the thirteenth century the holders of tenancies of this size were the representative villagers of the time: representative by virtue of the existence they led rather than by virtue of their numbers. Villages where customary holdings of this size predominated could of course be found in most arable regions, but in the large majority of thirteenth-century villages known to historians these holdings constituted no more than a large minority. In his classification of villein holdings in the four counties covered by the surviving portions of the Hundred Rolls, Kosminsky allots to the holders of half-virgates 36 per cent of the total. Kosminsky's demarcations are somewhat different from ours, while his sample as a whole is somewhat distorted by the predominance of Oxfordshire (a third of the total) with its untypically low numbers of smallholders. Nevertheless his figures are not far removed from those to be found in manorial documents. Table 1 shows that on the predominantly arable estates of the bishops of Winchester and Worcester, or the abbeys of Glastonbury and St Peter's of Gloucester, or the canons of St Paul's, as well as on the southern and East Anglian estates of the earls of Lancaster or the fully manorialized possessions of the earls of Cornwall, the numbers of customary tenants holding little more than a quarter-virgate but less than a full virgate, i.e. approximately more than eight and under thirty acres, was somewhere near the 30 per cent mark, seldom falling below 20 per cent but seldom rising above a third of the total. But whether they were or were not in the majority, their mode of existence, their standards of life, indeed their entire social condition, approached nearest to the characteristic type of medieval peasant.

This type is of course something of a theoretical abstraction, but its relevance to real peasant existence is implied in most sociological definitions of peasantry. Most of the current definitions assume the 'peasant' to be an occupying owner or a tenant of a holding capable, but only just capable, of providing his family with a 'subsistence income'. Subsistence income, in its turn, is commonly understood to denote an income large enough to make it unnecessary for the family to depend on regular employment for wages, yet not so large as to permit the family to live wholly on the proceeds of rents or to enable it to work its holding entirely or mainly by hired labour.

This conventional criterion will also be employed here. We shall accordingly try to grade the peasant holdings by their ability to sustain typical peasant existences or by their failure to do so. What had to be the size of a holding capable of providing in the thirteenth century a 'typical' income and a typical standard of life? This question does not admit of a precise answer, but can be answered approximately. Our estimates of average yields per acre, or of the essential outgoings of a peasant farm, or of the material needs of an average peasant family, may all be variable and uncertain; they are nevertheless sufficient to justify the conclusion that in most thirteenth-century villages holdings of the size we have allocated to our middling group—that of half-virgates—would provide a family of five with about 2,000 calories per head per day in average years, i.e. just enough to keep body and soul together. To do this, it also had to be provided with other attributes

TABLE I

DISTRIBUTION OF HOLDINGS[3]

Estates	*Manors*	*Date*	*'Top rank' tenants*	*'Middle rank' tenants*	*Small-holders*
Shaftesbury Abbey	17	late twelfth century	285	209	242
Canons of St Paul's	14	early thirteenth century	175	366	501
Bishops of Winchester	15	mid-thirteenth century	268	645	713
St Peter's, Gloucester	17	mid-thirteenth century	264	158	363
Glastonbury Abbey	32	mid-thirteenth century	359	593	1094
St Swithun's Priory Winchester	4	mid-thirteenth century	14	104	65
Bishops of Worcester	7	end of thirteenth century	132	188	120
Berkeley Estates	2	end of thirteenth century	16	17	43
	104		1053 (22%)	2280 (33%)	3141 (45%)

of a true peasant household, and above all the use of family labour and a high degree of independence of 'bought in' supplies.

Of the various variables entering into computations of peasant incomes, the weight of compulsory outgoings was probably the most important. All our computations have been based on the assumption that a very large part, perhaps more than half, of the gross produce of customary land had to be earmarked for various manorial payments. If so, in places where manorial payments were not heavy, i.e. where tenants held for money rent, and especially where the rent had been anciently fixed, e.g. on the Lincolnshire estates of Peterborough Abbey or about half the estates of the bishops of Durham, a holding might yield correspondingly larger net incomes than it would in the hands of villeins subject to full labour dues. It is thus possible that in regions like the Danelaw or Kent, where free tenures were numerous and payments for land relatively low, our middling group would in the thirteenth century be largely composed of holders of quarter-virgates or of cotlands that would rank as mere smallholdings elsewhere.

Similar allowances have to be made for the predominantly pastoral areas where villagers derived the bulk of their income not from their arable acres but from sheep and cattle; or for industrial and trading villages in which a large proportion of the population engaged in non-agricultural employments.

Yet none of these allowances invalidate our initial generalization about the middle group and its half-virgate holdings. Free tenants may have been more numerous in English villages of the thirteenth century than the founders of economic history knew, but in the anciently settled core of medieval England taken as a whole they were no more than a sizeable minority; the predominantly pastoral areas were smaller in the thirteenth century than the topography and the geology of England or the later history of its land utilization might lead us to expect; industrial villages were few and far between. In general England's population in the thirteenth century was predominantly agricultural, her agriculture was in the main arable, her arable villages were in the main composed of customary tenants. The social group characteristic of the customary population of arable England in the thirteenth century would therefore be roughly representative of English rural society viewed as a whole.

IV

Below the middling group lay the great mass of smallholders, i.e. men whose holdings were as a rule too small for true subsistence farming. Judged by their holdings alone, the men whose economic status was the lowest were to be found among the all-but-landless villagers possessing little more than the cottages in which they lived. Some of the men in this layer were servants who resided under their masters' roofs, and could not be considered as smallholders in the strict sense of the term. In its strictest sense the term may not apply to many of the villagers of the smallholding group whom the documents might describe as 'ferlingers', i.e. holders of quarter virgates of customary land. Many villagers with ferlings need not have fallen much short of the 'middling' villagers in output and in standard of life. But our lines of demarcation are bound to be faint as well as arbitrary, and the groups marked off by them are bound to merge at the frontiers.

Taken as a whole, the smallholding population of thirteenth-century villages was very numerous, frequently more numerous than the middling group and sometimes more numerous than the rest of the village taken together. In the random sample of manors tabulated above (Table I) tenants with ten acres and less formed more than one half of the population on all estates except those of St Peter's, Gloucester, where manorial sources conceal from our view large numbers of tenants' sub-tenants. What this means in human terms is that about one half of the peasant population had holdings which, taken by themselves, would as a rule be insufficient to maintain entire families in the bare minimum of subsistence.

In fact, an average smallholder had to supplement his income in other ways if he was to maintain a family. Industrial activities, such as leathercrafts or woodworking, might sustain entire villages of smallholders in areas especially suited to such pursuits.[4] Petty traders and artisans with smallholdings could also be found in predominantly agricultural villages. Almost every sizeable village had its smiths, carpenters, tilers, millers' assistants, and even hucksters and chapmen. Most thirteenth-century villages also contained spinners, or rather spinsters, and some might harbour a few fullers and weavers. In the second half of the fourteenth century weavers and other cloth workers proliferated in the newly grown cloth-working areas. In addition, smallholders could find employment as communal employees, i.e. village shepherds, herdsmen, or swine-herds, or eked out additional income by other non-agricultural pursuits—as carters, building labourers, seasonal quarrymen. Some families added to their income by brewing ale. Judging by the fine paid for the breaking of assize of ale, alewives were numerous in most villages.

Most of the opportunities for employment must, however, have lain in agriculture. In the thirteenth-century villages containing or adjoining manorial demesnes, numbers of villagers were employed as full-time labourers, or *famuli*. On demesnes as large as that of the Bishop of Winchester's manors of Downtown or Bishop's Waltham, the numbers of manorial officials and *famuli* could approach thirty. In addition the demesne might occupy considerable numbers in seasonal tasks. Grain was threshed and winnowed, wholly or in part, by the seasonal labour of hired men, and men were also hired to build and to roof the lord's farm buildings, to carry his building material or to supplement with hired labour the labour services available for ditching and dyking.[5]

Substantial villagers also employed hired labour. Our sources leave little doubt that in almost all the villages some villagers worked for others. Manorial and village by-laws recorded in court rolls abound with injunctions designed to safeguard the lord's supply of hired labour in harvest time against the competing claims of peasant employers. In fact manorial surveys and other documents occasionally refer to the villeins' servants. In the assessments for the Poll Taxes of 1379 and 1381 the names of the more substantial villagers are frequently followed by those of persons described as their *servientes*, presumably their resident labourers. Judging from modern examples, those of eighteenth- and nineteenth-century England, eighteenth-century Prussia or nineteenth-century Russia, the cultivation of holdings as large as a medieval virgate of thirty acres might very frequently require hired help. Bishop Latimer's father, a prosperous fifteenth-century villager farming the equivalent of two to four virgates, gave employment to six men. And it has already been shown here that the exaction of labour services from customary tenants could necessitate the employment of hired labour on customary holdings. It is therefore obvious that a certain number of smallholders must have earned or supplemented their income by working for peasant masters.

These and other openings for employment in a thirteenth-century village did a great deal to make it possible for smallholders to subsist on holdings too small for true subsistence farming. The extent of the outside employments should not however be overestimated. Some, if not most, smallholders were in all probability under-employed, and we must assume in the over-populated thirteenth-century countryside some under-employment must have been as inescapable as it has been in most peasant societies in modern times. Even the roughest of computations would be sufficient to demonstrate that in many a thirteenth-century village where the number of smallholders was no more than average, e.g. on the Abbot of Peterborough's manor of Kettering with about fifty smallholders, employment available on the 300 acres of demesne or on its few holdings in excess of one virgate would be insufficient to absorb all its idle hands all through the year. It is not therefore surprising that such populous places as the Abbot of Glastonbury's villages of Brent and Zoy should have sent out every year hundreds of *garciones*, unmarried young men, in search of employment elsewhere.

The failure to realize how incomplete and discontinuous the employment of village labourers was vitiates some recent statistical attempts to compute the income of the medieval village labourer by multiplying his daily wage by 250 or some other figure representing the total number of working days in the year. The calendar as well as the nature of agricultural operations were bound to make most rural employments intermittent and often no better than casual. We must therefore conclude that the supplementary income from wages could not wholly compensate smallholders for the acres they lacked, and that, taken as a group, smallholders occupied the lowest position in the economic scale of the medieval countryside.

V

There remains to consider the topmost layer of the thirteenth-century village. This layer, like the two lower ones, is marked off by frontiers so faint and so widely spaced as to admit great variations in acreages and in incomes; but in general the bulk of the holdings of this group will be found bunched at its bottom, since its statistical mode did not much exceed the holdings of a single virgate. The numbers of truly wealthy peasants (those holding two virgates or more) within the group would be very small, but the group as a whole might be fairly large. By comparison with villagers of lower rank most of these men could be regarded as well-to-do. If in the arable regions of England and on land of average quality a customary holding of half a virgate would be just sufficient to support a self-subsistent peasant household, a holding twice that size could provide a substantial surplus over and above the family's most essential needs.

Some households in this group could therefore afford economic outlays beyond the means of typical peasants. We do not know how much of the additional outlays went into the purchase of luxuries or semi-luxuries. But what we can guess about the preferences of medieval peasants as consumers strongly suggests that other outlays ranked more highly in their preferences than consumable luxuries. Additional land probably ranked highest. Not all the buyers of land recorded as such in our documents were rich villagers, but where the evidence of villagers' transactions—mostly in court rolls—is sufficiently detailed to reveal the social condition of the parties, it invariably suggests that the wealthier villagers bought more than others.

The high preference for land was, of course, part and parcel of the mode of life and of the scale of values characteristic of peasants of most ages and most countries. To a peasant, whether wealthy or poor, the ownership of land was an object to be pursued in all circumstances. To him land was not only a 'factor of production', the means towards higher output and income, but also a 'good' worth possession for its own sake and enjoyed as a measure of social status, a foundation of family fortunes, and a fulfilment and extension of the owner's personality.

The outlays on land purchases by wealthier peasants can therefore be taken for granted. What cannot be taken for granted is the use to which the land they newly acquired was put. Was it invariably run as a 'home farm' to augment the household's supply of food? Our answer must be a qualified affirmative. Holdings of the wealthier peasants as a rule differed from those of semi-virgaters mainly in their somewhat larger scale of operation. It was on holdings of this scale that the poorer villagers would presumably be employed as servants and labourers; and it is from such holdings that a large part of marketable agricultural supplies must have come.

Yet other possibilities must also be taken into account. Our sources make it quite clear that in the thirteenth century the more substantial villagers sometimes sub-let portions of their holdings. Needless to say not all the sub-letting was done by the wealthy. Villagers of more modest substance—widows, invalids, old folk—sometimes found themselves unable to cultivate their land; our records abound with references to holdings of this kind 'ploughed', i.e. cultivated, frequently on share-cropping terms (*ad campi partem*), by other men, usually lessees for a term of a year or two years. But the same records also contain numerous references to wealthy lessors. Where we find a large peasant holding made up of widely separated blocks of land, sometimes in different villages, or containing numerous habitable houses with several identifiable cotlands, the presumption is that the land could not have been exploited otherwise than by sub-letting.

Sub-letting, however, was not confined to composite holdings. We frequently find sub-leases which appear in surveys as single tenancies. Such holdings could contain 'under-settlers', i.e. tenants' tenants, even though their existence may be concealed from view. Now and again our documents reveal by indirect signs the existence of 'under-settlers'. On the estates of St Peter's of Gloucester or the bishops of Ely, the surveys, in defining the tenants' obligations, lay claim on the services (especially harvest services) of their sub-tenants, thus revealing their existence. Similar revelations, however fleeting and indirect, will be found in other sources: the bailiffs' accounts, court rolls and assessments to taxes.

It is thus possible to regard some of the larger village holdings as peasant 'mini-manors' of which portions would be directly cultivated by the principal tenant, while the rest would bring in rents and possibly some services. Sub-manors of this type were most likely to be found on the very large holdings of three, four or more virgates in the possession of freemen or *francolani*.

However, the wealthier peasants in the thirteenth century did not apparently confine the use of their surpluses and savings to purchases of land on their own account, but may also have helped to finance the land transactions of other men. Direct evidence of these, so-to-speak, banking and financial uses of the money surpluses of the wealthier peasant is very scanty. But their prevalence is indirectly suggested by one of the most puzzling features of village life. The puzzle concerns the provenance of the large sums which were laid out on the buying of land and other similar transactions. It is indeed difficult to understand how some of the villagers were able to find, without much apparent delay, the large sums of money required as entry fines or purchase price for land they bought. Abroad the problem was frequently solved, if solved is the right term, by loans advanced by money-lenders. But the curious and unique feature of the English village in the thirteenth century is the rarity of the professional money-lender, comparable to the *Wucher* or the *usurier* of the German and French villages. The Jews before their expulsion in 1290, and the Italians both before and after that date, do not appear to have operated in villages or to have sought or found many peasant customers. It is possible to argue that what kept them away from the villages was the difficulty of using the villein land as a security for loans. But why should they have not been lending money to smaller peasant freeholders?

An answer to this question, albeit a conjectural one, is that the villagers in need of money drew upon the resources of their wealthier neighbours. That money was borrowed left and right is evidenced by numerous pleas of debt on the manorial court rolls. Yet except for some parsons dabbling in a little money-lending it is as a rule impossible to single out among the creditors any professional usurers. Most of the substantial villagers will be found among the creditors: the function of money-lending thus appears disseminated through the upper ranks of the village society.

Further evidence of disseminated money-lending can also be descried among the names of men cited as pledges for various land transactions guaranteeing the payment of the purchase price by the buyer. But in that case why have they not been called upon to find the money in the first instance, at the time of purchase? In fact judicial records contain some cases in which men acting as pledges claimed to have advanced the purchase money. Admittedly such cases in the surviving documents are very few, but there is nothing in the record to suggest that in the thirteenth-century village they were in any way exceptional.

And even if further study fails to find the richer peasants operating at providing finance in every village, in those villages in which they did operate their local power and influence would truly be greatly enhanced. Men who, as we have seen, could operate as employers of their neighbours' labour and the lessors of their neighbours' land, would also acquire a stake in other people's lands and holdings. Even if so placed they might still remain members of the village community and peasants in outlook and social behaviour, but, judged by purely material tests of their economic activities and resources, they stood at the furthest possible remove from the ideal type of medieval peasant.

VI

The demarcations that we have so far drawn across the village society delineated the economic stratifications in the thirteenth century; they do not necessarily correspond to the economic stratifications both before and after that period. On the whole, however, the configuration of rural society probably remained very nearly the same. There were always large number of smallholders, a small group of village *kulaks* and an intermediate mass of middling peasants.

These persistent economic differentials are clearly visible in the Domesday Book. Some 10 per cent of the Domesday villagers were *cottarii, cotsetti* and *servi,* smallholders or wholly landless men. And it is quite possible that the *bordarii* (another 20 per cent) were also smallholders of one sort or another. Yet even these figures may overestimate the regularity and the size of individual holdings in 1086. Within each of the main Domesday categories, and especially in that of *villani,* i.e. fully-fledged customary virgates, the holdings might at first sight appear to be very uniform in size. The presence of virgaters and the regularity of their holdings may however be wholly fictitious. In the county of Middlesex, for which the Domesday Book happens to provide somewhat more detailed information of villeins' holdings, villeins are shown to hold not only entire virgates, but also considerable numbers of half-virgates and multiples of virgates. Mr Lennard has also shown that in the Domesday of the lands of the bishops of Ely, in which manors are described more fully, the holdings were distributed less regularly than they appear to be in the corresponding entries of the main, the Exchequer, Domesday. Similarly in early twelfth-century surveys available to us, such as those of Peterborough or Shaftesbury, the distribution of holdings is also less regular than in the Domesday Book; and the interval of time between their compilation and the date of the Domesday Book was not long enough to permit any wholesale change in sizes of holdings. We may therefore suspect that, had the compilers of the Domesday Book been interested in the actual holders of land and not in the units of land-holding, they might have recorded inequalities in the actual occupation of land concealed from our view by the uniform formulae of the inquest.

However, no matter how we interpret the Domesday evidence for the eleventh century, there should be little doubt about the evidence of the twelfth century. All the records of that period reveal the existence of the same differences which we have noted in the later period: a large body of smallholders, a small number of wealthy villagers, and a mass of men of middle substance holding the economic equivalent of more than a quarter but rather less than a whole of a virgate of land of average quality.

Nevertheless the persistence of the demarcations observed in the Domesday Book must not be misunderstood. Social shifts were bound to take place in the four centuries after 1080. The change most characteristic of the thirteenth century was the decline in the average size of holdings. The comparisons of the Glastonbury surveys of the late thirteenth century with those of the late twelfth, or of the accounts of Peterborough estates of the beginning of the fourteenth century with the accounts and surveys of the mid-thirteenth century, or of the abbey of Ramsey evidence at several points of time, show smallholdings proliferating; and, what we already know about the soaring demand for land in the thirteenth century and its dwindling supplies, makes this proliferation intelligible.

The changes at the other pole of the social scale are more difficult to trace or to account for. Wealthy villagers with two and more virgates were to be found everywhere, but whether their numbers grew or declined is impossible to say. As we shall see presently, the evidence of land transactions in the thirteenth century suggests that the main source of land which the persistent land buyers of this period—the greater landowners and the church—acquired were most frequently the lands of petty landowners or of the substantial peasant freeholders. This might predispose us to expect that the numbers of such freeholders would decline in the thirteenth century. Yet there were some such men to be found on most manors in the thirteenth century, and the evidence is insufficient to tell us whether these numbers grew or declined.

At first sight the evidence about the distribution of land and sizes of holdings might appear to be much more explicit in the closing centuries of the middle ages—the late fourteenth and the fifteenth. In almost every village for which information is available men with large or very large holdings, i.e. the equivalents of two virgates and more, were becoming more numerous in the late fourteenth and fifteenth centuries. From this some historians have concluded that the English village in the fifteenth century suffered—or would 'benefited' be the right word?—from a kind of economic 'differentiation' similar to that which Marxist writers have discerned in some continental villages in the late nineteenth century. According to this view village societies were at that time undergoing a 'capitalist' or 'pre-capitalist' transformation. The old equality of land-holdings, and the middling rank of peasants representing the older equality, were breaking up, while the class of 'kulak' capitalists grew at the top and a mass of proletarized agricultural labourers were accumulating at the bottom.

This scheme will not fit the evidence of English villages in the later middle ages. Whereas the increase in the English 'kulak' class is unmistakeable, the decline in the numbers of the labouring poor is equally unmistakeable. In most villages their numbers were lower in the fifteenth century than they had been in the thirteenth. The decline is easily accounted for by the downward trend of the population as a whole and by the promotion of the poorer villagers into higher ranks.

Economic promotion may provide a truer and more convenient description of fifteenth-century changes than 'differentiation'. In most fifteenth-century villages average holdings of all villagers grew, and as a result the largest holdings became larger and the smallest holdings became fewer. As for holdings of middling size, they would appear to increase or decline according to the positions of demarcation lines. If the number of acres per household were the same as that we assigned to the middling group in the thirteenth century, i.e. more than a quarter virgate and no more than a half virgate, the proportions of men in the group would appear to increase in some of the villages so far studied. In many villages the middling mass of villagers, the 'semi-virgaters', gained more recruits by promotion into it from below than it lost by promotion from its own ranks into the 'kulak' class above it. But, on the other hand, if our demarcation lines were so re-drawn as to scale up the size of the 'middling' holdings to accord with the increase in the average holdings of villagers, the structure of rural society as represented by the distribution of landholding in the fifteenth century would not differ much from its structure in the thirteenth century. The 'kulak' rank might be slightly larger, the small-holders less numerous, but the statistical 'mode' would still be represented by villagers of middle rank.

However, the actual economic condition of the different ranks of village society may have changed more markedly than their relative position in the scale of landholding. It is obvious that a villager with the equivalent of several virgates on his hands could both benefit and suffer from the new economic dispensation. Like all other villagers, he would benefit from greater opportunities for acquiring land, yet, like all other landowners, he would suffer from higher wages and—if he sub-let his land—from lower rents. His balance of advantages would depend on the proportions in which he combined the two sources of agricultural income. A village 'kulak' who derived most of his income from rents (probably an uncommon figure) might find himself on the losing side.

At first sight the villagers in the middling ranks should to some extent have shared the fortunes of wealthier peasants. For they too could benefit from lower land values and suffer from higher wages and somewhat lower food prices. Many more of them were now able to 'thrive' into the condition of 'kulaks' by enlarging their holdings, but whether their income was thereby greatly enhanced would also depend on the extent to which they were involved in sheep farming or cereal growing, employed labour or let their land. We must however assume that middling men did not depend on hired labour to any great extent and that only a few among them regularly sublet any of their land. If so, we should be justified in concluding that on balance most of them stood to benefit from the late medieval transformations.

More unmistakable were the improvements in the condition of the lowest category of villagers, those with very small holdings or cottagers with no field land at all. The smallholders and cottagers should have benefited from the greater opportunities for acquiring land. The presence of large numbers of smallholders and landless men previously under-provided with land explains why manorial lords were able to re-let many of the holdings left vacant after the Black Death—an ability which surprised some historians and led them to play down the effects of the Black Death itself.[6] The ranks of the village smallholders were thus reduced twice over: by the direct effects of the Black Death and by promotion into the ranks of tenants above them. And we have already seen that the economic condition of those who still continued as agricultural labourers benefited from higher wages accompanied by stable and/or falling food prices.[7]

Between them the peasant in the middle ranks and the smallholder formed the great majority of the rural population. The improvement in their economic condition must therefore colour our entire view of the late fourteenth and fifteenth centuries. If in the past medievalists were inclined to disagree in their estimation of popular wellbeing in the later middle ages, their disagreement was largely due to their failure to distinguish clearly enough between the performance of the rural economy as a whole and the condition of individual villagers. We are learning now from the experience of the under-developed countries that, when populations increase at a very fast rate, it is possible for national economies, measured by their aggregate products and incomes, to rise steeply, and yet for the economic conditions of individuals to improve very little or even to decline. In the same way, the agricultural boom of the thirteenth century was wholly consistent with the impoverishment of the lower ranks of village society, while in the late fourteenth and fifteenth centuries the contraction in the total area of cultivated land and the fall in the aggregate output of agriculture went together with an improved economic condition of the majority of the villagers. We can therefore justifiably consider the late middle ages both as a time of economic decline and as the golden age of English peasantry.

References

1. Sir William Ashley, *The Bread of our Forefathers* (1928). In spite of the controversy in which the author was engaged the evidence in the book in fact supports both his view of the preponderance of inferior grains in the villagers' diet and the alternative argument stressing the importance of wheat as a peasant crop.

2. J. Z. Titow, *English Rural Society*, pp. 80–93. His computations on pp. 80 and 89 are highly pertinent and are substantially the same as mine, though they may be subject to some correction in detail.

3. The villages and sources from which the data in this table have been drawn are specified in M. M. Postan's chapter in *The Cambridge Economic History*, Vol. I, pp. 619–620.

4. J. Birrell, 'Peasant Craftsmen in the Medieval Forest', *Agric. Hist. Rev.*, Vol. 17 (1969).

5. M. M. Postan, *The Famulus: The Estate Labourer in the Twelfth and the Thirteenth Centuries* (Supplement No. 2, *Econ. Hist. Rev.*) (1954).

6. A. Elisabeth Levett, *The Black Death on the Estates of the See of Winchester*, Oxford Studies in Social and Legal History, V (1916).

7. For a general survey of the subject of this chapter, see M. M. Postan in *The Cambridge Economic History*, Vol. I, 2nd ed.

9 The Villagers: Serfdom and Freedom

I

Our story of the changing economic conditions in village society and our conclusions about the way in which different groups within the villages fared during the middle ages is complicated by the parallel changes in the legal status of villagers. In the older writings the differences in status of villagers were as a rule represented as the decisive factor in the wellbeing of individual peasants. In the previous chapter we showed how the condition of villagers depended on the purely economic factors: the size of smallholdings and the income they yielded. There is some evidence to suggest that the villagers themselves did not rate the differences of status as highly as the amount of land they cultivated.

The evidence is largely negative, and mainly that of manumissions. A villein could always improve his economic condition by buying from his lord a charter of manumission releasing him from the disabilities and payments of unfree status. And high as the price of manumission sometimes was, it was seldom so high as to be beyond the means of more substantial villagers, and not higher than the prices they sometimes paid for additional land. Nevertheless, purchases of freedom were by no means frequent. Grants of manumission occurred more often on some estates than on others and were probably more numerous in the documents of the bishops of Winchester than in the documents of the abbots of Peterborough or Glastonbury. Yet, except for five or six years in which the total number of manumissions was ten or more (these were as a rule years in which free burgage status was conferred on inhabitants of towns newly created on the bishop's domains), the average annual number of manumissions on Winchester estates taken together was little more than five, and it is doubtful whether their cumulative total over the 150 years since 1209 was much higher than 250. In any one year at the end of our period, in the 1340s, the total number of bishop's free tenants who had obtained their freedom by manumission or descended from manumitted villeins was smaller still, probably no greater than seventy or eighty, or about 2 per cent of the bishop's entire tenantry.

The evidence of manumissions does not stand alone. It is corroborated by surviving references to cases when free men married well-endowed villein women for the sake of their land, even though they may thereby have prejudiced the status of their progeny and perhaps also their own condition. The documents have also preserved a few cases of free men accepting from the lords villein tenements with villein obligations attached to them.

In short we are driven to the conclusion that freedom was not always estimated more highly than, or even as highly as, material possessions. This does not however mean that personal status did not affect the lives of villagers and that freedom was not valued by them. On the contrary free status was appreciated and serfdom resented for a variety of reasons. We have already seen that in theory the villein's land and his livestock belonged to his lord and could not be alienated without his consent. A villein could not change his place of residence or give away his daughter in marriage without the lord's permission. He was not permitted to sue his lord in king's courts; his right to enter into agreements concerning his goods and property, to bequeath or inherit land and livestock, were in various ways limited to the lord's rights over his person and his property. Above all the services he owed to the lord were in theory uncertain, and could be increased or changed at the lord's will.

In practice, however, these disabilities were much less oppressive than they appear in legal theory. Titles to villein holdings were protected by manorial custom, so that villein tenants were hardly ever deprived of their land by the arbitrary action of their lords. Labour services were also fixed by custom. Where and when lords attempted to re-define the custom governing labour services to their own advantage, their ability to do so was rooted not in the purely legal disabilities of villein status but in the economic conditions of the day. Villeins were also able to buy free land without let or hindrance. They also bought, sold, pledged and hired livestock; and acquired and parted at will with movable goods. The lord's permission to marry, to move away, or to enter into agreements was purchasable by fine, and hardly an instance of the lord's refusing to accept the fine has so far come to light.

In fact the main weight of the villein's disabilities was economic.

The customary ('assized') rent of villeins was as a rule considerably higher than that of freeholders. And although the licences for marriages, migrations, sale and contracts, were all purchasable, purchased they had to be. Similarly labour services were often discharged by hired substitutes, or remitted for a consideration, from year to year. But both the hire and annual remission of services required an outlay of money on the villein's part.

So great in fact was the purely economic burden of villein status that in comparing the economic worth of a villein with that of a free peasant we must assume that, in order to maintain the same standard of life, the villein required a larger, sometimes a much larger, holding than a freeholder in the same village.

This does not, however, mean that free tenants, considered in the aggregate, were necessarily better off than customary tenants similarly considered. There were perhaps more freemen than villeins in the topmost layer of village society, i.e. among the few villagers with holdings of two or more virgates. On the other hand, smallholders were also relatively more numerous among the freemen, especially in counties and hundreds in which free tenures were widespread. In the Hundred Rolls free tenants holding quarter-virgates and less formed 59 per cent of the freeholding tenantry, whereas among villeins smallholders similarly defined formed only 27 per cent. The numbers of free smallholders were highest of all in regions, such as the Danelaw or East Anglia, where freeholders or near-free sokemen formed the bulk of the village population. Thus in the parts of Lincolnshire studied by Mr Hallam —Sutton, Spalding and Pinchbeck—holdings under five acres accounted for 70 to 75 per cent of the total. The population on some Suffolk manors, e.g. the abbey of Bury St Edmunds, was little different.[1]

It may be that the recorded numbers of smallholdings among freeholders and sokemen are greater than the numbers of villein smallholders simply because manorial documents happen to be more communicative about the former than about the latter. But even when full allowances are made for this particular bias in our documents, the numbers of free smallholders will still appear large enough to require an explanation.

The explanation generally given is that free land underwent continuous fragmentation because it was fully exposed to the action of the land market and also because it was subject to partible inheritance. Rules of inheritance varied from place to place more than almost any other feature of rural society; but overlaying these local variations was the broad distinction between the impartible inheritance of bond land and the partible inheritance of much of free land. Free land of the peasants and most of their sokeland could be transmitted to all the surviving children and be held by them in joint tenancy or—a much more widespread practice—be divided among them in equal portions. We have seen that, when and where the shortage of land was very acute, the rules of succession to villein holdings may have become somewhat irrelevant since, in times and places like these, the great majority of villeins—perhaps as many as 75 per cent—succeeded to land either by purchase or by marriage to heiresses and widows. Yet even in these cases the holdings were handed down whole or—as in the case of widows—nearly whole. By contrast, free appendages to villein holdings or entire free holdings would often be divided among heirs or alienated in parcels. It is for this reason that free land was more fragmented than villein land and that the 'free' societies of Danelaw or East Anglia or Kent contained relatively larger numbers of small holders than the fully manorialized counties of the Midlands or the Thames valley.

Our conclusion thus must be that, judged by the size of their holdings, freemen were not necessarily the best-found group of village society. Their holdings were more disparate, i.e. more unequally distributed; but if averaged out they would not be larger than those of the villeins. The true economic difference between the free and the unfree was not in the average numbers of acres they held but in their greater command over the income which their acres yielded. The unfree had to part in favour of the lord with a far greater proportion of their output than the freemen. To repeat: such was the burden of villein payments that an individual villein would be poorer, perhaps much poorer, than an individual freeholder with a holding of the same size.

The unfree villeinage and the free peasantry were distributed very unevenly over the face of medieval England, and their relative numbers changed from century to century. In some parts of the country the bulk of the rural population was free. One such free region was Kent. Even in Kent it would be possible to find manors conforming to type and containing large numbers of unfree villeins. Most of the Kentishmen, however, were freemen and held their land in free tenure. The customs which defined their titles to land and enshrined the prevailing forms of landholding (mostly those by joint family groups) and rules of succession (frequently to younger sons) were both ancient and local. According to Mr Jolliffe they had been brought over from the continent by the Kentish Jutes; according to tradition they were protected from violation in later centuries by a grant of protection from William the Conqueror. But whatever its origin and whatever the causes of its survival, the Kentish freedom was widespread and clearly set the region apart from the rest of England.

Equally apart from the rest of manorialized England was another free area, that of the eastern counties, which included the whole of the Danelaw and stretched from Suffolk to north Lincolnshire and from the North Sea coast to the eastern parts of Leicestershire and Derbyshire. Here too the freedom may have been imported from their continental homeland by the Angles who occupied East Anglia, or by the Danes who invaded the region and settled in some parts of it three or four centuries later. It may have owed its persistence in still later centuries to the progress of reclamation which created belts of new and free holdings on the fringes of the fens. But whatever were the forces behind the freedom, its prevalence is unmistakeable. Needless to say unfree peasants were to be found in some numbers, more especially on older monastic estates, such as those of Bury St Edmunds, Ramsey or Peterborough, but in the region as a whole unfree villeins were relatively much fewer than elsewhere in England. The majority were freemen, or else sokemen, men of free status owing some non-servile service over to feudal lords.

In the other parts of England, and more particularly in the west Midlands, in the southern counties and in the south-west on the English side of the Tamar, serfdom in its various degrees was the lot of most of the countryfolk. Free peasants holding freely were of course to be found even in this servile core of England. There was hardly a village without some free members, and some counties, especially Oxfordshire, Warwickshire and Derbyshire, contained large enclaves, sometimes entire hundreds, of predominantly free population. According to Kosminsky's calculation men holding freely or for money rent formed more than one third of the population recorded in the surviving portions of the Hundred Rolls of 1273.

Thus generally speaking the medieval countryside was not uniformly the land of the unfree. Serfdom was the lot of most people in the greater part of England, but not of everybody everywhere. Moreover its incidence and its burdens changed from period to period. These changes are well known to historians, and have figured prominently in historical writings. They will be recounted here in greater detail.

II

The initial phase of rural serfdom has already been discussed in an earlier chapter; its history need not therefore be recapitulated here at any length. What is important to note here is that, however much medieval historians differ about the origins of medieval serfdom, they all agree that on the eve of the Norman conquest serfdom was widespread all over that part of England in which it was to predominate in later centuries. That by the eleventh century it had become part of the social order is shown by the remarkable blueprint of English society in a document (*Rectitudines Singularum Personarum*) listing and defining the various grades of society. That it was also so widespread as to engulf the bulk of the rural population is shown by the Domesday Book in which some two thirds of the tenantry at the time of Edward, i.e. in the third quarter of the twelfth century, are described as villeins and holders in villeinage. The term villein in this context need not necessarily denote a peasant of servile or semi-servile status, but other near-contemporary documents leave no doubt that men so described could no longer be ranked as fully independent of the manor and its lord.

It is the general opinion of historians that what the first century of Norman rule contributed to the growth of the servile or semi-servile condition was to generalize and define it. In the course of the twelfth century legal theory and practice made the status of villein clearer, more uniform and more rigid. The changes in legal theory were probably associated with the political changes in the reigns of William I, Henry I and Henry II, when the feudal system itself was, so to speak, redefined and reorganized more uniformly and precisely than before. The great lawyers of the time, Glanville and Bracton, are commonly associated with this work of definition; but the work was also done by the humbler lawyers of the twelfth and early thirteenth centuries and by the legally trained clerks who drew up the manorial custumals and surveys of the great estates. The concept of villein status and villein service, as defined by lawyers, was to prevail until the end of the middle ages, and has coloured all historical accounts of medieval society. Thus considered, the twelfth century appears as a time when the villeins' condition worsened, or, in more dramatic terms, the time of intensified feudal oppression of the free.

This view however is insufficiently related to everyday facts to be wholly true. While in theory villeinage may have been getting more rigid and more oppressive, the actual position of the villeins may have improved as a result of wholesale relaxation of the manorial rule in the middle decades of the century. We have seen that during that time the manorial system was suffering from lax administration and manorial depression in general. At the cost of yet another repetition we must recall that the direct management of the demesne during the period was difficult, that in most estates demesnes were farmed out and that on some estates the acreages of demesne arable contracted. This alone would have reduced the demand for villeins' labour and made the lords more willing to commute or sell annually many of the labour serviates due from their villeins. Even more important was the inability of the landlords to enforce labour dues in places where they might still have wished to use them in full. Indeed so unenforceable was the landlords' authority over some of their estates that there was apparently little to prevent some villein tenants from taking the law into their hands or else inducing the lords to commute their labour services for rents. Hence the remarkable increase in the numbers of *censuarii* and *molmen*, all of them erstwhile villeins who had held by full bond service, but who now held for rent or rent plus some very light seasonal labour dues.[2]

We should thus be quite justified in concluding that in the twelfth century England took a long step away from serfdom and towards greater independence and freedom. The step may even have been longer than the numbers of rent-paying tenants in the surveys and custumals indicate. If we are to judge from later thirteenth-century sources it appears that, in addition to the men who had succeeded in converting their holdings to rent, a very large number of villeins, perhaps the majority, had achieved a *de facto* lightening of their obligation, the significance of which has so far escaped the attention of most medievalists. Thirteenth-century documents reveal the prevalence all over England of a form of peasant tenure under which tenants were subject to alternative sets of dues, either rent or work (*ad opus* or *ad censum*). In theory it was in the lord's power to decide which of the two options he would choose, but the manorial accounts and surveys strongly suggest that in fact only the rent option was exercised.

How and when the practice was established may still be in doubt; but on the whole it is probable that it owed its spread, and bore witness, to twelfth-century commutations. We have seen that the latter often took the form not of a complete change-over to rent, but of a partial release whereby the heavier weekly services were commuted and only the lighter seasonal tasks were retained. This lends support to the contention that the 'either-or' terms were, like the holdings of the *molmen* and *censuarii*, the product of the twelfth-century relaxations in the manorial regime.

Whether we accept this contention or not, the fact remains that large numbers, perhaps the bulk, of thirteenth-century villeins held their holdings in this manner. If so, the actual condition of villagers at the end of the twelfth century was much less servile and less burdened with heavy labour dues than it would have been had the law of villeinage been applied with full vigour. While the legal theory hardened, the actual manorial practice softened to an extent that would justify our regarding the twelfth century as a period in which serfdom was in retreat.

III

As far as we can judge it turned to the offensive again in the thirteenth century. On a few estates—e.g. those of the earls of Cornwall—the commutation of services continued; while on some other estates manumission and similar concessions may occasionally have released individual villagers from servile burdens. The general movement of commutation, however, appears to have come to an end. The records give an unmistakable impression of a halt. Where labour services still survived, such services as were due were exacted in full. Not all of them were necessarily taken in kind. Some manorial estates were entitled to more labour dues than they could profitably employ on their demesnes; on these estates a proportion of labour services were 'sold' from year to year. But where and when the lords did so, they acted not under pressure from their tenants but, so to speak, from strength. Here and there we find them even trying to raise the labour services, either in order to procure additional supplies of labour or as an indirect means of raising rents. Occasionally the lords even tried to reimpose services on the men who had succeeded at an earlier epoch in converting their holdings into 'mollands'.

The reason why landlords were now not only desirous to maintain the weight of labour dues but also 'got away with it' are not difficult to guess. With the growing scarcity of land, and with the restored powers of landlords over the management of their estates, the pressure of landowners was more difficult to resist. This does not, of course, mean that the lords' encroachments were not in fact resisted. Judicial records of the thirteenth century abound with references to proceedings initiated by villagers in defence of what they considered their ancient right of holding for rent or for lighter services. In most of these cases the law sided with the landlords; and this attitude of the law may of course be nothing more than a manifestation of the feudal influences at courts or of the class bias of the judges. But there is little doubt that in most of these cases the letter of the law was on the landlord's side; that most of the rebellious tenants were in fact villeins who had in an earlier period obtained their release from labour services without the lord's concurrence, or at least without a formal charter of enfranchisement or manumission. And this is of course further evidence of the twelfth-century origin of the relaxations as well as of the difference in the economic and political climate of the twelfth and thirteenth centuries.[3]

IV

However the thirteenth-century reaction itself did not endure for very long or spread to every estate. In the course of the fourteenth and fifteenth centuries releases from labour dues again became as general and as frequent as they had been in the twelfth. During these closing centuries of the middle ages commutations were resumed and continued at such a pace that in the end labour services finally disappeared, as did also most of the personal disabilities of villein status.

The final break up of medieval serfdom may or may not have provoked some reaction from the landlords. Old writers frequently depicted the half-century following the Black Death as a period of social unrest generated by the lords' endeavours to put the clock back, to reimpose labour services and to keep wages down.

This version of the fourteenth century's history and of its

conflicts accords ill with facts. Employers of labour put up a resistance to the soaring rise of wages after the Black Death, and the fourteenth-century Statutes of Labourers, imposing maximum rates of wages, were the result of this resistance. The probability is that the main pressure behind the legislation came not from feudal landowners, who by now derived the bulk of their revenues from rents, but from the smaller men still cultivating their home farms. This at any rate is how the clash of interests is presented in the only contemporary discussion of the issues available to us: that in a parliamentary petition of 1368. But whether the demand for wage curbs did or did not come from the feudal landlords, the curbs themselves proved ineffective. As we know now, the laws of supply and demand proved stronger than the employers' pressure and the legislation it produced; and wages continued to rise until some time in the fifteenth century.

Apart from the abortive agitation against the wage rise, the fourteenth-century attempts to restore labour services or to exact them in full, or otherwise to undo the commutations and the relaxations of the previous epoch, were very few and far between and were nearly all confined to the immediate post-Black Death years. Even then they left fewer marks in our records and were presumably less frequent than the earlier, the thirteenth-century, attempts of the landlords to restore in full or to increase the labour services of the villeins. Somewhat more widespread may have been the attempts of some landlords to compel their villeins to take up vacant holdings, but on the whole these were also relatively ineffective. Flight, competition among landlords anxious to attract settlers, and the downright refusal of villeins to obey, defeated both the compulsory regulation of wages and the compulsory resettlement of vacant lands. In the end economic forces asserted themselves, and the lords and employers found that the most effective way of retaining labour was to pay higher wages, just as the most effective way of retaining tenants was to lower rents and release servile obligations.

The spirit of restlessness and revolt did not strictly speaking accord with the economic situation. What with the improved prospects of all the lower ranks of village society and the rapid withering away of servile dues and disabilities, a conventionally disposed observer, whether a contemporary witness or a modern student, might have expected the age to be one of universal and growing contentment. Yet this was a period of gathering discontent and rebellion. Discontent showed itself largely in movements of religious heterodoxy, represented by Lollards, by John Wycliffe or such popular preachers as John Ball. The rebelliousness of the time culminated in the Peasant Rising of 1381.

The bare history of the rising is plain and presents no problems. The first violent outbreak occurred at the end of May in Essex, and was apparently triggered off by the allegedly oppressive levying of the Poll Tax. The main outbreak however occurred a fortnight later in Kent and East Anglia. Two eventful days in June, the 11th and the 12th, saw a rebellious multitude of Kentishmen, led by one Wat Tyler, invade London and temporarily take possession of the city streets. Almost simultaneously multitudes rose in rebellion in various parts of the country but mainly in East Anglia and Cambridgeshire, invaded local town-centres, seized and burned manorial rolls and, in doing so, gave expression to a variety of discontents, some local, some directed against royal taxation or manorial disabilities.[4]

The revolt was at first met by promises of concessions from the King and the nobles, but was soon suppressed by force. Within a week of the June event the rising was over, and passed away without having seriously affected the social and economic conditions of the country. It nevertheless survived in historical tradition, and has throughout the subsequent centuries been remembered and discussed, not merely as a unique incident in English history, but also a landmark in social development and as a typical instance of the working class revolt against oppression.

The actual events after the revolt fit badly into the traditional picture; least of all do they fit into the story of villeins up in arms against the landlords who tried to re-establish and to enforce in full their rights to compulsory services. In the first place the rising was not purely rural: some of its most famous incidents, i.e. the riots at St Albans, Norwich, Yarmouth, Bury St Edmunds, Ipswich, Winchester, Scarborough, Beverley and York, did not involve rustics, or at least rustics alone, and were not primarily concerned with labour services. Secondly, the hotbeds of rebellion included Kent, East Essex and Suffolk and Norfolk, where free tenure predominated and where villeins were in a minority and were less bound by manorial ties than in most other parts of England. And although the outbreaks spread as far as Yorkshire and the Wirral peninsula, they largely by-passed regions where villeinage was most widespread and oppressive, such as Somerset.

The rebels are reported to have attacked and ransacked manorial muniments and to have burnt court rolls, but this does not necessarily signify that manorial records were now unusually oppressive, or that they were now cited against villeins more frequently and unjustly than in centuries before.

In fact it is very difficult to find a direct economic case behind the rising. An economic historian concerned with the Peasant Revolt can therefore do little more than warn other historians against too naive or too economic a sociology of rebellion—a sociology which considers every rebellion as a direct reaction to intensified oppression or deepening poverty. A more sophisticated view of the Peasant Revolt would present it not as a reaction to poverty returned or to serfdom revived but as a demonstration that men were now so far advanced on their road to freedom and prosperity as to resent more than ever the surviving vestiges of old oppressions. An even greater degree of sophistication would be to plead against an undue emphasis on economic causes, whatever they were. Were the religious and moral ideas of John Ball and the other seditious preachers mere vehicles of discontents they did nothing to generate, or were they and their ideas in themselves a source of unsettlement and unrest for which the manorial records, the machinations of lawyers and the manorial reaction were little more than convenient pretexts?

However, irrespective of their preferred interpretations of the Peasant Revolt, historians are now in general agreement that it was a passing episode in the social history of the late middle ages, and that it did very little to speed up and nothing to arrest the general movement towards commutation of labour services and the emancipation of serfs. This movement was not wholly completed by 1348, or by 1381, but it was finally wound up in the last century of the English middle ages. Some legal rudiments of old serfdom survived in the terms of customary tenures, mostly 'copyholds', of the sixteenth century. But in general rural serfdom had gone out of the land, and was all but forgotten by the time Queen Elizabeth ascended the throne of England.

References

1. Kosminsky, *Studies*, pp. 203–23; Hallam, *Settlement and Society*, pp. 196–222; R. H. Hilton, *The Stoneleigh Leger Book* (Dugdale Society) (1960), pp. xxxviii–xliv.

2. M. M. Postan, 'The Chronology of Labour Services', in E. Minchinton (ed.), *Essays in Agrarian History* (1970); for earlier discussion of the extent and the chronology of medieval commutations, see T. W. Page, *The End of Villeinage in England* (1900) and H. L. Gray, 'The Commutation of Villein Services', *Eng. Hist. Rev.*, XXIX (1914).

3. R. H. Hilton, 'Peasant Movements in England before 1381' in E. M. Carus-Wilson (ed.), *Essays in Economic History*, Vol. II.

4. Writings on the Peasant Revolt, mostly popular, are very numerous, but the account in E. Powell, *The Rising in East Anglia in 1381* (1896), is still the best, even though restricted to the eastern counties.

10 The Landlords

I

Considering how ubiquitous was the presence of the manorial feudatories and how heavily it weighed upon the lives of the countryfolk, it is surprising that so little should have been written about them as a class and about their changing fortunes in the middle ages. It may well be of course that the landlords have not been studied separately merely because historians have been under the illusion that they could understand them without studying them. The social demarcations which separated the landlord class from the rest of medieval society and enclosed them as a separate social group were so obvious and so sharply defined that historians might perhaps be forgiven for believing that they could always recognize a medieval lord when they saw him. Indeed the lines of division between the feudal landlords and the rest of society were cut more deeply and were more fixed than all other divisions in medieval society. From this point of view medieval England was a highly stable and wholly polarized two-class community wherein a much elevated class of feudal magnates and knights was confronted with a much inferior mass of rural humanity.

Needless to say even a society as stable and polarized as that was bound to harbour some intermediate groups. What distinguished the men in these groups was not only their position on the boundaries between classes but the greater ease and frequency with which they were able to cross the boundaries on their way up. Such men could be found in the Church, Benedictine houses included, in the upper ranks of the merchant class and above all among lawyers.

Historians have always believed that entry into the landowning class was easiest for wealthy men who had amassed their wealth in commerce. The more conspicuous medieval instances of such entry are well known, and none are known better than that of the de la Poles, a fourteenth-century merchant family which within two generations rose to the position and title of earls of Suffolk; but among their humbler contemporaries there was also a large number, perhaps more than a score, of gentlemen descended from merchant families of London and of the main provincial cities. On the other hand many of these merchant families were themselves of gentle origin (in this respect Dick Wittington was no exception), since apprenticeships in a high-ranking branch of trade was not beneath the dignity of young sons of landed families. The known instances of merchant families wholly unrelated to the gentry rising into it are by comparison few; and on the whole fewer in the fifteenth century than they appear to have been in the heyday of war speculation and war finance during the opening phase of the Hundred Years War. For these and other reasons some of the popular notion of the bourgeois inflow into the nobility may well turn out to be exaggerated.[1]

On the other hand it is difficult to overestimate the continuous social advancement of lawyers and their ability to break into the upper ranks of society. All through the middle ages, but perhaps more in the late centuries than in the earlier ones, legal education and the opportunities it offered for bureaucratic and political employment provided the easiest and best-trodden path to the advancement of individuals. Lawyers, not all of them necessarily men of good birth, filled the offices of state, acted in judicial capacities, served on baronial, episcopal and abbatial councils, represented powerful men and interests at courts of law, at the Exchequer, in business transactions and in transfers of property, and even administered royal armies. Their opportunities for enrichment, political influence and social rise were accordingly great. It is not therefore surprising that lawyers descending from families of merchants or petty landlords or of even humbler provenance should have been able to climb into the upper reaches of society more frequently and with greater ease than most other men. The ability appeared to grow from century to century, since clerks or descendants of clerks appear to be more numerous and more prominent in government, parliament and baronial households of the late fourteenth and fifteenth centuries than they were in the society and government of earlier periods.

So much for the intermediate groups on the higher levels of society. Some intermediate elements could also be found along the lower divide that separated the gentry from the peasants immediately below them. The topmost layer of free peasantry—some wealthy freeholders or *frankolani*—possessed holdings and enjoyed incomes at least equal to those of lesser knights. The differences between them and knights were sometimes purely formal. By a royal prescription of 1247 all freeholders worth 40*s*. per annum and more were to be knighted. But it appears that in the thirteenth century many freeholders of substance avoided the honour and the obligations of belted knighthood. In order to remedy the shortage of knights in the shires the crown had to admit to knightly duties—mostly those of serving on inquests—men who had not been knighted.[2]

These intermediate groups apart, landowners were a remarkably undifferentiated group. They formed what a sociologist would recognize as a single 'unit of social intercourse'. All the important social ties and contacts, in the first place marriages, but also trusteeships, executorships, sureties in lawsuits, warranties in debt and in landed transactions, were confined to men within this unit. Within it promotions and demotions—or what sociologists would describe as 'social mobility'—were unimpeded. There was nothing to prevent a gentleman of modest fortune from rising by marriage, by royal service or by good fortune into the topmost feudal ranks, nor was there anything to prevent younger sons or impoverished descendants of great families from sinking to the position of humble knights. A family like the Pelhams of Sussex, though of relatively modest condition to begin with, could in the course of the fifteenth century rise to equal the magnates without acquiring a noble title; whereas the family of Fitz Lambert, which at the end of the twelfth century held the barony of Redbourne, was by 1321 reduced to a near-peasant holding of some sixty acres without apparently losing its knightly rank. Knights were often educated in baronial households, were attached to them as retainers and served as baronial functionaries. Professor Roskell has also shown that in the fifteenth-century parliaments the knights of the shire of knightly origin and status shared the attitudes of the magnates, represented them on public bodies and generally formed part of the same 'interest'.[3]

II

So clear and incontestable was the social unity of the class that historians might be forgiven for believing, as many of them do, that within it no differences could ever be so great as to give rise to internecine conflicts. Hence the uncertainty—an uncertainty bordering on confusion—with which so many historians have dealt with changes in the position of the landowning classes and with the manner in which these changes affected the different sections within it.

This uncertainty first came to the notice of students in the course of the familiar controversy about the landowners of the sixteenth and early seventeenth centuries. In this controversy some historians tried to distinguish two separate layers within the landowning classes, the magnates and the gentry, reacting differently to economic circumstances, prospering or declining at different times and sometimes at each other's expense. Other historians, however, have argued that the relative positions of the greater and the smaller landowners, considered as groups, remained roughly the same at all times. Individual fortunes rose and fell but the balance of economic power as between the great families in the aggregate and the smaller ones, also in the aggregate, was not thereby altered.[4]

The same clash of hypotheses is also possible in the study of medieval landownership. Were the changes in the landowning class between the eleventh century and the fifteenth merely cellular, i.e. mere replacements of some great families by others, or were they also structural, i.e. capable of altering the relative weight, the wealth and power, of entire groups within it?

Until recently this conflict of hypotheses has remained concealed from casual viewers and perhaps from the disputants themselves. It is however obvious that the history of landownership during the revolutionary decades of the Norman Conquest has been treated as a purely cellular process, and told as a story of how the personnel of the landowning class changed as a result of wholesale replacement of Anglo-Saxons by the Norman or other followers of the Conqueror. The subsequent history of the landowning classes has been told in the same manner. Yet on *a priori* grounds it appears highly improbable that major economic changes, such as those which English agriculture and rural society underwent during the middle ages, could have occurred without affecting the fortunes of the landowning classes as a whole or of different groups within it.

Needless to say the fortunes of the greater landlords did not solely depend on the vagaries of agricultural production and values or of other purely manorial profits. As I shall have to stress repeatedly later, the landowners were a 'feudal' class entitled to the non-agricultural revenues and bearing the non-agricultural charges inherent in the contracts of tenure and in the public functions they performed. Yet however fully we allow for these non-agricultural revenues and charges we should still find that manorial profits formed the main source of noblemen's and gentlemen's incomes. As manorial profits rose and fell, so did the aggregate revenues of the landowning classes expand and contract.

At the same time different groups within the landowning classes were bound to differ in their ability to benefit and in their liability to suffer from changes in the economic situation. Thus in considering the agricultural expansion of the late twelfth and thirteenth centuries we must presume that whereas all owners of land must have benefited from rising outputs, from expanding settlement and from higher land values, some must have benefited more—indeed much more—than others. We now know that the two sources of landlords' income—that of rents, and that of demesne produce—combined differently in different lordships, and that whereas some landlords depended mainly on rents, others involved themselves deeply with direct cultivation and with production of crops for sale. Smaller lay estates possessed limited opportunities for exploiting the rising land market; the smaller monastic houses and small lay landowners themselves consumed the greater part of their demesnes' output, and were therefore unable to reap the full benefits of the buoyant market for agricultural produce. The economic situation should therefore have favoured the magnates rather than the smaller owners.

The possibility that different strata of the landowning class fared differently in the thirteenth century has occasionally occurred to writers concerned with the political conflicts of the time. They could not fail to note that the baronial wars of the thirteenth century and the constitutional changes which accompanied and followed them were somehow involved with social changes and economic fortunes. Historians have as a rule taken the view that in summoning the knights of the shire to parliament in 1295, and thereby establishing the parliamentary tradition of English government, Edward I was responding to the changes in the position of the smaller landlords. It has been similarly assumed that Edward's wish to exploit the changed position of smaller landlords prompted his various acts of legislation in the second half of the century.

Yet what this changed position was is still subject to doubt.

Historians usually define it in political or constitutional terms, though now and again they have tried to link it with social facts. Bishop Stubbs, the fountain-head of the current ideas of medieval government, went so far as to admit that, considered 'as a political estate', the smaller landowner 'had class interests and affinities', and that 'the growth of these in contrast with the interests of the baronial class might form for the investigator of social history an interesting if somewhat perplexing subject'.[5] Yet his own historical account of the thirteenth-century gentry is confined to the story of how the knights had been drawn into the machinery of government, especially into the inquests and commissions, and had become an indispensable element in country administration. Some historians however have gone further than that and have argued that knights were able to play an increasing role in local government because their wealth and their hold over land were also on the increase. These historians have had no difficulty in finding wealthy knights in the thirteenth century. If we define the knightly class by its tenurial and personal status, and consider as knights all non-baronial feudatories holding land by knight service, we shall at all times find among them a few men as wealthy if not wealthier than many a nobleman. The Pelhams of Sussex, still a knightly family at the beginning of the fifteenth century, were worth at that time £500 per annum and more. Sir Thomas Wykeham, an Oxfordshire knight and a great-nephew of Bishop William Wykeham, was even wealthier, as in all probability were also several north country knights, like Sir William Eue.[6]

Yet neither the great wealth of these men in the fifteenth century nor the growing wealth of the class as a whole in the twelfth is necessarily relevant to the wealth and position of knights in the intervening periods. The professional soldiers in William the Conqueror's host gained in wealth and status as they were settled on land and converted into holders of knights' fees; they gained more still in the twelfth century when the warring parties recruited military support by endowing their followers with military fiefs. This was also the time when men in possession of arms were able to seize lands, often entire manors, belonging to the Church or the magnates. Yet none of these happenings will allow us to conclude that smaller landowners *en masse* continued to grow in wealth all through the period of Edward I's legislation in the thirteenth century.

Any such conclusion would not only be inconsistent with what we know of the economic changes of the time but would also conflict with what we can glean from the surviving records of land transactions in the thirteenth century. These records bear witness to the accretions to the estates of lay magnates and of nearly all the great abbeys: accretions which were almost invariably made at the expense of smaller landowners. It is these accretions that Stubbs must have had in mind when he wrote about the times 'when the greed for territorial acquisition is strong in the higher class', and when the smaller man is 'liable to be bought out by the barons'. It is precisely in this manner that families of gentry were losing their lands and coming near to extinction in some parts of the country. Numerous small landowners in the vicinity of the Glastonbury manors were ceding lands to the abbots intent upon rounding off their possessions. In those eastern counties in which the abbots of Peterborough were interested, and especially in the Soke of Peterborough itself, the catalogue of families selling land to the abbot or to his villeins—the Giminges, the Peverells, the Tots, the Gargates, the Southorps, the Solomons, the Thorolds—comprise a large proportion of local gentry and yeomanry. Some of them, such as Geoffrey of Southorp and Robert Paston of Castor, appear to have parted with large parts of their property in the Soke.

True enough, genealogists and students of manorial descents could quote instances of smaller landowners in the thirteenth century thriving into the higher ranks of the nobility by marriage, inheritance, royal favour or profits of baronial or monastic offices; and here and there smaller private cartularies, such as those of the Brays, tell the story of small knightly estates formed anew or enlarged. This contrary movement of rising fortunes was not however strong enough to cancel out the downward movement of declining knightly families. The numbers of families on the rise so far brought to light by historians are smaller than those on the decline, though not perhaps to an extent sufficient to support a purely statistical argument.[7] But the statistical case, slight though it is, finds strong support in several considerations of a more general character.

In the first place most of the rising families owed their rise to factors which had little to do with the economic trends of the time. Some of them, like those whom Mr King found prospering in the vicinity of Peterborough Abbey, were functionaries of the abbots of Peterborough benefiting from the perquisites of office; others were followers of great magnates, or lawyers with access to the great offices of state. Families of such provenance were rising all through the middle ages, and their relative numbers did not appear to be any greater (they were more likely to be smaller) in the thirteenth century than earlier or later.

The other reason why the evidence of declining families should weigh somewhat more than the evidence of the rising ones is its historical consistency. Not only is it consistent with what we know of the uneven impact of the economic boom on landlords of different degrees, but it agrees with what we know of land transactions. As I have just indicated, most of the abbeys of which the records have been preserved, and some of the great baronial families whose fortunes are known, were enlarging their landed possessions in the thirteenth century by purchase. Yet we know of hardly any instance of land alienated in their favour by other magnates of abbots, while innumerable references to land sales of smaller men—knights and freeholders—abound. We are thus driven to the conclusion that the smaller men were losing their hold over land and thereby also their collective share in the landed wealth of the country.[8]

These land losses of the smaller men may have been due to many causes, but until these causes have been discovered we must assume that smaller landowners sold land under the pressure of economic necessity. What the necessity was and how it originated is not difficult to observe; it has in fact been inferred in recent studies dealing with military fiefs and their holders. Most of these studies have brought out the high and rising costs of the military equipment required for knightly service. In the early twelfth century when most military fees were created and their obligations were defined it was reckoned that the knight's equipment cost 15 shillings. By the end of the thirteenth century the cost appeared to have risen nearly fourfold: to 50 shillings. The wages of hired professional soldiers rose correspondingly: from 8*d.* in the middle of the twelfth century to 2*s.* in the early thirteenth. Yet the income of an average knight, who stayed on his land and did not hire himself out as a full time soldier, did not rise to anything like the same extent or may not have risen at all. The income petty landlords derived from rents was relatively small, a fact fully brought out by Kosminsky's study of Hundred Rolls. Moreover rents were as a rule customary and could not be easily increased to keep pace with rising prices. But the main economic disadvantage of small landownership was its size. A small manor meant a small demesne; and a small demesne could not leave a large marketable surplus, or indeed any surplus at all, over and above the needs of the owner's household. A disparity between the average knight's income and his military outlay was thus bound to develop at any time in the thirteenth century. If to this regular disparity we add the burden of various irregular imposts, above all of feudal payments like 'reliefs' and 'aids', we shall find it easy to see why so many of the knights were in debt and had to part with land.[9]

The evidence of debts comes wholly from the records of the Exchequer of the Jews. It makes it quite clear that among the Jews' debtors smaller landowners predominated, and that their land formed the bulk of the landed property mortgaged with money-lenders. On the other hand there is hardly any evidence in the Jewish records of large-scale indebtedness on the part of the greater manorial landowners. Some evidence of Jewish debts for the earlier period, such as the surviving records of debts to Aaron of York in 1188, contain among debtors some religious houses and some twelve large landlords including Earl Robert of Leicester: a great magnate indeed. This however was a time when religious foundations were heavily burdened with papal and royal imposts and when landlords of every degree, including men of baronial rank, were raising liquid funds for their crusading expeditions. It is also probable that at the beginning of the thirteenth century a number of magnates were subjected to great financial exactions from King John and, in some years, by Henry III, and consequently contracted debts to the Jews. But as the thirteenth century advanced, the small landowners were becoming very nearly the sole clients and the chief victims of Jewish finance, while monastic houses and greater barons appear as its indirect beneficiaries. The chronicler may or may not have been right in alleging that the influence of the magnates was on the side of the Jews because the latter in their dealings operated with magnates' money. But there is little doubt that many of the estates pledged to the Jews eventually found their way into the hands of the magnates. According to a submission to the Oxford Parliament of 1258, 'the Jews transfer their debt claims and the land they held in mortgage to the magnates, who thereby accumulated lands of the smaller landlords'. (*Judaei aliquando debita sua, et terras eis invadiates, tradunt magnatibus et potentioribus regni, qui terras minorum ingrediuntur ea occasione.*) The surviving evidence of Jewish obligations (*Starrs*) fully supports the contention that the Jewish mortgages provided the mechanism whereby great men were getting hold of the smaller men's land. The story how Robert and Henry Braybrokes or Queen Eleanor pursued their policy of taking over lands pledged to the Jews has been told several times; numerous abbatial acquisitions of lay lands are also known to have involved lands of Jews' debtors; and there is every probability that further researchers will uncover many more similar instances.[10]

Thus viewed, the summoning of knights or *minores* to the successive parliaments betweeen 1254 and 1294, ending with the final establishment of the practice in 1295, must be considered together with a whole series of enactments in the second half of the century, beginning with the clause in the Provisions of Westminster of 1259, which protected freeholders from the abuse of power by barons, and ending with the statute of *Quia Emptores* of 1290, which put an end to the continued formation of mesne tenancies. These enactments also link up with the expulsion of the Jews in 1290, which must be viewed not as an isolated act and a mere concession to anti-semitic sentiment, but as one of a series of measures designed to deal with the economic grievance of smaller men. In other words, if what Simon de Montfort and Edward I tried to do was to win the support of the knightly class, they did so not by bowing to its new strength but by coming to its relief.

By contrast with the knightly class, the great landlords appeared to prosper in the period between the Domesday Book and the Black Death. As we shall see presently their apparent prosperity may belie the real situation at both the beginning and at the end of the period, i.e. before 1200 and after 1300, but there is no ground for doubting and no student of the period would question the good fortune of the magnates in the thirteenth century itself. Yet, paradoxically enough, in this as in other periods it is even more difficult to observe the fortunes of the magnates than those of the *minores*. For various reasons the condition of the greater landlords does not lend itself to conventional statistical measurements. In the first place the topmost layer of the landowning class, the magnates, was too small to be usefully analyzed with the help of conventional statistical averages. There were no more than 1300 tenancies-in-chief in the Domesday Book and possibly as few as 700; and not all tenants-in-chief were magnates. Professor Painter put the number of barons in 1160–1220 at a mere 160. Indeed so few they were that a change in the condition of one or two great families could distort the statistical image of the group as a whole.[11]

In the second place the wealth and income of individuals within the group were disparate to a degree. Whether we define the class as that of tenants-in-chief or as that of owners of multiple knights' fees, it would still comprise feudal estates differing greatly in size and wealth. In 1086 the Conqueror's brother, the Count of Moraine, owned estates worth some £2,500; yet the the class also harboured men like Gilbert de Breteuil or Robert d'Aumale, both tenants-in-chief holding multiple fees, whose annual income from land was still little over £50 per annum. The disparities may not have been equally great in the immediately following periods when some great estates of the king's relatives were split up, but become pronounced again in later periods. In 1245 William Marshall had a total income from land of just under £4,000 per annum of which about half came from his English possessions. In the late thirteenth century Isabelle of Aumale enjoyed an income which Denholm Young puts at £2,500. Richard Earl of Cornwall's income in 1301 was evaluated at £3,800 of which about two-thirds was income from land comparable with corresponding possessions in the Domesday Book. In the late fourteenth and early fifteenth centuries, the Earl of Lancaster enjoyed an income of similar size, as did also the Earl of York in the 1430s. These vast landed incomes, like the highest fortunes of 1086, were many (perhaps as much as six) times higher than the average income of, say, twenty tenants-in-chief in the lowest ranges of the samples available to us.[12]

Disparities in landed wealth and income on this scale would by themselves make it difficult to generalize about the economic conditions of the group. What makes such generalizations all the more difficult is that magnates derived some of their income from various sources other than land which were also widely disparate and could in some cases be very high. In the middle of the twelfth century William Earl of Gloucester commanded, in addition to his regular revenues from land of about £700, a somewhat less regular income from 300 knights' fees capable of yielding in feudal aid and relief the equivalent of more than £300 per annum. At the same time there were to be found among the substantial tenants-in-chief landowners with less than five fiefs each. Some great landowners drew profits from tolls and imposts on towns and fairs within their franchises. At some times in the thirteenth century the great wool fair of Boston yielded between £200 and £300 to the owners of the Honour of Richmond; the earls of Gloucester derived from the town of Bristol nearly a quarter of their total income, while the profits of the town of Leicester could yield the equivalent of 30 to 35 per cent of the total income of the earls of Leicester. The profits of the stannaries of Devon and Cornwall provided a fluctuating but always very large proportion of the total income of the earls of Cornwall.[13]

Some of the non-manorial payments were fixed by feudal custom or were otherwise standardized and remained for very long periods unchanged. But even if and when they happened to change they seldom did so in direct response to economic factors or otherwise reflected the general movement of economic change. Merged with the manorial revenues they were therefore apt to mask the fluctuations in the baronial incomes from land.

Measured separately, the purely agrarian incomes changed in a fairly regular and continuous, so to speak trend-like, manner, closely corresponding to the secular changes in agricultural economy. In fact, at first sight the long-term changes in manorial profits of the greater barons appear more pronounced, i.e. to rise and fall more steeply, than they did in fact.

The study of purely manorial revenues, i.e. those of demesne produce, rents, mills and manorial courts, is served by a wealth of evidence and has enabled several historians to attempt to measure them. The best-known measurements, those of Professor Painter, are based on a sample of 272 baronies, drawn largely from the returns of royal officials, and show that manorial profits rose very abruptly, more particularly in the late twelfth and early thirteenth centuries. In 1200, they stood at 60 per cent above their Domesday level; they grew by a further 60 per cent before 1250 and by some 30 per cent between the middle of the thirteenth century and the 1330s.[14] As Professor Painter's figures are derived from returns of royal officials they are apt to be biased; and as they are given for single years separated by long intervals they cannot be used to reconstruct the movement of manorial profits in the intervening years. These shortcomings are to some extent avoided in the measurements derived from private and fairly continuous accounts of certain great estates or households. Unfortunately the estates which can be so studied are very few and the samples based on them are apt to be disappointingly small. My own sample draws upon the evidence of not more than eight estates comprising about 400 manors. It is therefore all the more significant that inquiries so differently conducted should agree in their general verdict of rising profits. The rise shown by the smaller samples appears to be less continuous and above all less steep than that exhibited by Professor Painter's figures, but it agrees with the latter in bringing out the relatively higher rate of growth in the early part of the thirteenth century and a marked deceleration in the first half of the fourteenth century.[15]

Neither series, however, can by itself reveal the true path followed by the baronial incomes during the period. In the first place, the incomes they aggregate are given at current prices, and to that extent reflect the rise in prices and the fall in the purchasing power of money which, as we shall show later, continued all through the pre-pestilence era. Undoubtedly rising prices of agricultural produce of land helped to boost the profits of manors, but they were also bound to reduce the real worth of the lords' manorial revenues. If we try to get at their 'real' worth by deflating them with such price indices as we are able to construct, we shall find that the price rises at the turn of the twelfth and thirteenth centuries were so high as to wipe out most of the recorded increases in manorial revenues in that period, and that in the subsequent 150 years, the price rises, though much more gentle, were nevertheless sufficient to reduce by 1300 the cumulative increase in manorial revenues to about 25 per cent above their level in the 1230s.[16]

Yet even when expressed in 'real' terms the figures cannot faithfully reflect the true changes in the economic condition of great lordships in that they do not take into account the non-manorial revenues or the changes arising from the various rights and dues of feudal tenancy, and the fiscal impositions of the king. Some of the feudal rights and dues brought, or at least promised, profits; others, more particularly royal taxes, entailed costs and resulted in financial losses. They could therefore both supplement and detract from the purely manorial revenues of feudal landownerships. The important question, therefore, is whether their movements were sufficiently general and consistent to influence baronial revenues in the same direction, i.e. to enhance them or to reduce them in the aggregate.

Needless to say the movement cannot be tracked with any certainty. But, allowing for exceptions and deviations, its main course was in the barons' favour. The tendency was for feudal charges to lighten and for the corresponding feudal revenues of barons to 'stay put'. The story of the burdens, and of their lightening, can be illustrated by the changes in most of the royal imposts on feudal tenures, both those arising from the customary feudal incidents and those imposed as taxes pure and simple.

The most important feudal incidents affecting the economic position of the greater feudatories were 'reliefs', 'aids', military service and wardships. As I have already explained, 'relief' was an entry fine paid by an incoming tenant at the inception of his tenancy. The greater landlords stood to derive income from reliefs in so far as their estates comprised feudal sub-tenancies, e.g. knights' fees; and their income appeared to have remained fairly stable in money terms, since relief on knights' fees appeared to stay at the 100*s*. level most of the time. On the other hand they themselves owed relief to the king. This relief could on some occasions be very high. In 1214 William Fitz Allain had to promise the king 10,000 marks as relief: a sum equivalent to the income from his estate for an entire generation. At about the same time John de Lacy was required by the king to pay 7,000 marks for his father's estate. These were however exceptionally large properties and exceptionally extortionate periods in the history of royal finance. For most of the subsequent period the reliefs were not only standardized but also declining. Like all fixed feudal payments they were gradually eroded by the price rise; in addition the rates themselves were apt to be scaled down. Until the early thirteenth century they stood at or near the £100 level: about three to four times the annual value of an average knight's fee. Later, in Henry's time, the rate was scaled down to 100 marks or about £69 and finally fixed at this level in 1297.

Of the other purely feudal liabilities none was more important than the military obligation of the *servitium debitum* and the fiscal dues levied in its place. While the military services were still exacted in full or near-full measure, i.e. in the twelfth century, the tenants-in-chief stood to gain or to lose according to the difference between the number of knights' services they owed to the king and the number of fees from which they could themselves claim service; and in this respect baronies were apt to vary a great deal.[17] The greater feudal baronies provided for their military obligation by creating military fees, i.e. by letting out ('sub-infeudating') estates to knights who made themselves avilable for duty in certain periods and on certain occasions. To an overlord a knight's fees so established could bring both a gain and loss. Gains would comes from feudal dues of knights other than their military service: losses would result from foregoing the economic yield of the land sub-infeudated as a fee. In cases in which a lord had not created sufficient knights' fees to cover his entire military liability to the king he kept the profits of the land but had to bear the costs of equipping and paying the knights serving for the king. In the end, largely as a result of the wholesale infeudations of the twelfth century, the total number of established fees came to exceed the number of knights required by the king from his tenants-in-chief. There was still some deficiency in 1166, when more than half of the tenants-in-chief owed more knights than the number they had established upon their land; but by then also, the overall balance of dues and benefits, whatever it may have been in the earlier period, was beginning to shift to the barons' advantage. To begin with, knights' service had by the end of the twelfth century been commuted for fixed money payments, the so-called 'scutage'. In the end what remained of the knights' purely military service was the obligation of some barons to provide the residuary number of knights for which they were still responsible. How small this number had by then become is shown by the exiguous muster on some mid-thirteenth-century occasions. Whereas in Henry II's time the total number of knights owing by the barons under the *servitium debitum* was about 6,500, there were apparently no more than 375 knights serving in Edward's Welsh War.[18] If much larger numbers of knights in fact fought in some major campaigns abroad, more particularly in the Hundred Years War of the fourteenth and fifteenth centuries, this was because most of these knights were soldiers under a wage contract to their captains. Such soldiers were not in short supply since the lure of soldiering never lost its attraction for gentlemen, and drew larger numbers of them into military expeditions than were still liable to *servitium debitium*. But hired companies of soldiers, even mounted knights, were not necessarily a charge on the resources of individual magnates.

The main charge was fiscal: that of scutage paid in commutation of military service in person. To begin with, it was quite heavy. In the course of the twelfth century it was levied on at least seven occasions; and from the middle of the century onwards it also carried additional surcharges or fines which raised it above its conventional rate of £1 per fee. By the turn of the century, however, it was already on its way out. By then the greater magnates appeared to have been exempted from it as were apparently the more recently created knights' fees.[19] These exemptions may have occurred on occasions on which the magnates provided knights serving in person, but we have seen that the numbers so serving were well below the numbers for which they were liable under their *servitium debitum*. Moreover, the unit on which the scutage was assessed, the knights' fee itself, was rapidly disintegrating through subdivision into fractions, often minute ones. For this and other reasons the scutage as such ceased to be levied in the thirteenth century. On the few occasions on which it still appeared to be claimed, it was treated as part of the more general taxes, chiefly as a basis for assessment. Its later history thus merges with the history of the general taxes of the time.[20]

A somewhat similar sequence—high imposts in the twelfth century followed by the gradual lightening of the burden, from the second quarter of the thirteenth century onwards, and an eventual absorption into more general taxes—can be traced in the history of most other feudal dues, and more particularly that of the feudal 'aid'. In its original conception 'aid' was an *ex-gratia* donation by a vassal to his lord (in the case of a tenant-in-chief, to the king) on occasions of special need, such as ransom or the marriage of a daughter. But it could also be asked for in times of military necessity, and was in fact repeatedly levied on this pretext by the kings in the course of the twelfth century. This was, however, only one of the ways by which the kings converted the aid into a general and more regular tax. Its eventual function came to be that of a pretext and a vehicle for the taxes ('subsidies') on incomes and movable goods about which more will be said presently.

The only major economic burden of a feudal nature which did not appear to change in favour of tenants-in-chief was that of 'wardships' and 'marriage', more particularly the former. In essence wardship was the right of the overlord to administer his vassal's estate when the latter happened to be a minor. The estates of wards were as a rule administered most rapaciously, but even in the hands of considerate royal administrators royal ministrations could be a cause of heavy losses to tenants and of great profit to the king. Not surprisingly the barons pressed hard for the abolition of wardships, while the kings obstinately clung to it. In the Parliament of Oxford in 1257 the barons petitioned for its abolition, but without success. Right through the late middle ages and well into the Tudor era wardship was to remain an important source of royal revenues and a constant object of baronial resentment.[21]

The barons had less cause for resenting the many ways in which the burden of other non-feudal impositions, mainly royal taxes, was shifting in the middle ages. In general the earlier taxes were becoming progressively less heavy as the thirteenth century wore on; while the later and newer taxes, those on movables, distributed the burden so widely as to shift its main weight off the barons' shoulders. The earliest and, for a time, the heaviest of the king's taxes was the Danegeld. It had been imposed to finance resistance against Danish invaders and was, to begin with, heavy enough to affect (or to be thought by historians capable of affecting) the course of social and economic development in the closing centuries of the Anglo-Saxon era. Even in the middle of the twelfth century it could still yield well over £3,000, or the equivalent of one-quarter to one-third of Henry II's annual revenue. By that time, however, its yield was on the decline. It was imposed infrequently and was collected at an ever lower rate: that of 6*s.* per hide in 1083, 4*s.* per hide in 1096 and 2*s.* per hide in Henry I's time. It was eventually abolished altogether by Henry III in 1162. As the barons had consistently opposed the tax we must assume that its abolition was a royal concession to the baronial party.[22]

As I have already indicated, most of the earlier taxes—Danegeld as well as its short-lived successors—which had all been levied on land or on tenures, were eventually replaced by taxes on incomes and movable goods. Together with the much later duties on imports and exports of merchandise these taxes were to become the mainstay of royal finance in the later middle ages. Their introduction however was gradual, and can be traced back to the twelfth century or even earlier. Until the first quarter of the thirteenth century they were increasing in frequency and weight. From that point onwards, until well into the fourteenth century, their growth was arrested by the opposition of the barons, and they were not imposed except at rare intervals.

The taxes on movables originated and were throughout their history represented as 'aids' and in fact grew out of the feudal aids of the earlier period. The earliest of such generalized aids was probably that of 1166, but a first heavy imposition to be presented as an aid but to be in fact a general tax on movables was the famous Alladin's Tithe levied in 1188 to finance an unusually great contribution to the cost of the Crusades. Even greater, and similarly borne by the whole mass of Englishmen, was the aid imposed in 1193 to pay for the ransom of King Richard imprisoned in Germany. Thereafter general taxes under the guise of aid were imposed repeatedly; and while some of the impositions were levied on real property or on tenures and were assessed either on units of land (hides or carrucates or plough teams) or on knights' fees, some were levied on movable goods and on incomes of all and sundry.

By 1237 a whole series of scutage and aids, including three aids on movables, were levied in quick succession. They inevitably met with baronial resistance and were to become one of the main issues in the baronial opposition to the King. The resistance first came to the surface in 1213–19, even though it was as yet confined to the King's tenants in northern counties. It came to a head in 1237 when the barons of the entire country flatly refused to agree to any further aids. This refusal marked the final success of the baronial struggles against the King. In the subsequent forty years the barons were to enjoy what by comparison with earlier years was a veritable 'tax holiday'. After 1272 the King was able to obtain somewhat more frequent and more liberal grants, though it was not until well into the fourteenth century that the taxes on movables grew into becoming a regular and well-standardized source of royal revenue.

The transition, though slow and uneven, was from the economic and social point of view a radical one. Not only did the weight of the taxes for a long time remain relatively low, but the tax itself ceased to be feudal in everything except name. It was no longer borne by the king's tenants-in-chief or their vassals, but fell squarely on the backs of all the men in the country in possession of goods and incomes. Although we know little about the actual incidence of medieval taxes, the assessments which have survived strongly suggest that the lords were able to pass much, perhaps even the whole, of their liabilities on to tenants of every kind including their villeins, and that it was the common folk who became the main payers of the new taxes.[23]

Thus on a broad view the general trend was for the royal demands on barons to lighten. For one brief interval at the turn of the twelfth and thirteenth centuries, Richard and John squeezed their barons hard, and a financial pressure equally hard was for a brief period applied by Henry III. But eventually the pressure rebounded against the kings themselves. The grievances against royal impositions were one of the main issues in the baronial struggle against the Crown; and in the end it was on this issue that the barons won their most conspicuous successes. For whatever may have been the constitutional outcome of the struggle—and on this verdicts may differ—in matters purely fiscal the barons appear to have won. The effect of their victory was to ease their fiscal burdens, at a time when purely feudal dues were also on the decline while manorial incomes were rising.

III

Arguing on the same lines it should be possible to formulate a working hypothesis concerning the fortunes of the greater and smaller landowners in the subsequent phase of English economic history, that of the agricultural crisis of the fourteenth and fifteenth centuries. This was a time of falling land values, declining rents, vacant holdings and dwindling profits of demesne cultivation. We may therefore presume that the class whose income from land took the form of rents or farms must have suffered from the new dispensation: indeed must have been its main casualty. By the same token the smaller landowners may have suffered less, since most of them consumed a large proportion of their produce and presumably farmed out little, if any, of their land. Those of them who specialized in sheep and cattle must have suffered least, since pastures were now abundant and labour costs of sheep-farming relatively low. Their position would be comparable to that of more substantial villagers who suffered from rising costs but were favoured by the greater abundance of land and by new opportunities for adding to their acreage.

Gentlemen of this rank also stood to profit from other economic features of the time, such as the revived tendency to farm out manorial demesnes. The farmers of the demesnes were men of every condition—better-off villagers, townsfolk and lawyers—but country gentlemen were also to be found among them. Of even greater benefit to them were some of the non-economic developments. If any section of society profited from the 150 years of war in France, the smaller men directly engaged in the business of fighting stood to gain most from the opportunities for loot and ransom. But it was the internecine conflict at home that appears to have brought them most profit. In the party strife culminating in the Wars of the Roses the rival interests, like the two sides in the Civil War of the twelfth century, measured their strength by the size of their retinues; and they recruited their retinues by methods which *mutatis mutandis* corresponded to the sub-infeudations of the twelfth century. The magnates may no longer have been able to create new feudal sub-tenancies valid in law, but they could still let estates on lease or carve out wholly new estates to be held or leased on terms favourable to the lessees; and this became one of the ways of remunerating the allegiance of followers. Mr MacFarlane termed this development as 'bastard feudalism'. In so doing he also argued, I believe rightly, that the development of the bastard feudalism was bound to improve the fortunes of the country gentry at the expense of the greater landlords.[24]

It is indeed much easier to diagnose the good health of the late medieval gentry than to demonstrate the ailing of the magnates. Considered as a group, the magnates of the fifteenth century are no easier to handle statistically than their prototypes of the thirteenth century. Their numbers were equally small and perhaps even smaller. The separately held earldoms were certainly fewer after 1340, since hardly any new earldoms were created under Edward III, and their numbers were not fully restored in the fifteenth century. The topmost ranks were further thinned out in the dynastic struggle of the Wars of the Roses. It has even been argued that there were fewer great men sharing the landed wealth in its baronial ranges, and that the individual shares of some exalted few might have grown sufficiently to raise their wealth above its previous levels, even though the aggregate profits of landownership declined.

However, this like other verdicts about the collective fortunes of the magnates must rest, not on direct measurement of their wealth and income, but on deductions from what we know of the general economic and social situation. It is not that direct measurements are wholly impossible or have not been attempted. The evidence of manorial profits in the late middle ages has already been discussed and will be considered again presently. We also possess some contemporary valuations of baronial incomes, compiled mostly for taxation purposes, from which Professor H. L. Gray has been able to derive a valuable estimate of baronial wealth in 1436. The evidence of these valuations, being official, may not be as reliable as the evidence of private accounts; it is, moreover, incomplete in that it does not apparently make allowances for mandatory or fiscal charges borne by feudal landords. Above all, it represents the conditions in the first quarter of the century before the political and economic malaise of the time set in and the greatest shift in baronial fortunes occurred.[25]

It is not, therefore, surprising that the evidence should not have brought out any great changes in the wealth of the barons, though it suggests that there were fewer topmost incomes, in the £3,000 plus category, and that the size of the group with incomes of high but not topmost size—those of about £2,000—increased. But changes like these in all probability reflect the reshuffle in the ownership and composition of great estates rather than a change in the economic fortunes of large-scale landownership.

By comparison with these contemporary estimates of the barons' total income those of their agricultural income derived from their private records present a fairly clear picture of declining fortunes. The picture comes out clearest from the evidence of such huge and well-scattered estates as those of the earls of Lancaster whose agricultural incomes appear to have fallen by at least 50 per cent between the beginning of the fifteenth century and its third quarter. The evidence of the Lancaster estates finds its parallel in that of most, though perhaps not all, other estates. Some landlords were placed so favourably and were so enterprising and efficient as to be able to move against the trend. An abbot or lay landlord near London could still profit by the proximity of the Great Wen. A landlord well provided with investable resources and able to concentrate on sheep farming was thereby able to compensate for the falling of profits from smaller farming. The Hungerfords, who rose in wealth and throve to a baronage in the service of the Lancaster family, derived much of their income in the second half of the fifteenth century from their pastures in Wiltshire, and altogether managed their estates so well that their profits suffered much less than those of most other landlords. Sir John Fastolf, as multifarious a profiteer as ever there was, found himself in a position to indulge in some purposeful agricultural investment and also to exploit the prosperity of cloth-working villages on his land. And one wonders how much the resilience of the bishops of Winchester's agricultural profits for a decade or two in the late fourteenth century and again in the middle of the fifteenth could be ascribed to the personal qualities of the bishops at these two periods—William of Wykeham in the earlier period and Cardinal Beaufort, a grasping bureaucrat and financier, in the later periods.[26]

However, opportunities for moving against the economic tide were not given to most landlords. The estates of the Benedictine abbeys which happened to retain their grain-growing demesnes to the last possible moment suffered from high wages and sagging prices more than most other landowners. Great lay lords, not only the earls of Lancaster, but landlords like the Percys or the earls of Stafford, who depended on rents and on manorial farms for the bulk of their agricultural income, were badly hit by the falling land values. They were either insufficiently provided with good grazing land or incapable of aggressive estate management.[27]

Needless to say in the fourteenth and fifteenth centuries, as in other periods, agricultural incomes by themselves cannot give a full measure of magnates' income. No less than their predecessors before 1348 the feudal landlords of the later middle ages were a political and a military class, sustained by miscellaneous seignorial revenues, profits of war and fruits of office, and also likely to suffer from political disbursement and losses of every kind.

On the whole it is doubtful whether all, or even most, of the fifteenth-century magnates would be in a position to make up for the shortfall in their incomes from land by purely feudal revenues. In the fifteenth century as in the thirteenth benefits of feudal revenues were not equally distributed among the great estates. On some, like those of the earls of Cornwall, feudal profits provided a very large share of the total revenues; on others (surprisingly even on such estates as those of the earls of Lancaster) rents and other agricultural revenues were by far the most important source of income. But even on the estates on which feudal revenues were very important, they do not appear to have risen in the fifteenth century. On the contrary such non-agricultural revenues as entry fines from lands held in fee and possibly also the yields of markets and fairs, where non-conventionalized or farmed, showed a tendency to decline.

On the other hand, the weight of the various royal impositions and taxes no longer appeared to lighten with time as it had done in earlier centuries. As far as we can judge, the older taxes, inherited from the previous periods, had by the beginning of the fifteenth century all been fixed by established convention, and were as a rule merged with the annual farm of the shire rendered by the sheriffs. We have however seen that these older taxes were overshadowed by newer impositions on movable goods. These taxes, usually described as 'subsidies' of tenth and fifteenth, were levied on the movable goods of all and sundry. In theory they were 'aids' to the king for his military necessities and were on this formal pretext regularly voted in parliament. But eventually they developed into all but annual taxes, halfway between income tax and property tax, capable of yielding considerably more than the land taxes of the twelfth or the thirteenth centuries. Who bore their main weight, however, is not certain. The ecclesiastical tenth fell squarely on the ecclesiastical foundations. There is some evidence to suggest that the main burden of the fifteenth payable by laymen was borne largely by the villagers, but some of it may have also been carried by the landowners even if indirectly. Above all it can be argued that the very heavy customs and subsidies on the exports of wool frequently voted by parliaments jointly with subsidies on movables penalized the wool growers, even if the main penalty was paid by the foreign users of English wool. We must therefore conclude that although the changes in the burdens of taxes were uncertain and in any case not very great, such changes as there were did not appear to have benefited the feudal landlords and certainly could not have compensated them for the decline in their agricultural revenues.

The same conclusion also applies to the other possibilities of compensation. It has been argued that the magnates made up their falling land revenues not so much by regular and traditional incidents of feudal tenure, as by the less formal perquisites of power and status, and above all by the fruits of political office and military leadership. There is no doubt that in the conditions of the fifteenth century fruits of office could be a powerful lure. Men were drawn to the seats of government, especially to those of royal government, partly by the power and glory they conferred but mainly by the profits they promised. It is not however certain that the offices, be they as close to the public purse as the Exchequer or the King's Chamber, were as profitable as they may have appeared to the various contenders. A number of smaller men certainly made their fortunes in various clerkships in and around the great offices of state. We also know of one or two greater men—Cardinal Beaufort above all—who did well out of the offices they held. The fame of a few fortunes so made may have excited and lured many others who hoped to do equally well. It is therefore quite arguable—though unprovable—that as the agricultural revenues of the magnates worsened so their eagerness to compensate for them by the fruits of office grew; and that the fifteenth-century struggle for power and the persistent tug-of-war between the two feudal parties and the War of the Roses itself were prompted by the magnates' greater need of fruits of office.

All these, however, are mere hypotheses for which very little evidence can be adduced. What may have fed the warfare between feudal parties was the weakness of the Crown under the later Lancastrians, the strains and misfortunes of the Hundred Years War, and the imbalance of local power in the northern and western counties. The profits of office were an additional prize, but considered as a prize they may have proved highly elusive. Their lure dazzled and deceived the contestants in the fifteenth century as they have sometimes misled the modern student of the fifteenth century.

Both contemporaries and some modern historians may have been equally deceived by the lure of war profits. It has been forcibly argued by some very well-informed medievalists that the one source of baronial revenue of the fourteenth and fifteenth centuries which could make up for the deficiencies of agricultural revenues was that of the Hundred Years War. From the economic, as well as the military and political, point of view it was a 'bigger and better' war than any other medieval conflict. Indeed so long and so good was it, and the profits it yielded from ransom, booty and offices and fiefs abroad were so high, that England's landowning class, and especially its upper crust, emerged from the war richer than it had been 120 years earlier.[28]

The argument has never been subjected to a proper statistical analysis, and until it has been it must be judged by a simple test of historical probability. Will it pass it? No doubt some men prospered in the war, and the hope of doing equally well must have made the war highly popular with some of its leaders. But whether the promise of the war was wholly borne out is very doubtful. Medieval wars were lotteries in which all noblemen and gentlemen were eager to participate but only a few could be certain to succeed. And of all the medieval wars the Hundred Years War, with its victorious phases alternating and ending with phases of defeat and retreat, would be the least likely to set the profits of war always flowing in the same direction.

Ransoms are a good example of profits flowing both ways. More prisoners were taken by the English than by the French, but until their names have been listed and paired off we shall not know how much more numerous or profitable were the French prisoners than the English ones. It is moreover certain that in the business of ransoms both parties might lose. Ransoms as a rule passed through many hands, were subject to deductions in favour of superiors and of the king, were frequently discounted with merchants, and bore heavy charges for collection and interest.

The profits of booty were little more certain. Booty would be the most remunerative on the occasions when it came from collective tributes from towns and fortresses. Such occasions did not, however, present themselves very often, and least often in the second stage of the war, when the English were losing territory. As for ordinary soldiery pillage, its chief beneficiaries must have been the lesser men who did the actual pillaging. The leaders probably benefited more the lower they stood in the chain of command.

More remunerative probably were offices and fiefs in occupied regions. But I have already warned against the assumption that all offices, at home or abroad, were invariably profitable. Surprisingly little is known about the foreign fiefs; we have only the vaguest notion as to how they were administered or how their profits were apportioned between great men and smaller grantees. In any case all these profits ceased the moment the occupied regions were abandoned, as they were between 1445 and 1453. By 1453 English rule also ended in Gascony—a province whence some English subjects of the king had drawn income for generations before the Hundred Years War. By the middle of the fifteenth century the net gain from this source must therefore have become very uncertain.

If to this uncertain residue of gains from ransoms, booty and offices we add the all-too-certain tally of costs—equipment and wages of soldiers unrepaid by the king, liveries of attendants, personal armaments and accoutrements of captains—the final balance of the war as a whole for the baronial class in its entirety may well turn out to have been negative.

Apart from the soldiers of fortune who 'struck it lucky' the men likely to come out of the war better off than they had been when they came in were the profiteers who took part in the war without sharing in any of the military operations—the clerks in charge of war chests and war supplies, the merchants and contractors who provisioned the troops and financed the payments and transfers of funds. Most of these men, like the successful soldiers and captains, eventually invested their gains in land; as did also the prosperous merchants, and above all lawyers of every type and origin. In this way new men were recruited to the upper ranks and, above all, the number of landowners of lower and middle rank was augmented. But the smaller landlords would in any case have gained, and in fact did gain, in both numbers and strength from the social and economic trends of the period, which as we have seen moved in favour of the small landowners and against the magnates.

References

1. Sylvia Thrupp, *The Grocers of London* (1949), pp. 20 ff.

2. L. Wood-Legh, 'Sheriffs, Lawyers and Belted Knights in the Parliaments of Edward III', *Bull. Inst. Hist. Res.*, XX (1943–46). Cf. M. M. Postan, 'The Costs of the Hundred Years War', *Past and Present*, April 1964.

3. J. S. Roskell, *The Commons in the Parliament of 1422* (1954), *passim*, esp. pp. 77 ff.

4. H. Trevor Roper, *The Gentry, 1540–1640* (Supplement, *Econ. Hist. Rev.*) (1953); L. Stone, *The Crisis of the Aristocracy, 1558–1641* (1965).

5. William Stubbs, *The Constitutional History of England*, Vol II, 4th ed. (1906), pp. 194-5.

6. For the Pelhams, see Roskell, *The Commons* pp. 208–11; M. A. Lower, *Historical and Genealogical Notices of the Pelham Family* (1896); and M. Clough, as in note 24, page 182 below. For Wykeham, see W. H. Williams, *Oxfordshire Members of Parliament* (1896), p. 29; *Dictionary of National Biography*, XLIII, p. 230; and Roskell, *The Commons*, pp. 239, 241; also pp. 78–9 (Eue).

7. Edmund King, 'Large and Small Landowners in the Thirteenth Century', *Past and Present*, No. 47, May 1970. For the evidence of Glastonbury acquisitions see Dom A. Watkins (ed.), *The Great Chartulary of Glastonbury*, vols. I–III, Somerset Rec. Soc. 1947–64.

8. See note 7 above and Appendix 2, p. 247.

9. Sally Harvey, 'The Knight and the Knight's Fee in England', *Past and Present*, No. 49 (1970); K. Mitchell, *Studies in Taxation under John and Henry III*, 2nd ed. (1951), pp. 309–311; J. H. Round, *Feudal England* (1895), pp. 271–2.

10. H. G. Richardson, *The English Jewry under the Angevin Kings* (1960); B. Siegschlag, *English Participation in the Crusades* (1939) (privately printed), cited by S. Painter, *Studies in the History of the English Feudal Barony* (1943).

11. H. Ellis, *A General Introduction to the Domesday Book* (1868), Vol. I, pp. 363 ff. Painter, *Studies*, p. 170.

12. Painter, *Studies*, pp. 170–78.

13. John Hatcher, *Rural Economy and Society in the Duchy of Cornwall, 1300–1500* (1970), Ch. VII; Hatcher, 'The Earl of Cornwall's Income from the Stannaries', *Econ. Hist. Rev.* (1971).

14. Painter, *Studies*, pp. 160 ff.

15. See below, page 247, Appendix 2.

16. For estimates of price movements by which the current prices are deflated here, see Ch. 13 below, pp. 224–46.

17. George E. Woodbine (ed.), *Bracton. De Legibus et Consuetudinibus Angliae*, Vol. II (1922), folio 84, p. 244; Painter, *Studies*, pp. 58–63.

18. J. E. Morris, *Welsh Wars of Edward I*, Vol. 1 (1901), p. 45.

19. K. Mitchell, *Taxation in Medieval England*, pp. 180–181; see also note 21 below.

20. Mitchell, *Taxation*, pp. 164–5; J. F. Baldwin, *The Scutage and Knight Service in England* (1897), p. 43 and *passim.*; Stenton, *English Feudalism*, pp. 179–185; Round, *Feudal England*, pp. 268 ff.; E. Miller, 'The State and the Landed Interest in the Thirteenth Century', *Trans. Roy. Hist. Soc.*, 3rd series, Vol. 11 (1952).

21. J. Hurstfield, *The Queen's Wards: Wardship and Marriage under Elizabeth I* (1958); Painter, *Studies*, pp. 65, 66.

22. See below, pp. 247–8, Appendix 3.

23. Mitchell, *Taxation*, pp. 168–71, 177, 190–220.

24. K. B. MacFarlane, 'Bastard Feudalism', M. Clough (ed.), *The Book of Bartholomew Bolney*, Sussex Record Soc. LXIII (1964), and the same author's unpublished history of the Pelham estates, provide good instances of fifteenth-century gentlemen risen in the world; other instances abound in our documents. On the increasing share of Knights in parliamentary representation see M. McKisack, *The Parliamentary Representation of English Boroughs in the Middle Ages* (1950) and Roskell, *The Commons*, pp. 106–12, 126 ff.; cf. Wood-Legh, 'Sheriffs, Lawyers and Belted Knights'.

25. H. L. Gray, 'Incomes from Land in England in 1436', *Eng. Hist. Rev.* XLIX (1934). For baronial income from land in an earlier period (fourteenth century), cf. G. A. Holmes, *The Estates of Higher Nobility in Fourteenth-Century England* (1957).

26. K. B. MacFarlane, 'The Investments of Sir John Fastolf's Profits of War', *Trans. Roy. Hist. Soc.* (1957). See also page 248 below, Appendix 4.

27. J. N. W. Bean, *The Estates of the Percy Family, 1416–1537* (1958); C. D. Ross and T. B. Pugh, 'Materials for the Study of Baronial Incomes in Fifteenth Century England', *Econ. Hist. Rev.*, 2nd ser., Vols. V1–VIII (1953–56). R. R. Davis, 'Baronial Accounts, Incomes and Arrears in the Later Middle Ages,' *Econ. Hist. Rev.*, 2nd ser., Vols. XX–XX1 (1967–68).

28. K. B. MacFarlane, 'England and the Hundred Years War', *Past and Present*, No. 22, July 1962; M. M. Postan, 'Some Social Consequences of the Hundred Years War', *Econ. Hist. Rev.* XII (1942); Postan, 'The Costs of the Hundred Years War', *Past and Present*, No. 27, April 1964.

11 Trade and Industry

I

A society like that of medieval England would nowadays be classified and described as 'pre-industrial'. Its income came mostly from agriculture, and by far the largest proportion of its people was engaged in growing food. The numbers occupied in trade and industry formed a relatively small proportion of the total; and even those so occupied often combined their industrial and commercial occupations with some agricultural pursuits. This does not, however, mean that industrial and commercial activities were wholly insignificant and played little part in shaping the economic geography of the country or in directing the course of its economic development. Throughout the middle ages medieval England required and obtained commodities which few or no regions of England produced, such as salt or spices. Moreover, some of England's villages and entire regions were so specialized that life within them would have been difficult or even impossible without some interregional exchanges. The ability of several regions to specialize in pastoral pursuits, above all in wool-growing, presupposed their ability to dispose of their products outside and perhaps also to make up for the specialized character of their agriculture by importing some of their food. Moreover, we have seen, and shall have to stress again, that within most medieval villages there were always to be found individual households incapable of growing all the food they needed, just as there were some households (to say nothing of the demesnes) which could, and almost invariably did, produce disposable surpluses. In other words, the pattern of English settlement and its social structure permitted deficiencies and surpluses met by purchases and disposed of by sales. Some opportunities for trade were therefore to be found in all places and, above all, at all times.

A conclusion like this might not have come easily to nineteenth-century historians and is still occasionally resisted by well-informed scholars writing in our own day. To scholars so minded trade is an activity characteristic of societies and economies in relatively advanced stages of development, and is out of place in societies as 'primitive' as that of the early middle ages. Some such view of trade followed naturally from the Victorian estimation of its own age. To men of that age its salient characteristics appeared as products of continuous and ascending progress. Trade was one such Victorian characteristic; indeed a characteristic they were most conscious and proud of. They consequently found it easy to assume that trade, like the other attributes of their England, had gradually progressed throughout the centuries of English history; that there was bound to be less trade the further back they looked; and that there was presumably next to no trade in times as distant as the earliest middle ages. It accordingly became the accepted convention of such little economic history as there was to begin the story of medieval trade with an account of its 'origin', i.e. the first emergence of what was then termed 'the exchange economy', and proceed to describe in terms largely imaginary how that exchange economy expanded in the subsequent centuries until it finally reached its fulfilment in the reign of the good Queen.

Nowadays, there is little justification in evidence or reason for holding this view. No society known to us, however remote in time or backward in economic development, was wholly incapable of exchanging commodities within itself or with other societies. The archaeologists and anthropologists have brought to our knowledge exchanges of commodities in societies and between societies primitive by most standards. It is of course possible to imagine a stage in human development when isolated families lived the lives of troglodytes and did not want or did not know how to swap their produce against the produce of other men. But for all the periods of prehistory in which men lived in social groups—the Bronze Age, the Neolithic and even the Paleolithic ages—the archaelogists have found evidence of men exchanging, sometimes over long distances, their surplus produce. The same is true of some of the primitive societies nearer our age, which happen to be similarly dependent on exchanges with outsiders. Needless to say, not all such exchanges would be conducted by the same means and the same technique by which men as a rule (not, however invariably) conduct their trade nowadays, i.e. with the help of money or organized markets or professional merchants. It is however import-art not to confuse the problem of trading methods and techniques with that of trade as a social and economic function, and not to identify the role which exchanges of goods played in economic life with any particular method of conducting these exchanges. What matters is the economic process itself, i.e. the ability of men to rely on each other's surpluses and to organize their lives accordingly. Regarded as an economic process trade has almost invariably been one of the essential functions of social existence, capable of greater or less development according to the economic circumstances of any given place or time.

By the same logic we must not assume that the more advanced or civilized by some other standard an epoch was, the greater was its need for trade and its ability to ply it; and that trade consequently grew from century to century. No doubt in some parts of the medieval world and at some points of time in the middle ages trade occupied a more modest place in men's existences than it was to occupy in the Western world in modern times. Indeed in some periods, above all in the hundred years immediately preceding or immediately following the Industrial Revolution in the eighteenth century, commerce expanded continuously and played an ever-increasing part in the English economy. Before that time, however, the changes in the regional geography of England and in its economic and social structure were not always conducive to commercial expansion. They were not sufficiently continuous or sufficiently uniform to swell and to go on swelling unceasingly the surpluses of some men and the deficiencies of others and, thereby, progressively to increase men's need to buy and their capacity to sell. The volume of English trade, its role in economic and social life and its organization changed from time to time, but the changes were not progressive or cumulative. The story of English trade in the middle ages is therefore told best not as one of continuous growth but as one of periodic mutations in response to the changes in the domestic and international setting of the economy and society as a whole.

II

The current of trade best known to historians and studied by them most is that which flowed across England's political frontier and is commonly termed as 'foreign'. Throughout its history it was closely linked with international politics and has therefore drawn the attention of political historians as well as that of economic ones. But the chief cause of its relative popularity with historians is its evidence. Commercial relations with other countries were frequently regulated and protected by treaties, and these have survived in sufficient numbers to bear witness to the trade which England conducted or expected to conduct with other nations. An even more important source of evidence is that of custom accounts. The kings of England learned quite early how to tax the goods crossing their frontiers, and in the later middle ages greatly relied on the revenue of their custom duties. The revenues were recorded in custom accounts which have survived in sufficient numbers to provide a continuous record of English foreign trade.[1]

Unfortunately this flow of evidence was not in full spate until quite late in the thirteenth or even the early fourteenth centuries, with the result that even for foreign trade our earlier evidence is very meagre. It is most meagre for the Anglo-Saxon period and the opening century of Norman rule. For this period we have little more than widely scattered and often uncertain indications of the commodities entering the trade and the men engaged in it. The 'commodity' mentioned most often and earliest are English slaves sold abroad.[2] There is however every probability that Anglo-Saxon England continued to export abroad the same commodities which we have seen Romans take out of this country, mostly minerals such as tin and lead and perhaps silver. There is also little doubt that from the late seventh century onwards, and possibly earlier, England exported a certain amount of cloth. The cloth sold at that time abroad under the name of 'Frisian' was probably English cloth imported from England by Frisian merchants, about whom more will be said presently. That this cloth had a well established market and uses abroad is shown by a famous letter from Charlemagne to King Offa complaining of the low quality of the English cloth used for the uniforms of the Carolingian soldiers. We hear nothing about the exports of raw wool or of other agricultural produce, although the high levels which trade in wool and grain had reached by the twelfth century suggest that its beginnings may have gone much further back, perhaps to the middle centuries of the Anglo-Saxon era. That the commodities exported from England were in the nature of 'essentials' is suggested by King Offa's alleged proposal to place an embargo on English commercial voyages abroad as a reprisal for Charlemagne's failure to carry into effect a project for a dynastic marriage. We are told very little, however, about the commodities which England took in exchange for its exports. All that can be said about English imports is no more than a deduction from what is known of the commercial activities of foreigners who traded to England at that time.[3]

The foreigners most active in the English foreign trade between the sixth century and the eighth were the Frisians—the inhabitants of the region round the multiple estuaries of the Rhine. The sandy and waterlogged flats of these estuaries attracted a population of German tribesmen at the very early period of Germanic settlement in the west. The physical character of the area made it most unsuitable to arable farming, so that from the very beginning the settlers engaged primarily in dairying and, above all, fishing, navigation and trade. We accordingly find the Frisians acting in the Merovingian and Carolingian epochs as the principal intermediaries between northern Europe and the countries further south. They shipped down the Rhine wine, timber and grain of south German provenance and carried up the Rhine or overland fish and other commodities of northern origin. English cloth may have been one of these commodities, and so were possibly other English goods about which our sources happen to be silent.

We find the Frisians trading in such English towns as London or York. Their hold over England's foreign trade could not, however, have been complete. We possess a seventh-century reference to other foreign merchants in London and York, and somewhat later references to merchants from all over Europe—Rouen, Liège, Flanders and Normandy—trading in London. Nor were the English themselves inactive. The Saxon merchants, who according to one of our sources visited the town of Quentovic (modern Étaples) in the eighth century, were in all probability Anglo-Saxons. Our records also contain a letter from Emperor Charlemagne to King Offa promising protection to English merchants visiting the imperial territories. We hear of at least one very wealthy English merchant, Godric of Fincham, the central figure of a well-known *Vita*, active at the turn of the Anglo-Saxon and Norman eras. We also hear of a Jewish merchant visiting his co-religionists in England in the ninth century, and we must also assume, for reasons I shall presently specify, that Scandinavian traders—if traders is the right way of describing them—were also trading with England in Anglo-Saxon times.[4]

Indeed the Frisians' pre-eminence in the English trade, like their pre-eminence in northern Europe as a whole, came to an end some time in the ninth century as a result of Scandinavian pressures and violence. Not only did the Scandinavian raids disrupt much of the Frisian water-borne trade, but the Scandinavian invasion of Frisian lands and the destruction of the Frisian trading emporia on the Rhine reduced Frisian commerce to a mere shadow of its former self. In the period immediately following the main wave of Norse invasions and conquests the Scandinavians themselves were to serve and perhaps to dominate the commercial channels of north-western Europe and above all the trade to and from England. The tenth-century life of St Oswald mentions Danish traders in London, and other Scandinavian sources abound with references to commercial voyages to England.

Such voyages were probably older than the Danish invasions themselves. Throughout their early medieval history the Scandinavians roamed the northern seas not only as robbers, pirates and conquerors but also as buyers and sellers, and may have established their earliest connections with Anglo-Saxon England as peaceful traders. At any rate, if the account of the chroniclers is to be trusted, it appears that in the earliest raid on the English coasts, that near Dorchester in 789, the invading fleet was met and welcomed by English officials presumably on the assumption that the Danes were coming to trade.[5]

How much trade was or could be done when the raids and invasions were at their peak is difficult to say; there is however little doubt that no sooner had the raids ended and a Danish society established itself in the eastern counties than the Scandinavians resumed—if they had ever wholly interrupted—their commercial traffic to and from England. The sources tell us very little about the commodities they exported or imported in the early stages of that trade. The few surviving articles of foreign provenance dating to that period added to what we know of the Scandinavian connection with Byzantium suggest that luxury goods of near-eastern origin figured prominently among Scandinavian imports to England. We must also presume that, to begin with, the Scandinavians took out of England very little beyond gold and silver. The hoards of Anglo-Saxon coins unearthed all over the regions inhabited or dominated by the Scandinavians may have come mainly from booty and proceeds of the Danegeld; but if some or any was acquired by trade (as some of it most probably was) this bears indirect witness to the inability of the English to pay for their import by equivalent exports of goods.[6]

The trade may, however, have ceased to be unilateral some time before the middle of the twelfth century. By that time English grain had become a highly valued source of Norwegian food supplies—*vide* the eulogy of English grain imports which the Saga puts into the mouth of a twelfth-century King of Norway, Hakon Hakonsen. There is, moreover, no reason for assuming that grain was the only important export. We are not told whether Scandinavia took much or any English cloth but they probably did so, since the tradition of cloth-making had been long established. We have already mentioned the cloth exports to the Carolingian Francia, and by the eleventh century English cloth was also to be found on several continental markets. Some cloth would therefore have found its way to Scandinavian markets as well. In return for its grain and its industrial produce, England now imported from Scandinavia fish and certainly timber, since by all accounts Norway was at that time England's chief source of tall timber.

However, by the end of the twelfth century and the beginning of the thirteenth, the Anglo-Scandinavian links, in their turn, greatly weakened. The weakening was to some extent a by-product of the general decline which Scandinavian shipping and trade suffered in the course of the twelfth and the thirteenth centuries. The causes of the decline have been much discussed by historians and are still in doubt. The very success of the Nordic conquests in Europe, resulting as it did in the formation of settled Normano-French, Normano-English, and Normano-Italian states, may have reduced the incentive for further raids and also enfeebled the connections between the Nordic settlers and their homeland. Very important changes were also taking place at that time in the economic and political geography of the Baltic regions. From the middle of the twelfth century onwards German settlers, peasants as well as merchants, were busy occupying and settling the Slavonic lands east of the Elbe. In the course of this colonizing movement, and as a result of it, the Germans gradually interposed themselves into the commercial exchanges between the Baltic and the regions further west. Their increased hold over northern commerce and navigation was bound to reduce the Scandinavian part in the trade. In fact, before long the Germans came to dominate commerce and urban life inside the Scandinavian countries themselves.[7]

Whatever the causes of this decline in Scandinavian commerce elsewhere, the Scandinavian connections with England were further weakened by the Norman Conquest, which reoriented England's foreign connections, political as well as economic, southwards. The Angevin Kings of the twelfth century brought with them a dynastic link with Gascony in the southwest of France; and before long this political link developed into one of England's most enduring commercial connections. From Gascony came wine, for which medieval England developed an unquenchable thirst; to Gascony went grain and industrial produce, mostly cloth.

However, the most powerful factor behind English commerce in the Norman and Angevin period was the ever-increasing pull of the fast-developing Flemish economy, just across the channel. The economic rise of Flanders in the twelfth and thirteenth centuries is one of the wonder-stories of medieval economic history; indeed the earliest casebook example of economic development as now discussed in relation to the so-called underdeveloped countries. What happened was that peace and orderly government established in the regions by the strong counts of Flanders enabled population and agriculture to grow very fast—the latter by means of continuous reclamations from the sea and elaborate defences against tidal waters. Before long, however, the population outgrew the ability of local agriculture to maintain it, and increasing numbers were drawn into industrial occupations of every kind, but mainly into the manufacture of cloth. Cloth became Flanders' most important industry for reasons which were partly traditional—the area had an ancient nucleus of cloth-making trades—but mainly geographical. The geographical proximity of England with its large and easily accessible wool supplies fostered a natural symbiosis between the two countries. A very large, by medieval standards a vast, textile industry sprang up in Flanders with exports reaching to every corner of Europe and even beyond, while England channelled to the Flemish towns a large, by medieval standards also vast, flow of raw wool.[8] Continuous statistics of wool exports from England do not become available until some time in the fourteenth century, but how great the exports were at the end of the twelfth and possibly earlier is revealed by several accidental pieces of evidence. The ransom negotiated at the turn of the twelfth and thirteenth centuries to redeem Richard Coeur de Lion from his captivity was calculated on the basis of a wool levy of fifty thousand sacks, equivalent to the fleeces of over six million sheep. The figure may have been over-optimistic and the levy may never have been collected in full, but other evidence from the early and middle decades of the thirteenth century also indicates that the possibility of exporting between thirty and fifty thousand sacks per annum was assumed by the kings trying to exploit the trade to their advantage, and by the merchants seeking licences for export.[9]

The size which these exports had reached so early in the thirteenth century strongly supports the belief that the trade was older than our earliest evidence of its full involvement with the Flemish cloth industry, since no country could have built up additional sheep flocks of six million and more in a few decades. The size of the exports and the sheep population in the early 1200s strengthens our suspicion that, for all the silence of our documents about wool exports before 1200, wool had been exported in the earlier centuries. There is however little doubt that the wool trade grew fast during the thirteenth century and in the first two decades of the fourteenth.

Needless to say, Flanders was not the only recipient and user of English wool. Other cloth-making regions, above all, Florence, also imported considerable quantities and, in fact, depended on English wool for the manufacture of their better cloths. But on the whole the Flemish market was far more important than any other, just as English wool was very nearly the sole source of raw material for exportable varieties of Flemish cloth. The mutual dependence of the English suppliers and the Flemish users of wool accounts for the almost simultaneous development of both the Flemish cloth industry and the English wool exports both of which appeared to reach their highest point at the turn of the thirteenth and fourteenth centuries. Neither, however, was destined to stay at this peak for very long. Before the second quarter of the fourteenth century was over difficulties in the way of the English wool trade and in that of the Flemish cloth industry developed, and both declined; although in the case of English wool the decline was to be largely made up for by a compensating industrial development at home.

Difficulties in the way of the English wool trade were inherent in the very advantages it had enjoyed and the length to which it had expanded. In the first place there was little room for scaling up the output of wool beyond the point it had reached by the middle of the thirteenth century. We have already seen how the shortage of pasture imposed a ceiling on the maximum size of flocks which even the most progressive ecclesiastical landlords were able to maintain. What is true of individual wool growers was probably true of the country as a whole. To put it into somewhat more technical terms the supply of wool was very inelastic. As the demand for wool stayed high and as no alternative source of high-quality wool was available, the English exporters were able to charge the foreigners a high monopoly price which was apparently much above the costs of production at home. At the end of the fourteenth century a sack of good Cotswold wool sold on the wool markets of the Low Countries at £12 to £15 per sack (and for much more than that in Italy), at a time when the home producers still found it profitable to grow and to sell it at £4 to £6 per sack. The monopoly price and the very wide profit margins it permitted were bound to excite the appetites both of the merchants seeking to secure for themselves the benefits of the monopoly and of the kings tempted by the possibility of diverting some of the monopoly profits into the state coffers. The appetite of the former led to a protracted tussle for and against compulsory 'staples': a term used for localized foci of trade monopoly, about which more will be said presently. The appetite of the Crown on the other hand led to the imposition of ever-higher taxes on wool which eventually rose to about 40 per cent of its selling price abroad and more than 50 per cent of the value received by the wool-growers at home.

A very wide differential was thus established between the prices which foreign clothmakers had to pay for their wool and those at which wool was available to clothmakers working in England. A differential like this was, in the end, bound to stimulate the formation of a large indigenous cloth industry. A further stimulus came from the tribulations of the Flemish industry itself. Some of these tribulations may have been due to the high cost of English wool, which was one of the reasons why the Flemish export industry had to concentrate almost wholly on highly priced luxury cloth with a limited potential for further expansion. For these and other reasons the Flemish clothmakers kept low the earnings of the men they employed, thereby creating in the Flemish cloth towns great disparities in wealth and power and much social friction. In most of them social discontents and explosive pressures grew until an urban revolution flared up all over Flanders in the 1320s, during the opening phases of the Hundred Years War. As a result of these troubles the Flemish cloth industry plunged into headlong decline. By the 1360s, within no more than two decades of its peak, the Flemish output fell by no less than one half, and a large proportion of its workers emigrated, setting up new and rival centres of the cloth industry. The nearby province of Brabant was one such new centre, North Holland another, and England the third and the most important.[10]

For this rise of England's cloth-making the chronicles and the historians following them found a simple and attractively dramatic explanation. They tell us that having realized the benefits which cloth-making could confer on the country, King Edward III simultaneously prohibited the export of wool and the import of foreign cloth and invited a Flemish master, John Kemp, to come to England. This Kemp apparently did, with the result that within a few years of his coming a flourishing cloth industry had come into being.

This story has some basis in fact though a very tenuous one. The export of wool was prohibited for a short while in the 1320s as it had been on several previous occasions when England and Flanders happened to be in conflict. Prohibitions like this were not, however, long-lasting or complete. As a rule they were little more than pretexts for levying payments for special licences to export. Taking the second half of the fourteenth and the fifteenth centuries as a whole, the exports of wool to Flanders and Italy proceeded unimpeded, though at a much lower pace than at the turn of the thirteenth and fourteenth centuries. As for John Kemp the important question is not why he was invited, but that he should have accepted the invitation. The answer is that with the domestic price of wool, compared to its price in Flanders, so low, England was now the clothier's promised land. This promise John Kemp was not alone to seize; in fact he and numerous other Flemings who came to this country merely reinforced the ranks of native cloth-makers who had been always present in some numbers in the English countryside. The numbers were now swollen not only by Flemish immigrants but also by additional labour drawn to the cloth industry from the general reservoir of men seeking employment. The effect on exports was great and quick. At the beginning of the fourteenth century British cloth exports were very small indeed: no more than a couple of thousands of cloths per annum, if that much; by the middle of the century they approached fifty thousand cloths per annum, and were to stay around that level for at least another sixty or seventy years.

The rise of the cloth industry and the upsurge in its exports entailed a wholesale shift of English wool supplies away from foreign markets. Some wool still continued to be exported both to the Low Countries (North Holland had now become an important customer) and to Italy, but the total wool exports declined steeply—from the thirty thousand sacks in the thirteenth century to little more than a third of that volume in the early fifteenth century—and continued to decline throughout the greater part of the fifteenth century.

The economy of the country, or at least what we should now describe as its balance of payments, was bound to benefit greatly from the shift, since the English receipts from foreign trade were now augmented by the 'value added' to wool by its conversion into cloth. The benefits of the shift were not however confined to the aggregate financial proceeds of foreign trade, but also brought about some very important structural changes in the direction and organization of English commerce. Hitherto English merchants played a largely passive part in the foreign trade of the country; since foreign merchants controlled most of its outlets. The wine imports from Gascony and exports to Gascony were largely in English hands; the English wool exporters also had a large share, perhaps more than a third, of wool sales abroad. They sold the wool they shipped in the wool markets of Flanders, mainly in Bruges or Antwerp, to local merchants or agents or to more substantial clothiers and did not themselves distribute it to smaller clothiers or transport it for distribution inland. But with the rise of the cloth industry and the growth of cloth exports their part in foreign trade became or at least promised to become less passive. They were now able to offer a manufactured commodity not requiring further handling by intermediaries and capable of being sold directly to consumers. This provided them with an opportunity and an inducement to serve markets in the continental interior into which they had previously not ventured.

The English merchants were now able to widen the range of their activities not only in the export trade but also in the movement of imports into England. In the past, the English wool exporters as well as other merchants, mostly members of the English mercantile gilds, such as mercers, fishmongers or vintners (more about them later) used the proceeds of the wool sales to buy miscellaneous commodities of foreign origin which they proceeded to import into England. These goods they bought mainly if not wholly on the great markets of the Low Countries. But now with cloth to sell, English merchants were able not only to buy and sell in various commercial centres in the Low Countries but also to establish themselves in Scandinavia, chiefly in Bergen, in one or two Baltic centres, such as Stralsund and above all Danzig, and possibly also in some West German centres such as Cologne. In some of these places, certainly in Antwerp and Bergen, they set up and maintained for a time fully-fledged trading stations with resident representatives ('factories').[11]

However English active trade and indeed English cloth exports did not continue to expand indefinitely. Like all branches of foreign trade English cloth exports were vulnerable to international conflicts and more particularly to interruptions resulting from naval warfare. Several such interruptions occurred in the northern sea waters in the course of the late fourteenth and the fifteenth centuries, but they were not sufficiently protracted or widespread to do permanent damage to commerce. Those which occurred in the second and the third quarter of the fifteenth century, however, were to prove more damaging to future prospects of commercial expansion and indeed to the continued progress of the English cloth trade. The chief actors in these conflicts were the merchants of north German towns who traded all over Europe as members of the Hanseatic League and were protected by the League's treaties with western governments and by its political and naval prowess. The Hanseatic merchants enjoyed trading privileges in various international centres, including England, and controlled a larger, perhaps the larger, share of English cloth exports to central and to eastern Europe. They were not unnaturally anxious to exclude the English merchants from this channel and, above all, from direct contact with the Slavonic markets served by the various Baltic cities and more particularly by Danzig. A protracted conflict over the English establishment in Danzig was therefore bound to ensue. In the closing stages of the conflict, during the 1460s and 1470s, the English government, weakened and disorganized by the Wars of the Roses, was unable to give the English merchants the political and military support they needed; and a political defeat was therefore inevitable. As a result of this defeat the attempts of English merchants to establish a permanent foothold in the eastern Baltic were frustrated, and by the late 1470s they were compelled to withdraw from Danzig and from the Baltic area as a whole.[12]

This defeat of English endeavours at expansion in the Baltic had been preceded and accompanied by similar setbacks elsewhere. The earliest outpost to go was in Norway, where the English factory of Bergen had been ousted by German pressures quite early in the century. The final defeat of the English in the Hundred Years War and their withdrawal from Gascony lost them their ancient hold over the wine trade of Bordeaux.[13] In this way, by the end of the fifteenth century the English-borne foreign trade was once again restricted to the Low Countries where the bulk of English-borne cloth exports and what remained of English wool exports had to be concentrated. As a result of this concentration, and as its *quid pro quo*, the English cloth exporters were called upon to make yet another adjustment. They had to fit their activities into the economic structure of the Low Countries and to the vested interests of the indigenous manufacturers; and this they did by importing into the Low Countries large and increasing proportions of unfinished cloth, and leaving it to the Flemish and Brabantine dyers and shearers to do the finishing work. In the end a large proportion of English exports came in this semi-manufactured form and a new symbiosis was in this way established between the Flemish and the English industries.[14]

With this change in the outlets and the make-up of English exports went also certain changes in their organization, as well as a general decline in their volume of cloth exports. The exports had climbed to their peak by the end of the fourteenth century, and still stood at or near it in the early 1420s. But, what with the recurrent political disturbances in Northern Europe, with naval hostilities and piracy on the main sea-lanes and with the gradual withdrawal of English merchants from a number of outlying markets, it is not surprising that the flow of exports should eventually have slumped to a much lower level. They fell to their lowest point in the late 1450s and 1460s, when the relations with the Hanse were at their worst; they recovered at the end of the 1470s when the peace with the Hanse was established, but did not regain their fourteenth-century summit until the 1480s. Even at that height they may have been of smaller aggregate value than earlier since, being in large part unfinished, they embodied a smaller 'value added' to the raw materials than the exports at the end of the late fourteenth century. It was not until the sixteenth century and more particularly until the coming of the so-called 'new draperies' that the forward surge of cloth export proceeded again at the same headlong pace as before 1420.

The extent to which the fifteenth-century slump in cloth export reacted upon the English cloth industry itself is still a debating point among historians. If it could be shown that the internal consumption of cloth remained stable, or still more if it also declined, it would necessarily follow that the contraction of foreign sales resulted in a corresponding decline in the total output of cloth at home. On the other hand, if we could show that while exports contracted the domestic market expanded, and that its expansion at home was on a scale commensurate with the contraction abroad, we could safely conclude that the English cloth industry sailed wholly unscathed through the troubles on the export markets. Our verdict thus wholly depends on what we know or can surmise about the condition of the domestic market.[15]

III

The history of internal trade in medieval England is not as well served by documentary evidence as that of foreign trade. Such little evidence as there is throws some light on the organization of the trade, above all on the institutions serving and regulating it. On the other hand, we have next to no evidence to reveal its changing quantities. All the historian may wish to say about the ups and downs of commercial and industrial activity, its long-term trends or the proportions of a national product drawn into domestic industry and trade must be deduced from what is known about the general economic conditions. These deductions are bound to be highly uncertain, but they must not be altogether disdained. Although they cannot offer any very firm answers, they can at least help to eliminate the most infirm of answers and to limit the range of likelihoods.

The conclusions easiest to draw by deduction from general considerations are the 'functional' ones, i.e. those derived from what we know of the economic and social functions of trade. In discussing the functions of internal trade in the middle ages it would be convenient to distinguish trade serving interregional and interlocal needs from that serving the 'infra-local' needs, i.e. exchanges within individual local groupings, whether villages, manors or towns.

Interlocal exchanges have already been mentioned elsewhere. They existed by virtue of such regional specializations—or, to use a more technical term, such regional divisions of labour—as medieval conditions made possible. We have already noted that the specialized economy of most pastoral areas of England presupposed the ability and the need to sell the local surpluses of wool and dairy produce. By the same token most pastoral areas were to some extent dependent on outside supplies of cereals, especially in years of bad harvests.

Areas of specialized economy cast on a scale smaller than that of the pastoral areas have also been discussed earlier in this book. There were mining areas, such as those of tin in Cornwall, coal and iron in the West Riding of Yorkshire or the Forest of Dean, or coal on the Northumbrian coast (coal was regularly shipped to London from Newcastle in the thirteenth century). There were sea-faring and fishing villages along the coasts, settlements of charcoal burners in the forest areas, and a localized manufacture of iron goods in the Midlands, around Coventry, in Yorkshire, Sussex, the Forest of Dean and elsewhere. In the fourteenth and early fifteenth centuries a number of villages and smaller towns in various parts of England developed into predominantly industrial centres occupied wholly or mostly in cloth-making. In addition England was covered by a network of towns which supplied the country with miscellaneous merchandise.

In a later chapter the rising towns, with their function and organization, will be discussed in greater detail. Here towns are mentioned as yet further examples of specialized localities capable of offering to outsiders their characteristic product and services. In exchange for their specialized offers the towns received from outside food and raw materials. Not all the specialized villages and regions, and not even all the towns, were wholly dependent on food supplies from outside; but some such *quid pro quo* must have underlain the willingness and the ability of the mining, fishing, cloth-making or urban populations to pursue their specialized occupations.

No doubt in many a mining or cloth-working village some of the food which an industrial worker might need came from his own small holdings, or else from other more purely agricultural producers in the village. These exchanges within villages bring us to the second, the 'infra-local', network of exchanges, those between households within individual villages, manors or towns.

Some of these 'infra-local' exchanges originated in the imperfections of the household economy in the middle ages. In discussing the production and consumption of a typical peasant family historians and sociologists invariably and rightly emphasize its self-sufficiency. The typical peasant family produced on its land and with its family labour most of the goods it needed, and was not, or very little, dependent on outside supplies. We must not, however, exaggerate the degree of self-sufficiency of which village households were capable. As I have repeatedly stressed there were in most villages numerous households wholly or largely dependent on the supplies they bought or otherwise acquired from others. But even the households whose holdings and family labour enabled them to cover most of their needs out of their own output still obtained some commodities by purchase. Salt was, as a rule, bought and so were articles made of iron and earthenware. Most households also bought small quantities of pitch, tar, and occasionally even such semi-luxuries as pepper or textile fineries. Some dependence on the outside also resulted from certain monopolies imposed by the lords. Most villagers were compelled to take their grain to the village mill to be ground into flour or gruel meal. These services were as a rule paid for by 'multure', a proportion of the grain milled, but occasionally also in money. Village ovens were not as widespread in England as they were on the continent, and the lords seldom imposed a monopoly of baking. But when and where a communal oven existed it provided yet another occasion for purchases outside the households.

These purchases sometimes included commodities and services which would as a rule be produced within households in modern times. It appears that even in places where manors did not operate village ovens and did not enforce a corresponding monopoly, individual households occasionally and perhaps even frequently bought some of their food cooked, some of their bread baked and some of their ale brewed by others. The reason for this was not only the most primitive character of the heating and cooking provisions in peasant houses, but the apparent dearth of fuel. The extent to which the medieval countryside in the arable regions was underprovided with wood has not been sufficiently appreciated by antiquarians and historians. By the end of the thirteenth century, woodland in most arable areas had been greatly reduced, and burnable timber appeared to be very dear and presumably scarce; but above all it was owned by the lords. Medieval accounts contain numerous references to villagers buying 'underwood' from their lords. When this 'underwood' was bought, so to speak, *in situ* and green, it may have been used as fodder, but most of it appears to have been gathered dry, and presumably used as fuel. Considered as fuel it was, compared to other prices, exceedingly costly. On some Glastonbury estates a bundle, apparently quite a small one, could be priced at one shilling, or about the price of a bushel of grain. Cooking must therefore have been an expensive operation, something of a luxury, and cooked food was not frequently eaten. Porridge and gruel were the commonest family dishes and it is quite possible that some of the porridge was taken as 'brose', as it was to be by Scottish crofters in modern times, i.e. uncooked.

There was thus in most villages some demand for bread baked by outsiders and for cooked food bought from professional cooks. In most villages ale was also provided by 'alewives' specializing in brewing. In weekly markets and above all in larger fairs, cooks and sellers of every kind of cooked or baked food were as conspicuous as they are nowadays in market places in India or in the Middle East, and for the same reasons.

However, much of the infra-local exchange was generated by and for the large number of households wholly incapable of self-sufficiency. One of the features of medieval life which accounts for the existence of such households was the inequality in the distribution of land. The other was the weight of compulsory payments, above all cash payments with which individual holdings were burdened. It has been repeatedly stressed here that a large proportion of the village population—a proportion which in most areas in the thirteenth century may have exceeded one third—occupied holdings too small to provide sufficient food for a family, and that most smallholders were therefore dependent for their sustenance on profits from non-agricultural occupations or on wages they earned as agricultural labourers. Some of the food the labourers needed they frequently received in kind. Manorial 'famuli' were frequently paid in 'liveries', quantities of grain to take away, and were also given meals on the manor while at work. Similarly labourers working for other villagers were as a rule fed by their employers. These payments in kind did not, however, cover the entire needs of the rural wage earners, and in most cases they were also paid money wages in addition to liveries. Presumably they laid out their money on additional food and other commodities, as well as on payments of rent.

Rent and other obligatory payments provided the other instigation to infra-local trade. We have seen that, even though the gross output of an average medieval peasant holding—a half-virgate—was sufficient to maintain the holder's family at the minimum level of subsistence, a proportion of its output had to be given over to cash crops, the proceeds of which went to pay the rent and the other dues to the lords, the state and the church. As a result on some holdings at least one half of the produce had to be market-oriented and was grown to be sold. Some of the produce so sold—especially in the areas of high arable output—was presumably exported into deficiency areas in other parts of England, the rest was presumably sold locally to households insufficiently provided with land.

The economic compulsion behind the infralocal trade, whether caused by inequalities, or made necessary by obligatory payments, could in some places draw into exchange a large proportion of the village produce. What the proportion was in any place or time depended on the aggregate output of local agriculture, and above all the degree of prevailing inequalities and the weight of obligatory payments. Hence the conclusion which students reared on conventional notions may find at first sight unexpected: that the places and times in which the inequalities were worst and the manorial and fiscal obligations heaviest, were also the periods and places in which men had the greatest need to produce for the market and to trade. From this point of view the infralocal trade should have been at its highest in the thirteenth century, since this was the time when population pressure was greater than at any other period and smallholdings proliferated, as well as the time when many lords tried to maintain the surviving servile disabilities and were busy collecting the rents and fines to which villeins were liable. More paradoxically still, and wholly contrary to one of the main propositions of Marxian historiography, is the possibility that the infralocal trade declined in the closing centuries of the middle ages. For this was the time when the demand for land slackened and when the number of underprovided smallholders thinned out, when land values including rents slumped and when servile obligations were relaxed. This should not, therefore, have been the time most conducive to market-oriented production but, on the contrary, the time when the output of cash crops should have contracted as the forced inducements behind it weakened.

What with various industrial occupations in the countryside and the economic specialization between different parts of the country and market-oriented activities within villages, we should be prepared to find all over the country large numbers of men active as artisans, traders and specialists of every kind. Their numbers were, of course, bound to be smaller than in other more fully commercialized or industrialized societies—than, say, in

Flanders at the same period or in England in the eighteenth century. Yet their numbers were large enough to affect development of the economy as a whole. The evidence to enable us to estimate the numbers is not, of course, available. In view of the part-time nature of so many rural occupations the evidence would have been extremely difficult to interpret even if it had been available. Some impressions of their numbers however could be gathered from the spread of family names denoting commercial or industrial occupations. Later in the middle ages these names, having been passed down to several generations of descendants, lose all their value as evidence. But in the early thirteenth century, the time when these names first came into general use, they can be assumed to reflect more accurately the actual occupations of men bearing them and the relative importance of individual crafts in the occupational composition of the population. It would thus be interesting but not surprising to find that whereas Smiths were the most widespread occupational surnames, those of building and constructional workers of every kind formed, in combination, the largest of all the occupational groups characterized by their family names. Carpenters, Tylers, Thatchers, Masons, abound in our documents, and their abundance can be taken as indirect evidence of their widespread employment in the thirteenth century. Judging from manorial accounts most manors in fact maintained and gave employment to numbers of carpenters and other building workers, who on some estates, such as the headquarter estates of the great bishops or abbots, outnumbered the agricultural labourers permanently occupied on the demesne. If to these specialized occupations we also add the labourers and the carters employed in building operations, and towards the end of the fifteenth century also the brick-makers, we should be wholly justified in concluding that building was by far the most important non-agricultural occupation in the countryside.

Judged by family names, and hence by employment, cloth-making and leatherworking were next in importance. The reasons why the various leathercrafts—the Skinners, the Tanners, the Tawyers, the Saddlers—abound among family names is easily accounted for by the vast numbers of livestock and hence also by the large quantities of skins capable of being worked up into leather goods of every kind. There was approximately one sheepskin available for leather workers to three fleeces annually shorn for wool. In addition, there were large numbers of cowhides and horsehides in which medieval England had built up a considerable foreign trade, but of which a large proportion were turned into leather articles for use in this country.

In this ladder of non-agricultural occupations cloth came very high. Judged by the employment it gave and the aggregate value of its product, the cloth industry may have come higher even than the leather crafts, more particularly in the later fourteenth or the beginning of the fifteenth century, when the output of cloth for exports was at its highest. If the known returns of English exports at the beginning of the fifteenth century are converted into their equivalent in working days embodied in them (the exercise is difficult and is bound to be imprecise, but is not impracticable), it would appear that the total additional employment the cloth exports created was at least the equivalent of fifteen to twenty-five thousand full-time workers. The actual number of individuals drawn into the industry was, of course, higher than that since large numbers of the cloth workers—all its spinners and a proportion of its weavers, though not probably its fullers and dyers and shearers —were smallholders devoting to their industrial pursuits only half their time, or even less. We should not therefore err much if, in estimating the additions which exports made to the number of individuals employed in the industry some of their time, we went as high as 50,000, which was perhaps 5 to 7 per cent of our minimum estimate of the total number of English smallholders and landless men. Considering that the medieval economy was predominantly agrarian, and that cloth-making was only one of the industrial employments open to workers, this proportion, though low in relation to the total number of potential wage-earners, nevertheless represented a very sizeable addition to the industrial labour force.

How permanent this addition was destined to be, or in other words how long and how well the industrial activity initiated by the exports of cloth held up, is a moot point. What makes this point impossible to settle definitely and finally is that all arguments about it must be wholly based on *a priori* reasoning, and above all on what we can surmise about the behaviour of the domestic market. Did the domestic demand for cloth decline in keeping with the decline of cloth exports, did it remain stationary, or did it increase sufficiently to make up for the shortfall in exports? Only if the latter could be demonstrated would it be possible to conclude that in spite of declining exports the total volume of cloth production and employment stayed buoyant or even continued to increase as heretofore. If, on the other hand, the likelihood was that the domestic market failed to expand sufficiently fast to compensate for falling exports, the inevitable conclusion must be that from the second decade of the fifteenth century until the third quarter of the century not only did exports slump but the cloth industry itself declined.

In discussing these alternative possibilities it is important to bear in mind that while some economic factors may have stimulated the domestic market of cloth, others may have depressed it. The most favourable factor of all was the somewhat greater prosperity of villagers in the later fourteenth and fifteenth centuries. With their prosperity higher, they should have disposed of larger cash surpluses, which they could if they wished lay out on luxuries and semi-luxuries, such as cloth. Their cash balances may also have been favoured by the slight fall in the food prices which occurred at the time. The fall would not have benefited the section of the village population which derived some of its income from sales of produce, but would certainly have redounded to the advantage of the poorer men, the smallholders and the landless wage-earners.

Against the factors favouring the domestic cloth market we must cite a number of unfavourable factors. In the first place there was an overall decline of population, and consequently also a decline in the total number of would-be buyers of cloth. The effect of the decline on the cloth market is however difficult to judge for several reasons. To begin with it is impossible to estimate to what extent were the depressing effects of the smaller aggregate of potential buyers offset by the increased purchasing powers of individuals. To add to our difficulties, we cannot be certain that the disposable cash resources of individuals increased *pari passu* with their prosperity. It is easy to think of many reasons why their cash resources should have actually contracted. With the decline in the relative numbers of smallholders incapable of growing their food the infralocal food trade should have also declined and the cash incomes of men supplying the markets with produce should have gone down. We must also bear in mind the seemingly paradoxical, and yet very high, probability discussed above: that with rents and other compulsory cash payments lower the compulsion to grow crops for sale greatly lessened. Above all we must not assume that even larger cash balances would necessarily have brought about a corresponding increase in the effective demand for cloth. The relation between cash balances and the demand for cloth depended on the current 'consumers' preferences', i.e. on how highly cloth ranked in the villager's order of wants. It may well be that the first call on their additional resources was not for more land or stock or agricultural equipment but for more and better clothes, but it is equally possible that the latter came low in the average villager's order of preference, and that increased prosperity and even an increased cash flow would not have led to a corresponding expansion in the domestic demand for cloth. Finally we must not lose sight of the demand for cloth which came not from the masses, the main body of villagers and poorer townsfolk, but from the rich, including the monastic houses. And if we are right in thinking that the incomes of the landowning classes fell in the late fourteenth and fifteenth centuries this would add yet a further argument against the hypothesis of an expanding domestic market for cloth.

The resulting balance of probabilities is thus very uncertain. The only certainty about it is that considering the weight of factors on both sides the final balance was bound to be very small. If we were to conclude that on balance the domestic market continued to decline, we would also have to admit that the increased prosperity of the rural masses must have kept the decline slow and small. Similarly if we believed that the domestic market showed a tendency to expand in response to rural prosperity, the various adverse factors were bound to keep the expansion in check. In other words, the expansion of the domestic market, even if proved, would probably have been insufficient to make up in full for the large and drastic decline in the cloth exports which occurred in the middle decades of the fifteenth century.

References

1. M. M. Postan, 'The Trade of Medieval Europe: The North', *The Cambridge Economic History*, Vol. II; E. M. Carus-Wilson and O. Coleman, *England's Export Trade, 1275–1547* (1963).

2. J. Brutzkus, 'Trade with Eastern Europe, 800–1200', *Econ. Hist. Rev.* Vol. XIII (1943); for the implication of regular sales of English or British slaves across the Channel, see D. Whitelock (ed.), *English Historical Documents*, Vol. I, No. 26, p. 364.

3. Whitelock (ed.), *English Historical Documents*, No. 197, p. 781; No. 20, p. 313; J. Raine (ed.), *Historians of the Church of York*, I, p. 454.

4. Brutzkus, 'Trade with Eastern Europe'.

5. *The Anglo-Saxon Chronicle*, fo. 789, in Whitelock (ed.), *English Historical Documents*, p. 186.

6. A. Bugge, 'Die Nordeuropäische Verkehrswege in frühen Mittelalter', *Viertelj. f. Sozial–u. Wirtschaftsgesch.*, IV (1906); A. Mawer, *The Vikings* (1912); C. R. Beazley, *The Dawn of Modern Geography*, Vol. II, pp. 17–111; A. Bugge, 'Norse Settlements in the British Isles', *Trans. Roy. Hist. Soc.*, 4th ser., IV (1921).

7. A. Bugge, 'Der Untergang der Norwegischen Seeschiffsfahrt', *Viertelj. f. Sozial–u. Wirtschaftsgesch.* (1904).

8. P. Grierson, 'The Relations between England and Flanders before the Norman Conquest', *Trans. Roy. Hist. Soc.* 4th ser., XXIII (1941); also H. Pirenne, *Histoire de Belgique*, Vol. I (1929), pp. 184–88.

9. E. E. Power, *The Wool Trade in English Medieval History*, Oxford (1941), pp. 63–85, and *passim*.

10. For the general course of wool exports and cloth trade and their interaction see E. E. Power, 'The Wool Trade in the Fifteenth Century', in E. E. Power and M. M. Postan (eds.), *Studies in English Trade in the Fifteenth Century* (1933); H. L. Gray, 'The Production and Export of Woollens in the Fourteenth Century', *Eng. Hist. Rev.*, XXXIX (1924); E. M. Carus-Wilson and O. Coleman, *England's Export Trade* (tables and charts). An account of the cloth trade somewhat different from the one presented here will be found in E. M. Carus-Wilson, *Medieval Merchant Venturers* (1954), Ch. IV.

11. M. M. Postan, 'The Economic and Political Relations of England and the Hanse from 1400–1475', in Power and Postan, *Studies.*

12. Postan, 'Economic and Political Relations', in Power and Postan, *Studies.*

13. For the history of the wine trade, cf. M. K. James, 'The Fluctuations of the Anglo-Gascon Wine Trade during the Fourteenth Century', *Econ. Hist. Rev.* 2nd ser., IV (1951), and James, *The Wine Trade of England in the Middle Ages* (1971). For local trade in general see L. F. Salzman, *English Trade in the Middle Ages* (1931). A wide-ranging discussion of the salt trade will be found in A. Bridbury, *England and the Salt Trade in the Later Middle Ages* (1955). Up-to-date accounts of the leather trade or the metal trades still remain to be written.

14. Gray, 'Production and Export of Woollens'; Carus-Wilson and Coleman, *England's Export Trade*, pp. 75–109. Some older writers may have exaggerated the extent to which English exports came to be confined to unfinished cloth: *ibid.*, p. 15. Nevertheless, undyed cloth appears to have formed a large part of English exports to the Low Countries at the end of the middle ages.

15. The impact of certain branches of the cloth industry on rural society in some localities in the south Cotswolds is illustrated in E. M. Carus-Wilson, 'Evidence of Industrial Growth on some Fifteenth-Century Manors', *Econ. Hist. Rev.*, 2nd ser., XII (1959).

12 Markets, Towns and Gilds

I

The bulk of medieval trade and industry was very highly professionalized and very largely confined to commercial towns. But before this urban concentration can be dealt with properly it is important not to lose sight of the other, more informal, ways in which trade could be conducted. Even at the height of the middle ages some of the trade and much of the industry were, so to speak, dispersed over the countryside and were frequently carried on as part-time activities ancillary to agriculture.

Many of these dispersed activities were served by markets functioning as centres of occasional commerce. Perhaps most occasional were the commercial operations of the village markets to which agriculture producers, like peasant producers of all times and countries, occasionally brought the surplus products they had to sell. Village markets of this kind are often concealed from our view by their very informal nature. It is only when a large village or a small town happened to receive from its lord a special right to hold and to regulate periodic markets that we are able to catch a glimpse of their working. Many others probably functioned unrecognized or at least unenfranchized by the authorities.

The local peasant producers were not, however, the only frequenters of the local markets. The latter also drew to themselves the travelling merchants whose function was partly to gather rural produce for subsequent resale and partly to retail in the countryside the merchandise of urban provenance. We find them in our documents described as broggers, chapmen, hucksters or just 'merchants' (*mercatores*). They were presumably the men who acted as woolmen, or 'wool broggers' as they came to be known later, who bought up wool and woolfells in small quantities from petty producers for delivery to wool wholesalers. The latter were men like the Midwinters and the Bushes of the north Cotswolds, who are repeatedly mentioned in the business documents of the

Cely family, a fifteenth-century family of wool exporters. They themselves lived in the countryside they served, and presumably employed a number of smaller men to travel about the countryside to 'collect' wool. In the earlier centuries, mainly before the end of the thirteenth, the function of 'collecting' the wool from smaller growers for resale to exporters devolved upon the greater wool-growing abbeys. We find a number of Cistercian houses undertaking to deliver to their merchant clients, as a rule Italian and Flemish exporters, not only the wool of their own growing but also wool described as '*collecta*', i.e. assembled in smaller quantities from other growers. There is some evidence to suggest that the grain trade was similarly organized. It was certainly run on these lines at the end of the middle ages and at the beginning of the modern era.[1]

Urban merchandise was often distributed over the countryside by the same men, although now and again we come across men who apparently operated wholly as travelling retailers of merchandise. Most of them apparently were agents of merchants in the towns. Judging from the evidence of urban documents, the more substantial London merchants operated as wholesalers, importing their goods from abroad or buying them at great fairs and distributing them over the countryside through the agency of their chapmen and hucksters. In all probability the village markets were the main scene of these men's operations; but, judging from some occasional references, a chapman or a huckster might also visit individual homes and run a veritable network of connections with local producers. In general the local village markets served as the main channel of their activities in the countryside.[2]

However, the small and scattered village markets were not the only places where professional and non-professional sellers and buyers met and where trade could be conducted at periodic intervals. In various places in England as in a number of centres on the continent a great deal of trade, wholesale as well as retail, flowed through great fairs, usually annual but sometimes semi-annual or quarterly gatherings of merchants at which goods were exchanged wholesale and financial settlements of some importance took place. In England much of the wool was thus sold to exporters and settlements for such sales were made at the great fairs, of which the semi-annual fair of Boston was probably the most important. In the late fourteenth and fifteenth centuries some fairs, such as that of St Bartholomew in London, of Northampton or York, functioned as cloth fairs. Other great annual fairs, like those of

Winchester, St Ives or Stourbridge, also functioned as channels of wholesale trade of every kind. Needless to say, however important these wholesale operations were, the great fairs drew to themselves customers of every kind by the opportunities for small sales and purchases and often by the diversions they offered to all and sundry.

The intermittent and highly scattered, and to some extent unprofessional, commerce flowing through the local markets and fairs did not, however, draw to itself the bulk of medieval trade. Most of the medieval trade eventually came to be conducted by professional whole-time merchants operating throughout the year from their places of business in towns. Within the towns trade was more highly regulated and controlled by organizations of every kind than it was to be in any subsequent epoch. Indeed so characteristically medieval were the urban concentration and control of trade, that the active history of medieval commerce and industry is inextricably bound up with the history of the town, its rise and development, its characteristic systems of government and its economic policies.

II

The rise of towns happens to be one of the perennial topics of medieval historiography. What historians have found necessary to explain is why the towns should have appeared and proliferated in the earlier middle ages and become one of the most characteristic of medieval institutions. Once upon a time English historians held the view that the invading Saxons were wholly ignorant of towns and shunned all urban institutions and pursuits. In that view all medieval towns, even where and when they happened to occupy Roman sites, were wholly products of later centuries. This view is no longer held in its simple and exaggerated form, since some urban life, however meagre, may have been handed down to the Anglo-Saxons from the Romano-British epoch. Moreover some indirect evidence of urban activities appears in sources sufficiently early in Anglo-Saxon history—certainly in the sixth century—for the view of the Anglo-Saxon society as wholly unurban not to be tenable. It nevertheless remains true that until the closing century or two of Anglo-Saxon rule the towns were few and their role in economic social life small. The time when towns multiplied and grew was the eleventh and twelfth and the early thirteenth centuries.

By, say, 1250 medieval England had come to be covered by a network of urban centres, most of them serving relatively small regions and occupied in commercial and industrial activities cast on a small and purely local scale.

The urban network and its formation in the earlier middle ages pose two related questions: why should towns have proliferated; and why should their proliferation have occurred at the time it did, i.e. between the eleventh century and the beginning of the thirteenth? The first of these two questions—that of the 'rise' of the towns—has occupied the attention of historians most, and a number of answers, all plausible, are now available to students. The best known to the general public is that associated with the name of Henri Pirenne, which links the rise of towns to men's striving after protection. In its Pirenne version, the theory accounts for the rise of the town on the continent by the tendency of population in general, but above all of the trading elements within it, to seek the protection of the feudal fortresses, mostly of the Merovingian and Carolingian counts, and to settle in 'suburbs' under the shelter of the burg walls. A more definitely military explanation, more precise and more, so to speak, technical than Pirenne's has been offered by several German writers and has been willingly and wittingly applied to late Anglo-Saxon England by Maitland. According to this view most of the main medieval towns arose as 'boroughs', the latter being fortified places created in each county during the Danish invasions to house the permanent county garrisons and to serve as rallying points of defense. The security which the boroughs provided drew to them the population of merchants and of other men seeking safety. Moreover, the need for security and peace and the general needs of garrison existence helped to establish within the borough a legal and administrative regime conducive to the pursuit of trade.[3]

These military theories have been countered or supplemented by a number of alternative hypotheses. Some historians have argued that there were many other opportunities and inducements for local conglomerations of people in general and of traders in particular, capable of developing into commercial centres. Such centres could appear on sites of the great pilgrimages, in the vicinity of shrines and cathedrals, or in places which offered purely geographical facilities for commercial traffic and intercourse—at the intersection of important roads, as in Cambridge, or at convenient river crossings, as at Oxford, or at estuaries serving as sea ports, as at London, Kingston-on-Hull or Ipswich.

Taken separately and, still more, in combination, these various hypotheses appear to be highly plausible. Unfortunately their relevance to our problem is not very close. What they account for is the reasons why medieval merchants preferred to frequent and inhabit some localities rather than others; in other words why medieval towns happened to be sited in places in which we find them in the twelfth century. What they do not directly answer is the question why the towns should have arisen at all and why their rise should have been timed as it was, i.e. in the two or two and a half centuries straddling the end of the Anglo-Saxon era and the early middle ages proper.

At first sight this question may appear to be so easy to answer as to be hardly worth asking. Was not the primary function of the towns to serve the needs of trade? Would not therefore the rise of trade and its growth between the tenth century and the thirteenth provide the most obvious answer to our conundrum?[4] In fact, however, this answer is too simple, and cannot be altogether true or full. We have seen that trade did not make its first appearance in the eleventh or even the tenth centuries and we do not know whether, if judged by its turnover or the numbers of men engaged in it, it grew at all fast or continually during the period in which England became urbanized. What is more, we must not assume that in all historical situations the needs of trade were and had to be served by conglomerations of merchants in urban centres. In some conditions trade could be conducted without towns. Prehistorical trade was certainly not conducted out of anything remotely resembling town settlements. Similarly we cannot be certain that the commercial activities of the Frisian merchants were focused in towns comparable to the urban centres of medieval and modern times. Their great emporium of Dorstadt proudly described by the chroniclers as a place with forty churches may well have been a cluster of forty fishing and dairying villages. Scandinavian, more particularly Norwegian, trading and raiding expeditions did not as a rule issue from towns of any kind. Much later in England the wool trade was frequently in the hands of merchants settled in villages in the heart of rural England; later still many a clothier inhabited small rural localities which frequently failed to acquire any of the attributes of town life and government. Similarly the very fast growth of trade in England in the seventeenth and early eighteenth centuries may have swollen the population of some of the existing towns, but very seldom gave rise to new commercial townships in the way growing trade is supposed to have done in the eleventh and twelfth centuries.

If so, the growth of trade could not by itself account for the emergence of the medieval network of towns. Trade was obviously an underlying cause, but there must have been something in the circumstances in which trade at that time grew that made it necessary for it to call towns into existence. What the circumstances were could only be guessed, but it would be a good guess that they were in the main political and constitutional. One of the circumstances was perhaps the political disturbances which led some people to seek the protection of fortified walls and of collective defense. But even more important than security itself were the political and military devices which medieval society evolved to deal with its problems of defence. These devices have been described elsewhere as elements of the emerging feudal order. Feudalism, its laws and practices, could indirectly affect the course of trade in more than one way, but two of its features had a direct bearing on commercial development. One was the restriction which feudal law put on personal mobility, on the disposal of property, and on the freedom of contract, and the other was the tendency of feudal society to professionalize men's occupations, or in other words to convert them into full-time vocations into which men could not easily enter, which they could not easily abandon and which they could not easily combine with other occupations. The two medieval occupations most fully professionalized were those in which the main body of rural society happened to be engaged: the working of the soil and the conduct of war and administration. In a society so conditioned the pursuit of trade was bound to be greatly impeded. It could best be conducted in places immune from the restrictions on personal status, on property and on freedom of movement and contract, and in the hands of men who were outside the feudal ranks of society, i.e. neither knights nor villeins. Medieval towns were precisely that. They were non-feudal islands in the feudal seas; places in which merchants could not only live in each other's vicinity and defend themselves collectively but also places which enjoyed or were capable of developing systems of local government and principles of law and status exempting them from the sway of the feudal regime. If so, the story of how and why the towns arose and proliferated should be told not only in economic but also in political and social terms. The story would then deal not only with the manner in which the trade or the population of this or that region or locality grew but also recount how a locality acquired its extra-feudal insignia, or 'privileges', which distinguished it from a feudalized village.

Most sizeable towns eventually received their extra-feudal privileges defined and assembled in charters of liberties granted to them by the kings or the great barons on whose land they happened to be situated. So crucial was the role of chartered privileges in the rise and development of towns that now and again medieval lords tried to conjure up wholly new towns or villages devoid of all urban attributes or even on wholly virgin sites, merely by conferring on them charters of urban liberties. Some of these 'new towns' remained stillborn, as for instance the new towns which the priors of Eynsham founded along the Oxford-Gloucester road, by carving out numbers of homesteads and conferring on them a charter of urban privileges. Most of the 'new towns', however, appeared to take root. In their case, as in that of the older towns, the charter and its liabilities embodied the essential pre-conditions of urban development.[5]

The surviving charters make it possible for us to define these pre-conditions and to trace their evolution. The most important of them were those of land and status. The householders in medieval towns, or burgesses as they came to be known, were deemed to be personally free and held their land by 'burgage tenure', a fully-free title which approached very closely the concept of full untrammelled ownership represented by the Roman *proprietas*.

The other liberty which most towns eventually acquired was fiscal autonomy, or freedom from interference and control by the royal or feudal agents. This exemption took, as a rule, the form of the '*firma burghi*' which gave the townsfolk the right to discharge their financial obligations to the king collectively, by a fixed annual sum which they levied themselves. The right to tax themselves was, in its turn, a step towards fuller and more general self-government. The English towns, unlike their counterparts in Italy or Germany, were never able to extend their autonomy to full political independence; the English kings were too strong for that. But within the precincts of the towns themselves their self-government became very real. Eventually most towns provided themselves with mayors, councils and other elected officials and with communal chests.

Finally most charters eventually conferred upon the towns the exemption from tolls and similar levies charged on mercantile traffic in other towns or on highways. These exemptions from tolls were sometimes mutual, in that they were contracted as between town and town, but more frequently they were granted by lords, whether kings or barons, in the form of freedom from tolls such as was already possessed by some other town, usually Oxford.

This freedom from tolls, and similar provisions for the freedom of trade between towns, appeared to run counter to one of the most important of the town privileges which is not always embodied in their charters, but yet formed one of the mainstays of the urban economy and a guiding principle of urban policy. The privilege was that of local monopoly. The *de facto* concentration of traders active in a region in that region's town had for its corollary the corresponding concentration of the region's trade itself. This *de facto* command which the townsfolk exercised over the commercial activities of their area was not, however, wholly informal. They frequently tried to formalize and to back it up by elaborate rules and regulations limiting the commercial activities of outsiders, such as rural residents or burgesses of other towns not able to claim reciprocal rights of free trade. These outsiders were usually excluded from trading with each other, but were allowed to buy and sell through the assistance of burgesses acting as intermediaries. Some towns did not enforce their monopoly very rigidly on such goods as wine, wool or cloth in which greater freedom of transaction was sometimes permitted. The reason for this relative laxity was the non-local origin or destination of the goods. For this reason it also appears that in England, as abroad, towns serving not local markets, as most of them did, but international ones, such as London and to some extent towns like Bristol, York or Southampton, did not impose on the main branches of their commerce the same detailed monopolistic limitations as they did on the purely local trade.

The chosen instrument of the monopoly was the gild. Although the monopoly of the local market was one of the principal aims of urban economic policy, in actual fact it was frequently administered not in the name of the town and not by the town government as such, but by specialized urban institutions which were, so to speak, the town government's commercial guise. The form this guise commonly took was that of the 'gild merchant' or market gild which, translated into modern English, would probably mean an association for the regulation and control of the market. Many towns of the twelfth century received by charter the right to set up a '*gilda mercatoria*' or '*hansa mercatoria*', an association of burgesses for common action in matters concerning their commercial activities and interests. The membership of the association was as a rule coterminal with the main body of the burgesses, but its functions were usually confined to the enforcement and the administration of the monopoly of the local market and to the regulations ancillary to it. Now and again, however, in towns which were large enough or sufficiently specialized to harbour substantial numbers of merchants or craftsmen specializing in certain branches of trade, these branches could themselves be organized into gilds performing functions similar to that of the *gilda mercatoria* but confined to one 'craft' or one branch of trade.[6]

The earliest of these craft gilds to be found in English towns were those of weavers in towns like London or Oxford. Eventually most larger towns came to possess craft gilds controlling the principal branches of their economic activities. Thus in the town of Coventry, which specialized in iron manufactures, several of the metalcrafts also had separate craft gilds of their own; the town of Newcastle had a separate gild in control of the coal trade; towns like York or Norwich or Bristol had separate craft gilds in a number of trades. But the town in which the function of commercial and industrial regulation and control was completely divided among craft gilds was London. London's commerce was always too great, and its interests too widely dispersed, ever to be controlled by a single market gild. From the very earliest times the regulation of its economy was in the hands of craft gilds large and small, some of which, like those of mercers, grocers, goldsmiths, fishmongers or vintners, were mainly mercantile; and others, like those of saddlers or tailors, were predominantly industrial. In the fullness of time, however, the London gilds came to be differentiated not only by the occupations they controlled but by their status within their occupations and within the economy of the town as a whole. Some of the gilds, mostly the mercantile ones, were large and rich enough, and harboured individuals wealthy enough, to form the upper level of the craft community, the so-called 'livery gilds' of London. The smaller tradesmen or craftsmen formed gilds of lower status, sometimes described as 'yeomen's' gilds. The 'yeomen' were frequently employees of greater merchant firms, and their gilds were in some respects not unlike the trade unions of modern times, since they devoted themselves largely to the business of representing and defining the interests of their members *vis à vis* the employers.

The purpose of the humbler craft gilds could thus be far removed from those of pure trade monopoly. In general, trade monopoly, for all its overriding importance, was not the sole object of the economic policy of the craft gilds, and sometimes not even of the market gilds. For one thing the existence and the enforcement of a collective monopoly on behalf of its members imposed upon the gild the obligation to safeguard the rights of individuals claiming a part in the monopoly. Most monopoly gilds had accordingly tried to protect the individual members' share in the total business of the town, or of the gild's occupation. Elaborate rules would frequently be worked out to make it impossible for individual members to 'engross', i.e. to get more than his due share of the business, or to 'forestall', i.e. to buy up goods before other gildsmen had a chance of buying, or in a more indefinite way to take an unfair advantage of other members. The limitation of the hours worked, of the prices charged and of the quality of goods were part and parcel of this system of safeguards, but they also protected the interests of the consumer whether they were primarily designed to do so or not.[7]

Closely linked with the gild monopoly functions, but not wholly identical with them, were the controls of recruitment and employment. If the monopoly was to be maintained the entry into the gilds had to be limited and regulated. Some of the gilds limited entry by imposing heavy entry fines; others gave preference to sons of members; but the chief limitations were those imposed by the apprenticeship rules. It was not always easy to be received as an apprentice. Apprenticeship itself was long, frequently as long as seven years. An examination—the 'master test'—had to be passed at the end of the period; and in the later middle ages young men without connections or funds often found it difficult to set up as masters even after they had passed their tests, and stayed on in their professions as 'journeymen' or 'yeomen'. In general the restrictions worked well enough to keep the intake of apprentices commensurate with the openings in it. Yet although the original purpose of apprenticeship was to control the entry into the trade and thus to buttress up the monopoly, it was eventually grown over with rules about the conditions, wages, hours of work and numbers employed. In this way, a veritable labour code grew up, only indirectly linked to the monopolistic purposes of the gild system.

The enforcement of the monopoly and the defense of the members' rights was thus the principal function of the gilds; the control of prices, of qualities, and of conditions of employment were their secondary functions largely derived from the working of the gild monopoly itself. The ceremonial and convivial activities were the least important, even though they were probably the earliest to develop. In general the order in which the functions of the gild have been expounded here is not the chronological order in which they in fact originated and evolved.

The chronology of the gild history and above all its origins is yet another of the debated problems of economic history. Some foreign historians derive the continental gilds from the *collegia* of craftsmen and traders established in the Roman cities in the closing centuries of the Empire. Others trace the beginnings of gilds to the groupings of artisans on the large royal and ecclesiastical estates. But the institutional roots of gilds easiest to trace in English sources are those which reach to the parish gilds, i.e. unions of parishioners organized round their churches for miscellaneous activities of mutual interest. We have seen that in some villages parish gilds could be used for activities which had little direct bearing on the church itself and often functioned as *foci* for combined action against the landlord, and as informal centres of local self-government. They could do the same in the quarters of the towns in which their parishioners resided. In urban conditions the territorial scope of the parish gilds could easily be professionalized, since medieval craftsmen belonging to the same occupation tended to reside in the same neighbourhoods. In dealing with matters of common interest urban parish gilds would therefore find it only too easy to take action in matters concerning the parishioner's occupation, and in this way provide the cell from which the craft gilds proper were to develop. Even in the large and fully developed gilds of later ages the genetic links with their parish cells frequently survived, bearing witness to the true descent of the gild organization. Some of the greatest London gilds, above all that of the mercers, preserved until our own age the name of the London parish around which they had once upon a time been organized. Here, as so often in other fields of economic history, the manner in which institutions originated and the purposes which they eventually came to serve were not, or at least did not for ever, remain identical.

III

In the closing phases of the middle ages, and more particularly in the fifteenth century, most of the English foreign trade was channelled through organizations of merchants which transcended the urban gilds in their scale of operations and power, yet partook of the economic purposes and methods of urban gilds. These organizations were, in the first place, the Company of the Staple of Calais, and in the second place the various English foreign-based associations which eventually formed the Company of Merchant Adventurers.

The 'staple' was an international term used by merchants and governments of most western countries to designate the compulsory concentration of certain branches of trade in specified localities. Most of the greater European towns with a large stake in certain commodities tried and were often able to compel all the trade in these commodities to pass through their territory and to be handled by their merchants. In England the possibility of establishing a staple for wool commended itself to all parties. To merchants and sometimes even wool-growers staples offered better facilities for regulating the trade and watching over its transactions and thereby enforcing 'fair' practices. To the crown staples offered greater ease of preventing evasions of dues, of enforcing official prices and regulations, but above all of collecting export taxes and managing loans on wool. Where the parties differed was in their preferences for the location of the staple. On the whole the growers and merchants not directly engaged in the export of wool favoured wool staples in England to which both foreign and English merchants would have access, and in which competition among exporters would keep the prices high. The English exporters, however, strongly pressed for staples in near-lying foreign markets, which would help to keep the foreign merchants out of this country, and would in fact force them to acquire wool only from the English exporters. The tug-of-war between the two parties continued throughout the greater part of the fourteenth century, and was closely involved with the endeavours of the kings to wring from the wool trade as much as possible in taxes and loans for their strained war finance. In the end the wool merchants were able to offer their cooperation in the levying and collecting of the high tax which wool exports had to bear, and above all to raise loans on the security of wool taxes. In exchange the Crown agreed to establish a wool staple in the town of Calais, reoccupied by the English at the very close of the fourteenth century. In that town the wool staple was to remain throughout the fifteenth century.[8]

The Company of the Merchants of the Staple, with a mayor and a council, came into existence concurrently in order to operate the Staple and to enforce the monopoly inherent in its very principle. The monopoly was directed not only against foreign traders but also against the English merchants who did not happen to be members of the Staple. The members were substantial merchants from most of the wool exporting towns, but mostly from London, and formed a fairly large but nevertheless a tight and exclusive circle. It was their established policy to prevent the circle from being broken into by indiscriminate entry or broken up by the rise of disproportionately large trading firms. The former object was easily achieved by the gild techniques of restricted entry and apprenticeship; the latter by a set of rules and proceedings directed against individuals trying to grab too great a share of the trade. The main function of the staple, however, was to enforce the principles of the Staple itself by watching over attempts by individuals to export wool through places other than Calais. A certain amount of wool, sometimes as much as a quarter of total annual exports, was taken out of England directly by Italian merchants operating under special royal licences, and the staplers could do little and seldom tried to do much to stop up this channel altogether. But all other attempts to smuggle wool out of England to northern Europe were rigorously policed and as a rule successfully scotched.

Some such vigilance on the part of the staplers was necessary not only to maintain their monopoly but also to safeguard the financial arrangements between them and the kings. In the first place the staplers regularly advanced to the Crown the eventual receipts from wool customs. The customs were collected in cooperation with royal officials, and their proceeds were eventually shared out among the members of the staple. The staple also collaborated with the Crown in operating a mint, probably the largest in the country, into which all cash proceeds of wool sales had to be paid and in which the bullion was reminted into English coin. In the course of the fifteenth century the Calais mint became the principal channel through which gold and silver generated in trade came into England, and a powerful agent in the management of English currency.

Different in origin, but in the end similar in its objects and methods, was the other organization of exporters and importers, that of the Merchant Adventurers. In the form in which it finally evolved in the fifteenth century the company was, so to speak, a residual legatee of several organizations formed in foreign countries by English merchants trading in cloth and other goods, mainly miscellaneous imports. The tendency to form such foreign-based organizations was general among merchants of all countries engaged in foreign trade. Much of that trade had to be conducted through agents resident abroad, many of whom were the merchants' employees or junior partners. Agents of this type were frequently lodged together under the same roof, under some sort of a common rule and under a collective protection. These purely residential and communal 'factories' also commended themselves to the 'masters' or the principal partners whenever they happened to visit the foreign places to which they habitually exported. Above all a communal organization with a mayor or governor could conduct negotiations with local authorities abroad, to represent the interests of English merchants in legal and other proceedings, and to act as a counter-party in treaties or agreements. The factories which the Hanseatic merchants possessed in a number of European centres in the fourteenth and fifteenth centuries, the 'Hanse of the German Merchants' as they were collectively known, were organizations of this kind; earlier still the Flemish merchants trading to England established in London a Hanse of Flemish Merchants. The English merchants apparently acquired some such organization late in the fourteenth century or in the early fifteenth in Norway (Bergen), in Brabant (Antwerp) and in Danzig. By the middle of the century, however, these outlying organizations folded up as the corresponding branches of trade they served withered away. The Scandinavian organization appeared to go first, and the Danzig one followed suit. In the end only the one, that in the Low Countries, based mainly on Antwerp, appeared to survive. In this way, just as the channel of trade to the Low Countries had come to draw to itself the bulk of English trade in northern Europe, so the Antwerp company eventually embraced the bulk of the English merchants, other than the staplers, regularly trading abroad.

The bulk of the merchants so represented were not, of course, all the merchants who in theory could or would have so traded had the organization of Merchant Adventurers permitted it. This it did not do. Although originally the various companies of merchant adventurers existed merely in order to provide the merchants with the various facilities abroad, in the end they, like the Company of the Staple and like all the gild organizations at home, found their chief *raison d'être* in the exercise of a monopoly power in the export of cloth. The monopoly developed slowly, in stages which are almost imperceptible, and was never to become as complete and perfectly enforced as that of wool exports. In the end the charter which the Company eventually received from the English crown and the privileges granted to it by some foreign powers, all came to recognize the monopoly and allowed the Company to act against 'interlopers', i.e. traders who were not members of the Company or who tried to ship goods in contravention of its rules and regulations.[9]

Both the Company of the Merchant Adventurers and that of the Staple were, to use a technical term, 'regulated' companies, i.e. organizations designed to regulate the trade of individual merchants, not to engage in trade themselves in their collective capacity. Companies of the other kind, trading with joint stock as single enterprises, developed well after the middle ages: in the sixteenth century and later. The only medieval exception, which in some way anticipated the joint-stock companies of the Elizabethan age, were groups of shippers periodically formed during the fifteenth century in Newcastle and Lynn for trading expeditions to Iceland. Measured by the physical volume of merchandise, Iceland was never a very important venue of English trade. But desirable commodities, mainly stockfish and a certain kind of very rough cloth, came from there; while for its part Iceland absorbed some English cloth and other miscellaneous commodities. So hazardous, however, were the Icelandic voyages deemed to be, that joint shipments by groups of merchants, sharing in the cost of the cargo and in its risks, were formed for each projected expedition. The sharing arrangements were apparently dissolved every time an expedition was completed and new partnerships were re-formed for subsequent expeditions.[10]

These partnerships and to some extent the regulated companies were from some points of view substitutes for the trading activities of very large firms. The regulated companies took care that such over-large businesses did not come into being, but their own rise was very largely to be accounted for by the absence of great firms in the late fourteenth and fifteenth centuries. They were not, therefore, true forerunners of what Marxian historians describe as the early commercial capitalism comparable to the great mercantile and banking firms in Italy and South Germany. These Italian and German firms were each individually large enough to operate with investments, to raise loans and make advances on taxes on a scale fully comparable with that in which the Company of the Staple operated collectively in the fifteenth century. They were also able to maintain staffs of agents and partners in foreign countries which fully matched the 'factories' maintained by regulated companies.

Nothing comparable to such firms was to be found in fifteenth-century England. Somewhat earlier, however, in the first half of the fourteenth century, several large enterprises made their appearance and began to develop in a way which, if continued, might have given rise to mercantile and financial units comparable to the great trading firms of Italy and Germany. These great businesses were called into being by the fiscal exigencies of the English crown in the earliest and costliest phases of the Hundred Years War. In order to raise the funds he needed for the war Edward III at first contracted loans with the great Italian houses of Bardi and Peruzzi, which were to be repaid from the proceeds of wool taxes farmed by them. When, as a result of Edward's temporary insolvency in 1325, the Bardi and Peruzzi went bankrupt themselves, their place was taken by syndicates of English merchants formed to carry out the same transactions in which the Italians had failed, i.e. to advance the king large loans repayable out of wool taxes, and on one occasion by an actual monopoly of wool exports. These syndicates also acted as joint-stock partnerships, but their most remarkable characteristic, which appeared to presage dramatic developments in the future, was the role played in them by a few very great merchants operating on a scale far greater than that of any stapler or merchant adventurer of fifty or a hundred years later. The most famous of these financial 'millionaires' was William de la Pole, the founder of the dynasty of the Earls of Suffolk, who as a result of his operations formed an immense fortune made up in part of great landed properties. Somewhat, but only somewhat, smaller fortunes were for a time amassed by men like William Melchebourn or Henry Philpot. If the promise of a precocious commercial and financial capitalism which these firms held out never materialized, the blame for this attaches not only to the flimsy foundations of their fortunes, which were mostly based on badly secured and expensive loans from others, but also on the highly risky character of financial and commercial transactions with kings, especially kings like Edward III. In the end every one of the English syndicates ended in bankruptcy, and William de la Pole and his successors ended in prison. The beginnings of English commercial capitalism were thereby nipped in the bud, and the place of the capitalists was taken by regulated companies which, for all the commercial and financial power they collectively represented, were still redolent with the medieval spirit of regulation and monopoly.[11]

References

1. E. E. Power, *The Wool Trade in English Medieval History*, Ch. III; Power, 'The Wool Trade in the Fifteenth Century', in Power and Postan (eds.), *Studies.* For an illustration of the activities of local wool merchants see H. F. Malden (ed.), *The Cely Papers*, Camden Soc., 3rd ser., I (1900).

2. The relations between merchants of London acting as importers and wholesalers and 'chapmen' acting as their country agents are well illustrated in the entries of debts in the records of the City of London, such as the series of *Calendars of Letter Books of London* (A to L), edited by R. R. Sharpe.

3. H. Pirenne, *Medieval Cities, their Origins and the Revival of Trade*, English trans. (1925); J. Tait, *The Medieval English Borough* (1930).

4. A. Ballard, *The British Borough Charters* (1913); M. Bateson, *Borough Customs* (1904).

5. C. Gross, *The Gild Merchant* (1890).

6. M. W. Beresford, *The New Towns of the Middle Ages: Town Plantations in England, Wales, and Gascony* (1967).

7. S. Thrupp, *The Grocers of London*; Thrupp, 'The Gilds', *The Cambridge Economic History*, Vol. III (1963); J. Toulmin Smith, *English Gilds* (1870); M. Dormer-Harris, *The Coventry Leet Book* (1907–1913); F. D. Watney and L. Lyell, *Acts of Court of the Mercers Company* (1936), Introduction.

8. Power, *The Wool Trade.*

9. Postan, 'Economic and Political Relations'; cf. Carus-Wilson, *Medieval Merchant Venturers.*

10. E. Carus-Wilson, 'The Iceland Trade' in Power and Postan, *Studies in English Trade.*

11. E. B. Fryde, 'Edward III's War Finance 1337-1341' (Oxford dissertation, 1947); *idem* 'The Last Trials of Sir William de la Pole', *Econ. Hist. Rev.* XV, No. 1, 1962; *idem* 'The English Farmers of the Customs, 1343-51', *Trans. Roy. Hist. Soc.* 5th ser., Vol. 9, 1959.

13 Prices

I

Throughout this study, prices and wages have been repeatedly invoked to account for changes in economic activity and in the well-being of the individuals. These references to prices would appear to have at least two important economic implications: first, that prices fluctuated in response to supply and demand, and secondly, that their fluctuations affected economic and social conditions. These implications will not bother an average reader familiar only with prices as they function in a modern economy. To a more sophisticated reader however the whole tenor of our references to prices may appear questionable. Sceptical questions about 'markets' and prices have in fact been raised by a number of sociologists and historians dealing with underdeveloped societies and economies. Students of simple pre-industrial societies are apt to doubt the importance, indeed the very existence, of exchanges operating in the same way and with the same effect as market exchanges do in modern societies. Prices are the essential mechanism of 'markets': the medium through which market forces reveal themselves and exercise their effect. It therefore follows that in places and times at which men sold and bought very little, and covered most of their needs out of their own outputs and disposed of only small parts of their produce, 'markets' and prices could not play the role they do now. We are told that what often passed for prices in conditions like these was nothing more than conventional valuations attaching to customary transactions and ceremonial exchanges.

These notions will be followed here for some distance, but not all the way. We may be justified in playing down the role of 'markets' and prices in truly primitive economies—those of the simpler tribes of Africa, South America or the Pacific in the nineteenth century—or of some prehistoric peoples of Europe. But a similar disparagement of markets and prices in the medieval economy would be highly distorting. In relation to the middle ages the notion of an economy immune from prices might apply to some situations but not to others; and even where it applies it does not necessarily justify an over-simplified view of an economy wholly insensitive to prices.

The over-simplification inherent in this view is due to its failure to distinguish between the existence of 'markets' and price mechanisms on the one hand and the economic and social impact of 'markets' and prices on the other hand. These are two distinct and largely independent problems. That in some fields of economic activity prices at which commodities changed hands were true 'market' prices determined by supply and demand, is not open to much doubt. The range of activities and products drawn into commercial exchanges was much narrower than it was to become in modern times; and many of the goods drawn into exchanges were bought and sold at prices which were purely conventional or customary. But we have also seen that even in the middle ages some sections of the population were engaged in pursuits dependent on produce which had to be marketed. The wool of the wool-growers, the charcoal of the charcoal-burners, all had to be sold; and when sold they commanded true market prices, i.e. prices determined by the interaction of supply and demand. We shall also see presently that even foodstuffs were influenced, sometimes very strongly, by supply and demand.

The prevalence of customary or conventional prices is easy to account for. In the medieval economy, most of the variables which influence price levels did not in fact vary much. Viewed over long periods supply and demand were relatively stable; their secular trends would therefore have been hardly perceptible to contemporaries, even if they may be visible to modern historians. Similarly the effective aggregate demand for goods might fluctuate from year to year, but over long stretches of time it also changed very slowly, as did also the standards of life and the make-up of daily consumption. In a society and economy as stable as this men came to expect goods to exchange at constant ratios, or to put it in simpler language they expected goods always to be worth the same.

Prices were therefore in fact harder than they might otherwise have been. What hardened them further still was the church doctrine and official intervention. The church doctrine was that of 'just price'. In the sense in which it was propounded by canonist writers the doctrine was much more than a mere injunction against overcharging. It linked the price system with the divinely ordained structure of society, by defining a 'just' price as that which would yield the makers of goods and their sellers sufficient income to maintain them in their respective social ranks. This however was not always the sense in which the notion of just price was invoked in daily transactions. Judged by references to prices in medieval sermons and a few surviving judicial proceedings, all increases of prices when demand was high or the supplies were short, and indeed all speculative exploitation of price changes, were deemed unjust. The underlying presumption was that all things had their 'natural' values, which was presumably that which had commonly attached to them in the past. In other words in its everyday sense the notion was one of customary prices.[1]

Some such assumption also underlay the official regulations of prices by medieval authorities. How effective these price controls were is difficult to tell: judging from the proceedings against transgressors, the medieval controls were frequently evaded. More effective could be the valuations embodied in various customary dues. As a rule, dues in kind were required from manorial tenants or other persons bound by feudal contracts. These renders, whether in foods or in personal services, were frequently evaluated in money equivalents. The valuations once fixed remained so for as long as the corresponding custom or tenurial contact itself lasted. Wide gaps between these values and the current market values were bound to develop, and as long as the underlying customs were still in force and continued to govern the actual payments of dues, they restrained the free play of supply and demand and helped to impose a hard crust of custom upon the action of market forces.

Yet the crust was frequently broken; and in places and times at which the reaches occurred, prices rose and fell, if anything, more drastically than they might have done in later periods. The customary barriers may have been strong enough to resist moderate changes in supply or demand, but they were apt to give way when the changes in supply or demand were great or continuous. Thus when the large shipments of leather from southern Europe, or wine from Gascony, arrived in London prices appeared to fall sharply.[2] Prices of timber invariably fell in the fifteenth century after heavy shipments of timber arrived from the Baltic. Gluts and shortages were even more frequent in the most important commodity and the most important markets of all—those of foodstuffs. Medieval harvests fluctuated frequently and sharply, with the result that the supplies available for sale varied greatly from year to year. On the other hand the demand for food was more or less constant and unyielding, or as economists would say 'inelastic'. Prices therefore soared every time harvests were poor and slumped every time they rose above the average. Grain prices responded to fluctuations of demand over periods even shorter than entire harvest years. Grains were at their cheapest in the early autumn, i.e. immediately after the harvests had been gathered, since the villagers then had some grain of their own to eat. But they almost invariably rose in the summer, since by that time many villagers had exhausted their own grain supplies and swelled the ranks of buyers.

Indeed it is probable that in the middle ages, as so often in modern times, the restricted size of the market, its 'narrowness', merely widened the amplitude of fluctuations; and that prices would not have risen or fallen as sharply as they did had the buyers and the sellers been more numerous, the volume of commodities larger, and the access to imported food easier. It is because the total quantity of marketable grain was small relative to the number of people to be fed in times of need, and because the number of people regularly buying their food was small relative to the number who had recourse to the market in times of scarcity, that the shortages and gluts had such a traumatic effect on prices. How traumatic it could be is shown by the short-term deviations of price movements from the secular trend. Whereas, as we shall see presently, the secular rise of prices between say 1225 and 1345 proceeded at a rate not higher than 0.5 per cent per annum, actual prices could be as low as 2*s*. 6*d*. (as in 1226) and 25*s*. a quarter (as in 1315–17).

The same argument also applies to the price of labour, i.e. wages. The notion that wages responded to changes in the supply of men available for employment may strike some readers as anachronistic. Most historians assume, on the whole rightly, that medieval wages, even more than medieval prices, were determined by customary valuations and expectations and could not therefore be expected to respond to fluctuations in the supply of hands or the demand for them. This custom-bound behaviour of wages must not however be exaggerated. It has already been pointed out elsewhere that at times when the supply and demand for labour changed very sharply and suddenly, customary wage standards, however firm and rigid, could collapse. A mortality following bad harvests could at times be so high as to bring about what manorial accounts call a *caristia* of labourers; and in this context *caristia* meant both scarcity and high wages. The supply of manpower and the demand for labour could also change over long periods so persistently as to induce a slow and gradual change in customary wage levels. Thus, taking on the thirteenth century as a whole, population grew and the supplies of labour increased continually, with the result that real wages probably declined. On the other hand the very high mortality of the Black Death and the sagging population trend from about 1325 onwards caused a continuous rise in wages. We shall presently see that on most estates money wages continued to rise until 1450 and stayed at approximately that level or very little higher until the last two or three decades of the century or even later. The real wages, however, i.e. wages expressed in the amount of food they were able to buy, probably continued to rise until well into the sixteenth century. Both real wages and the money wages of skilled and semi-skilled artisans—the smiths, the carpenters, the thatchers, the tilers—went on rising after the wages of agricultural labourers had reached their peak.[3]

The downward and upward trends of wages have been taken here as signs and consequences of demographic changes, though other explanations can and have been offered, and these alternative explanations will be discussed again presently. Here it will suffice to note that the 'other cause' commonly adduced by historians to explain the rising wages in the later middle ages is the greater demand for labour in the new cloth industry. This explanation, whether right or wrong, can only reinforce our general view of wage trend, since it assumes that wages were responsive to market forces even if the forces turned out to be not those of supply of manpower but those of demand for it.

To sum up, for all their limited range and customary constraints medieval prices and wages could in certain situations respond immediately and strongly to the interplay of supply and demand. This does not however mean that the reciprocal response—that of supply and demand to prices—was equally strong. In modern fully commercialized and profit-driven economies prices are expected to act as the principal transmitters of economic stimuli. The student of modern economies takes it for granted that in his decision whether to buy and how much to buy the purchaser is mainly influenced by prices: he will buy more when prices are low, and less when they are high. Similarly the producer's decision whether to produce and how much to produce is determined by what the prices for his products are or can be expected to be. Nevertheless even in modern economies prices do not perform their function as transmitters of economic stimuli or regulators of economic activity as perfectly as the theory would have it. In the middle ages their action as transmitters and regulators was bound to be much weaker still.

Some effect they doubtless had, since in most walks of life it was possible to find speculators who conducted themselves so as to profit from changes in prices. The medieval moralists inveighed against 'forestallers' and 'regrators', i.e. traders who tried to raise prices by buying up supplies of commodities or by holding stocks until prices rose. The latter was apparently a misdeed very common in the marketing of grain.

In general the economic activities most responsive to prices were those of industrial production, and in the first place cloth production. If, as seems probable, the production of cloth for export declined in the thirteenth century, the decline could best be accounted for by the relative cheapness, quality for quality, of Flemish cloth. But even if some doubt still attached to the decline of the English cloth industry in the thirteenth century, none are raised by the revival of the cloth industry and cloth exports in the fourteenth century. We have seen that at that period the English cloth producers reaped the advantages of the wide gap which had opened between the prices at which wool was available in this country and abroad.

These industrial responses to changes in prices were, however, in some ways untypical, since industry itself was somewhat untypical of the English medieval economy as a whole. In agriculture, which was responsible for the overwhelmingly greater part of the country's physical product and provided the livelihood of at least three quarters of its population, prices had a very limited effect on production. The pressures and incentives which moved agricultural producers to expand or to retrench were many and various, and were not confined to prices. On the commercialized demesnes, selling the bulk of their produce, the decisions whether and how much to grow, and above all the choices as between different crops or between wool and animal products on the one hand and cereal crops on the other, could be influenced by the way prices behaved. It has for instance been argued that the fourteenth-century taxes on wool exports lowered the domestic prices, and thereby discouraged some sheep farmers. It is doubtful however whether even the manorial managers in their year-to-year decisions could have been much influenced by the previous year's prices or the prices they were able to anticipate in the immediate future. The productive record of individual fields and the prospective supplies of labour had a more immediate effect on the decisions of manorial managers. Still less responsive to prices were the men who ran their demesnes mainly as 'home farms', i.e. to supply their households with food and fodder, and least responsive of all were peasant households.

We have so little documentary evidence of the manner in which villagers managed their holding, that all that can be said about them can be no more than a guess based mostly on a judgment of probabilities. One of the probabilities is that most villagers, like peasants of all times, consumed the bulk of their produce and did not produce for sale except in order to meet their obligations, mainly those to their landlords. As we have already argued elsewhere, the average holders of customary semi-virgates in the arable parts of the country had to earmark for obligatory payments as much as half of their output. But even on these holdings the producers' response to prices was not automatic and certainly not positive. It was more likely to be 'negative' in the technical sense of the term, i.e. to induce a decline of output when prices were high and a rise in output when they were low. For as long as cash crops were grown in order to provide for the payments which were obligatory and fixed, the necessity to grow more was greater when prices were low and *vice versa*. This in fact has always been the response of small farmers burdened with payments in most places and at most times, even in the USA before 1930.[4] Our conclusion must therefore be that whereas economic developments could at times exercise a powerful effect on prices, they themselves did not react to prices with the same frequency and strength as they would have done nowadays.

II

With these general considerations out of the way we can proceed to the story of the actual prices themselves, their periodic changes and other differences in their levels.

Our evidence of prices, though continuous and abundant, is at the same time highly restricted. It is mostly confined to prices of foodstuffs, extracted from manorial accounts of certain great estates. We also possess a considerable amount of evidence about wool prices and the prices of livestock. The greatest deficiency in our price data is that of industrial goods. Prices of timber and such iron goods as nails are to be found in large numbers, but the variations in quality, size, weight and other specifications are so great as to defeat all attempts at satisfactory price indices.

Our view of prices will therefore perforce be confined to those of agricultural produce, more particularly of wheat. The earliest information about these prices comes from the documents of the Royal Exchequer (the Pipe Rolls) which record the royal purchases of grain in the closing decades of the twelfth century.

In the opening years of our series, the last forty or thirty years of the twelfth century, prices were low compared to the height they were to reach in the subsequent two centuries, and may also have differed from region to region more pronouncedly than in later times. Judged by medieval standards the prices were also very stable, though their stability may in part have been due less to the inertia of the prices themselves than to the levelling effect of centralized buying. In 1165, at the very inception of our series, the royal agents were buying wheat at 1*s.* 9½*d.* per weight; allowing for a bulge between 1172 and 1174 and again between 1178 and 1184, the prices stood roughly at their 1165 level, fluctuating narrowly between about 1*s.* 7*d.* and 1*s.* 10*d.* per weight. The trend of prices for animals was almost equally stable and, compared to later periods, equally low. Oxen commanded about 3*s.* per head until 1192, except for the four years between 1182 and 1188 when they rose to over 4*s.* 2*d.*, probably in response to the heavy restocking of the Royal manors. Prices of sheep fluctuated a little more widely, but were also stable over long stretches of time. They were bought for about 4*d.* each in the first twenty years, rose to 6*d.* during the period of heavy restocking in the 1180s, and remained at this level until the end of the century. The prices of pigs were more stable still, and their prices stood at about the same level, usually 1*s.*, throughout the period.[5]

The evidence of regional variations is not as clear as that of relative stability; it is nevertheless sufficiently clear to be worth taking into account. Some of the regional variations were apt to be masked by costs of transport, for when the royal agents happened to buy grain cheaply in more distant regions, the difference in prices could be balanced by high costs of transport. How high the latter was on occasions is shown by the royal grain purchases of 1171, when the carriage of wheat from Oxford to Bristol raised its final price by over a third. Regional differences of agricultural prices were not of course confined to the twelfth century. So marked were they in the later centuries of the middle ages that an historian—N. S. B. Gras—was able to divide medieval England into a number of regional market areas each demarcated by a different price level.[6] But on the whole it appears that in the thirteenth and fourteenth centuries the local differences in prices were not as wide as they appear to have been in the twelfth century. Why the differences should have been so wide we can only guess. The twelfth-century slump in agricultural production and the disorganization of the demesne farming may have been greater in some cases than in others. It has also been suggested that the disorders of the mid-century continued to have their effect on the security of the roads until the end of the century.

The end of the century was in many ways a real turning point in the history of medieval prices: Lord Beveridge described the changes of the time as the 'price-revolution of the middle ages'. Prices of all agricultural products rose sharply and suddenly in the closing years of the twelfth and the opening years of the thirteenth centuries. Wheat commanded about 1*s*. 9*d*. per weight in the later 1190s but soared to well over 3*s*. 6*d*. in the four or five years between 1199 and 1203: a twofold rise. In the same period the price of oxen, which had stood at 4*s*. for several decades before 1199, rose to 7*s*. in the decade between 1201 and 1210. The price of sheep in the same period doubled from 4*d*. or 6*d*. before 1199 to rather more than 10*d*. in the first decade of the twelfth century. So also did the price of pigs.[7]

Having risen to their turn-of-the-century plateau prices stayed on or above it for the rest of the thirteenth and the early fourteenth centuries. In the nature of things prices fluctuated sharply from year to year owing to the vagaries of harvests and, in the case of animals, to the vagaries of currency. But underlying the year to year fluctuations it is easy to detect the swell of a secular tide. The latter rose slowly and gently but with sufficient consistency to bring the prices of wheat on the eve of the Black Death of 1348 to a height nearly twice as great as the point at which we find them in the first two decades of the century. For whereas in the twenty years from 1210 to 1230 the price of wheat fluctuated round 3*s*., it climbed eventually to a bi-decennial average of 6*s*., or little less than twice the price in the opening decades of the century.

The movement of prices in the course of these 150 years and for a long time after can be followed and even measured with some accuracy thanks to abundant evidence provided by the manorial accounts. Those of the bishops of Winchester's estates in southern England are the fullest and the earliest (they begin in 1209), and are almost continuous after the late 1230s. From that date onwards the evidence of the Winchester accounts can also be supplemented by the prices on some other great estates—above all Westminster Abbey and the abbey of Bury St Edmunds. The three series when combined—as they can be from 1345 onwards—are the basis of the figures represented in Figure 1. A glance at the graph will show two shallow troughs when prices rose very slowly, if at all, from about 1270 until the end of the century and in the early 1340s. However, in both cases the reduction in the rate of secular climb is very largely a statistical fiction. The prices in times of exceptionally good harvests, such as those of 1287–88 and those of the early 1240s descended so low as to bring up the statistical averages for entire decades. In the same way one or two very bad harvests, such as those of the early 1290s, could bring down the statistical averages for the mid-1290s as a whole. Indeed so disastrous were the harvests of 1315–17, and so great was the resulting rise in prices, that by including them into the decennial or bi-decennial averages we would have broken the trend by a wholly violent and untypical kink. The prices for these two years have therefore been excluded from our computations of the trend. At the same time their extraordinarily high level—nearly five to six times the average for the century—is a useful reminder of how dramatic and erratic the movement of medieval prices could be over short periods of time. It is only over periods as long as a century and more that the slowly mounting tendency of prices can be discerned.

The same difference between annual fluctuations and the trend can also be observed in the following period, that between 1350—the year following the Black Death—and the second half of the fifteenth century. In that period prices also fluctuated, though they were never again to rise as steeply as in 1315–17. On the other hand the trend moved even more gently than before, except that over the greater part of the century it did not mount but sagged, or at best remained stationary. Unfortunately our manorial price data for the fifteenth century are not as abundant as for the thirteenth, and such as there is has not been worked over by historians as thoroughly. Such conclusion as the fifteenth century figures have so far justified is that by the early 1370s the prices of all grains

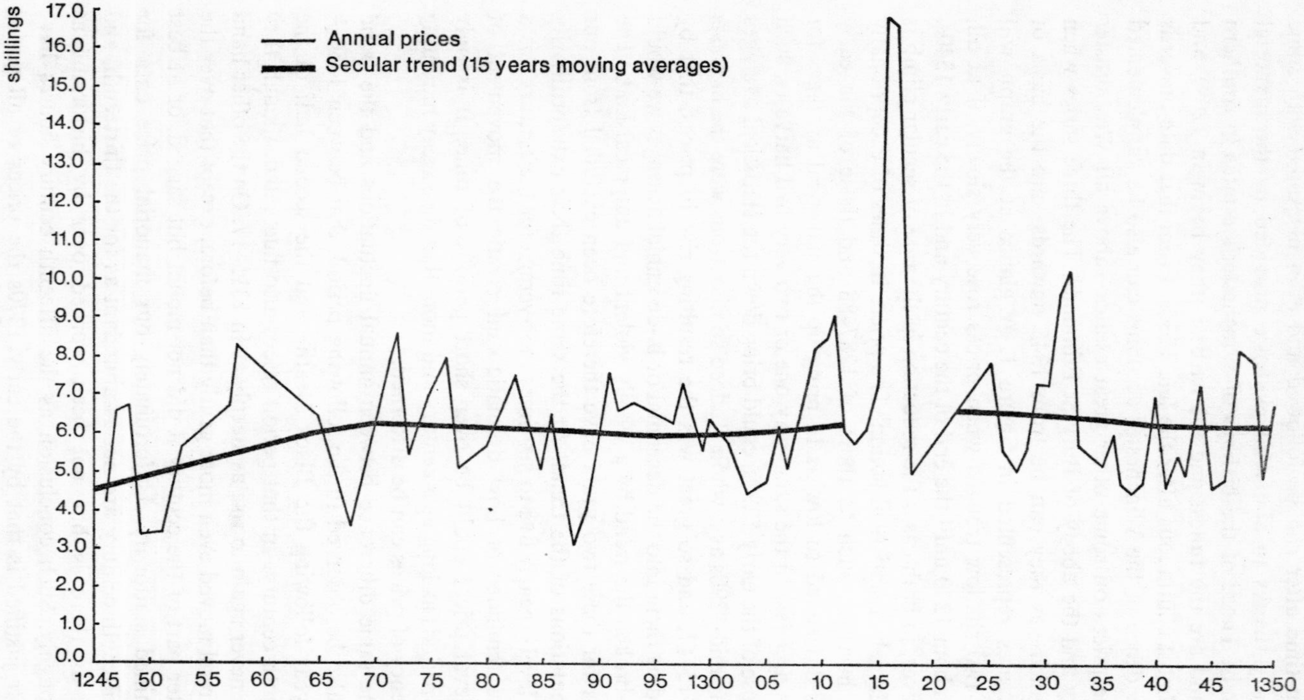

Figure 1. Prices of wheat, barley and oats (per qr.), 1245–1350.
Source: price data of the British Committee on Price History, extracted from the manorial accounts of the estates of the bishops of Winchester, the abbots of Westminster and the Bacon family (formerly of the abbey of Bury St Edmunds)

had apparently sunk some 10 to 15 per cent below the level on the morrow of the Black Death; that prices were relatively higher in the last quarter of the fourteenth century and during short periods in the early fifteenth century; and that they slumped rather markedly in the middle decades of the century and began to pick up again in the 1460s.

The prices of animals and animal products moved roughly in the same direction as the prices of grain. Yet the differences between the two both in the timing and the amplitude of price-changes for individual products may sometimes reveal the factors behind the medieval prices and help to identify the operative causes of the price changes.[8]

III

What were then the operative causes? The question is easiest to answer for the short term, i.e. year to year, fluctuations. The great, indeed overwhelming, importance of harvests on grain prices has been mentioned here. Some short-term movements of prices could also follow changes in currency: the debasements of coins by clipping, the reductions of their legal bullion content or the restoration of their full weight by recoining. The latter appear to have influenced the prices of animals, more particularly oxen. A student of medieval prices, Mr D. L. Farmer, has convincingly demonstrated how on several occasions on which currency was reminted or had its full bullion content restored, the prices of oxen fell. Such recoinages accompanied by a fall in prices of oxen occurred at least three times in the thirteenth century. On the other hand the effect of recoinages on sheep prices was not quite so marked, and the effect on prices of pigs, bacon and cheese was so small as to be almost imperceptible.[9]

The differential effect of revaluations of currency cannot be explained except by adducing some other non-currency factors. Thus one of the reasons why prices for oxen and to some extent sheep were responsive to currency is that they were what would now be described as 'capital goods', and that their prices were largely influenced by the decisions of landlords and other manorial managers capable of taking a commercial view of their outlays and of adjusting their buying and selling to the bullion contents of the currency. The same is to some extent true of sheep, as sheepfarmers whose main products—wool and skins—were so to speak 'cash commodities' traded on the highly commercialized markets in this country and abroad. Bacon and cheese probably owed their stable prices to their ranking as semi-luxury foods, for which the demand was, to use the language of economists, highly elastic. What this means is that a relatively small fall in their price could bring about a considerable rise in their consumption and *vice versa*. Price fluctuations, whatever their cause, as well as the additional supplies, could be quickly absorbed, and price changes would be small and brief.

Where the effects of coinage were purely subordinate, or even played no part at all, is in the long-term changes, since neither on theoretical grounds nor on those of evidence can secular trends be easily accounted for by changes in currency.

Currency and the supply of bullion have nevertheless been frequently adduced by historians and economists to account for the price trends of the thirteenth and later centuries. In its simpler form this explanation follows very faithfully the simplified version of the most traditional of economic theories of price changes—that which relates price changes to the supply of the circulating medium. It has thus been argued that prices rose in the thirteenth century in response to the higher output of bullion, mostly in central European mines. Similarly the declining or sagging tendency of prices in the late fourteenth and fifteenth centuries has been put down to the decline in the output of silver and gold during that period.[10]

The theoretical difficulties in applying this doctrine to medieval England are many, and all of them weighty. In the first place it was not enough for the silver and gold to be available in larger quantities abroad. Before the newly-mined bullion could affect English prices it had to reach this country. In other words what mattered was not the output of precious metals abroad but their influx into England; and the influx of silver or gold into this country depended on what we should now describe as national payment balances. If and when the English payments abroad happened to be larger than the foreigners' payment in England an outflow of bullion was bound to result, and the quantity of bullion in this country was bound to decline. Unfortunately we do not know enough about payments across frontiers to plot the changes in their balances; but the little we know is enough to throw doubt on the assumption that England always enjoyed positive balances on international account. The value of English wool exports may have been higher than that of foreign goods imported here, and may thereby have generated recurrent credit balances in England's commercial account. Yet very frequently these positive balances—if there were any—were apt to be dissipated by various non-commercial payments abroad. Throughout the thirteenth century English kings and ecclesiastical establishments frequently paid out large sums abroad in papal taxation, and above all in payments during military campaigns. Large amounts were also paid out in pilgrims' expenses. In these circumstances a constant credit balance in foreign payments and an uninterrupted one-way flow of bullion to England were very unlikely.

A flow of bullion could of course result from the condition of the currency itself. If and when the English currency was thought to be undervalued, i.e. could buy less of other goods than its bullion content justified, this set up an outflow of bullion to countries where it was more highly valued. The current would flow in the opposite direction if and when the English currency was thought to be overvalued. However, the periods of apparent undervaluation and overvaluation succeeded each other at intervals, and the flow of bullion could not therefore be expected always to run inwards. If contemporary opinion is to be trusted, the country appeared to suffer at most times in the thirteenth century from a shortage and dearth of silver.

In the third place, even if and when bullion came into this country it did not necessarily or always add to the amount of coinage in circulation. Such additions would have occurred if all the incoming bullion and gold were minted into coins or otherwise used as a medium of exchange. In the middle ages, however, not only were silver and gold used to manufacture jewelry or plate, but were also hoarded. What is more, the tendency to hoard was by no means constant; it notably increased in times of insecurity or in times when the undervaluation of the coins discouraged the holders of bullion from presenting it to the mints for coining. How large the private hoards could sometimes be is occasionally revealed by incidents like that of the recoinage of 1247, when the Earl of Cornwall undertook to contribute from his own resources 10,000 marks of silver to the bullion required to remint the currency.[11]

Finally it must be borne in mind that currency in the shape of gold and silver coins was by no means the only medium of exchange. At present we are used to the existence of paper money and bank money, i.e. of credits and other bank-made assets which enable individuals to settle their accounts without recourse to hard cash. The use of credit and the other equivalents of bank money was much smaller in the thirteenth century than the twentieth, yet it was quite widespread, more particularly in the main branches of international trade, such as wool, cloth and wine and in transactions involving the king and the king's debt. What is more, the quantity of 'bank money' was not stable, nor did it grow consistently in the middle ages. Most historians rightly assume that the use of various instruments of credit was more widespread and more sophisticated in the fifteenth century than it had been in the thirteenth. If so, the money-induced changes in the demand for goods and the rise in prices due to increased circulation should have been more pronounced in the fifteenth century than in the thirteenth—and we know that they were not.[12]

So much for the purely theoretical reasons why the currency could not be accepted as the sole or even the main factor behind the rise of prices in the thirteenth century and their decline in the fifteenth. In addition some difficulty also attaches to the facts adduced in the support of the currency explanations. If changes in the supply of silver content of currency were responsible for the thirteenth-century rises, why should a sudden upsurge of prices have occurred at the turn of the twelfth and thirteenth centuries? If recoinage and the restoration of the bullion content of currency had been responsible for the rise in prices, the rise should have occurred some twenty years earlier, since Henry II's great recoinage took place in 1180. If, on the other hand, the influx of bullion from the continent were to blame the price-rise should have occurred some decades later, since large inflows were not to happen until the opening years of the thirteenth century, if at all. The same puzzle attaches to the first quarter of the fourteenth century, from about 1310 to about 1335. During that period the trend was badly broken by the disastrous harvests and famine prices of 1315–17. But this break apart, the average level of grain prices was near-horizontal, and after 1320 appears to be lower than in the preceding two generations.[13]

Similarly the high prices for oxen in the period 1320–40 could not be explained, as some historians explain them, by the increases in circulation in the early years of Edward III's reign. The additions to purchasing power resulting from Edward III's disbursements were connected with the preparation of the launching of his French wars. Most of them occurred not in England but abroad, where most of his treasure was spent on buying allies and maintaining military establishments. But whatever is the truth about the king's inflationary finances, why should they have affected the prices for grain and those for animal produce so differently?

This disparity in fact conceals the very crux of the problem. The pure logic of the monetary explanation demands that the effects of changes in the circulating medium should be felt throughout the economy, i.e. in the prices of all the goods sold and bought, since changes in money must be, so to speak, 'neutral' as between different commodities. It therefore follows that, if the price movement for different commodities diverged, monetary factors could not have been the sole or the main cause of the price changes. To account for divergent paths of different price series for different commodities we must look for factors specific to each commodity and seek an explanation not only in monetary but also in the so-called 'real' processes in the economy. A glance at Mr Farmer's graph reproduced here (Figure 3) will show that the prices for grain on the one hand and those for oxen and other animal products diverged very significantly, especially in the early fourteenth century. The divergences were sufficiently marked to make a purely monetary explanation of the movement untenable. Could we then find any 'real' factors better able to account for the price trends?

An alternative 'real' hypothesis has in fact been suggested. The rising secular trend of grain prices could be accounted for by concomitant demographic trends. Population was increasing, or in other words the number of mouths was getting ever greater. The output of agriculture, though expanding, could not keep pace with the increasing numbers to be fed. The ever greater dependence on poorer lands and the impoverishment of some of the old lands raised the real cost of food in terms of resources which had to be devoted to the production of additional quantities of grain. Had the quantity of money in circulation remained stationary or declined, prices might have remained stable; but universal starvation would have resulted. Had the money supply kept pace with the increasing population prices would have risen very high, probably much higher than in the thirteenth century. The fact that price rise was very gentle, but that large sections of the population went short of food, indicates that the quantity of money in the hands of the people did not multiply as fast as the people themselves.

We have seen that real factors could be adduced for the

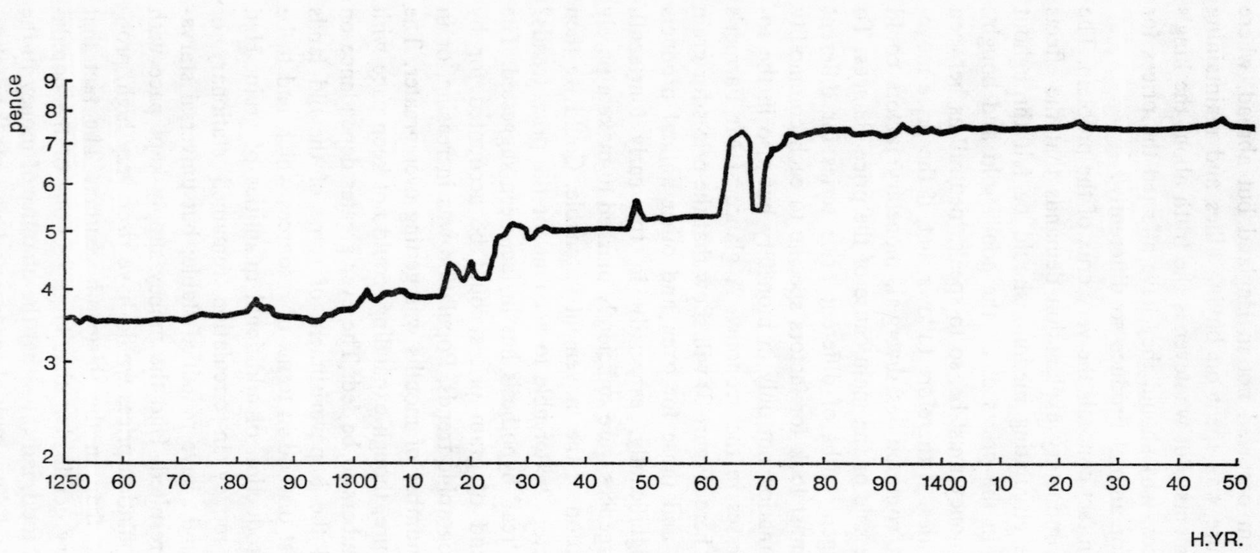

Figure 2. Mean cost of threshing and winnowing one raised qr. each on some manors of the bishops of Winchester and the abbots of Westminster (7 years moving averages). Source: price data of the British Committee on Price History

prices for oxen. Oxen were first and foremost the productive capital of agriculture; the demand for them reflected the demands of the expanding agricultural production; and enough has already been said about agricultural expansion in this period to make it unnecessary for us to account here for the rising demand for plough animals. On the other hand it has already been stressed here that cheese and bacon were semi-luxury foods whose price movements were bound to be greatly responsive to changes in supply and demand. Furthermore it is an accepted proposition of theory and an observed social phenomenon that when in poorer societies the prices for bread rise, the demand for it instead of falling also rises because its higher price reduces the purchasing capacity for luxury foods. The demand for luxury foods accordingly slumps in times when prices and demand for essential foods rise. And this is what might very well have happened in the opening decades of the fourteenth century.[14]

If this combination of factors, some monetary but others 'real', can be read into the upward movement of prices in the twelfth and thirteenth centuries it will also have to be read into the stable or sagging price trends of the late fourteenth and fifteenth centuries. It may be that the declining production of bullion abroad and the scarcity of minted bullion in circulation could account for the fifteenth-century reversal of the earlier price trends. On the other hand the fact that population had declined after 1340 or 1348 and may have continued to decline until the second half of the fifteenth century, and that the 'real' costs of cultivation were becoming lower or at least ceased to increase, would be a highly relevant reversal of the situation as we found it before the Black Death.

Neither the combination of circumstances we have read into the pre-pestilence facts, nor their inversion in the post-pestilence period, can be presented as fully established historical facts. They are no more than hypotheses, but they are working hypotheses, i.e. explanations most consistent with the facts as we know them and with the logic of economic change as we understand it.

IV

There is no need for us to 'rub in' the determining part which 'real', i.e. non-monetary, changes played in the movement of wages. As the graph above clearly shows (Figure 2) the trend of

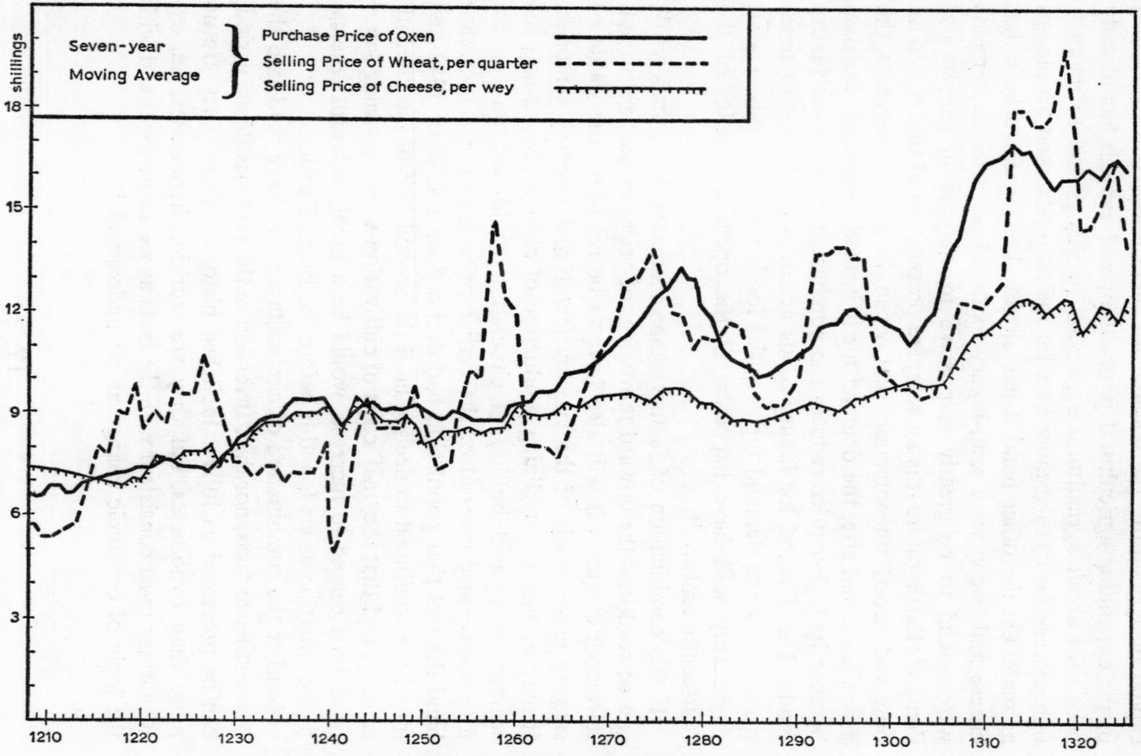

Figure 3. The price of oxen, wheat and cheese, 1208–1325

winnowers' and threshers' wages on the estates of the Bishops of Winchester and the Abbots of Westminster rose hardly at all between 1250 and 1310—at most by 10 per cent in sixty years; and in the preceding fifty years these wages appeared to be completely stationary. If these money wages are translated into real terms, i.e. their equivalents in ounces of silver, or better still into bushels of grain, they will reveal a clear downward trend culminating at a point in 1320 some 25 to 40 per cent lower than the starting point in 1210. From 1315 onwards the trend takes a decidedly upward turn rising in money terms by about 20 per cent in one decade. From this high level the wages continue their gradual ascent to the Black Death and beyond, reaching their peak between 1360 and 1370: a period which coincides with the outbreak of the second plague and the apparent collapse of attempts to keep wages down by legal prescription. From 1370 onwards these particular sets of wages represented in our graph retain their high place but do not exhibit any marked upward tendency in money terms. But expressed in real terms they appeared to rise much faster than our graphs indicate, and go on rising all through the fifteenth century. Other wages, especially those of artisans, continue their rise even in money terms.[15]

The movement of wages has already been discussed in connection with the population changes, and has been considered as a consequence and evidence of rising population before the second decade of the fourteenth century and of the declining population after it. This particular explanation has however been challenged, though this time the challenges invoke not monetary factors but other, 'real', causes. Two alternative explanations have so far been offered to account for the rising wages of the fourteenth and fifteenth centuries. It has been argued that in the fifteenth century wages rose as a result of increased investment and of a general expansion in labour-intensive arable farming. Many, perhaps most, historians of the later middle ages also appear to believe that wages were boosted by increased industrial employment, above all by the expanding cloth manufacture. Both hypotheses, plausible as they appear to be, are difficult to substantiate. Increased demand for agricultural labour is difficult to reconcile with what we know of the changes on the demesnes. The use of labour on the demesne was declining, and the decline was unlikely to be compensated for by increased employment in peasant households. In all probability the total acreages under plough—that of the demesne and the villagers put together—contracted, and the contraction in the acreage should have reduced the employment of agricultural labourers. But even if the acreage had remained stable, the transfer of land from the demesne to the peasants could by itself be expected to reduce the demand for labour. It is in the nature of peasant households of small and middling size to draw their labour as much as possible from within the family itself. It is also in the nature of most peasant households to harbour under-employed men and women and thus to possess reserves of labour sufficient to deal with additions to holdings. For these, admittedly *a priori,* reasons, additional employment on the villagers' land would have been most unlikely to compensate for reduced employment on the demesne.

Almost equally implausible appears the hypothesis of industry compensating for the reduced employment in agriculture. The cloth industry grew very fast in the fourteenth century, and we must presume that whilst it grew it set up an additional demand for labour. The size of the additions must not however be exaggerated or mistimed. In recounting the story of the cloth industry I emphasized that while the industry certainly grew in the fourteenth and early fifteenth centuries, we cannot be certain that it continued to grow throughout the fifteenth century. The only thing we know for certain is that the exports of English cloth, which had expanded very fast before the 1420s, grew hardly at all between 1430 and 1470. Our belief in the continued growth in the English cloth industry in that period must therefore hinge on what we know of the domestic market for cloth. Unfortunately our evidence of the domestic market and of its size is very meagre. What the historians believe and write about it is a mere play of probabilities, and the probability that during that period the domestic market declined is at least as great as the probability that it grew.

What is more, the additional employment which the cloth industry could at the best of times have given was, compared to agricultural employment, rather small. Even in the late fourteenth century and the beginning of the fifteenth when the export of English cloth was at its highest—slightly above 50,000 cloths per annum—the number of full-time workers required to produce these exports would not have been much greater than the equivalent of 20,000 full-time workers.[16] True enough, many of the workers—nearly all the spinners and a proportion of the weavers—were occupied in cloth-making only part of their time, so that the numbers drawn into the cloth industry and deriving some income from it was greater than 20,000. But however much multiplied, this figure will still be small compared with the numbers of smallholders available and offering themselves for employment in the period when total population was at its highest. Even at its minimum estimate the total population at that time exceeded 3¼ million, while the number of smallholders, at 35 or 40 per cent of the total, must have approached a million-and-a-half. It might have exceeded two-and-a-half million if the population had been as great as our maximum estimates suggest. We are therefore driven to the conclusion that however effective may have been the additional demand for industrial labour, it was not as important a 'real' factor behind the movement of wages as the changes in population.

References

1. G. LeBras, 'Conceptions of Economy and Society', in *Cambridge Economic History of Western Europe*, Vol. III (1963). However, the best account of the theory of just price in English is still in W. Ashley, *An Introduction to Economic History*, Vol. II (1925).

2. M. K. James, 'The Fluctuations of the Anglo-Gascon Wine Trade', in E. M. Carus-Wilson, *Essays in Economic History*, Vol. I (1951).

3. See below, pages 241-4.

4. For a comparative and largely theoretical discussion of the problem cf. Marc Nerlove, *The Dynamics of Supply: Estimation of Farmer Response to Price* (1958), and Robert M. Stern, 'The Price Responsiveness of Primary Producers', *Review of Economics and Statistics*, XIV (1962).

5. D. L. Farmer, 'Price Fluctuations in Angevin England', *Econ. Hist. Rev.* 2nd ser., IX (1956). The prices cited in some Anglo-Saxon codes of law were at times so near those of the middle of the twelfth century as to suggest the possibility of prices stable over several centuries. Laws of Ine (688–694) paras. 23, 55–59; also Aethelstan's ordinance of c. 924, para. 62 in Whitelock (ed.), *English Historical Documents*, pp. 364, 388, 389.

6. N. S. B. Gras, *The Evolution of the English Corn Market from the Twelfth to the Eighteenth Century* (1915).

7. Farmer, 'Price Fluctuations'; see also Figure 1, p. 234. An older but still usable collection of prices from the thirteenth century onwards will be found in J. E. T. Rogers, *History of Agriculture and Prices* (1866).

8. D. L. Farmer, 'Some Livestock Price Movements in Thirteenth-Century England', *Econ. Hist. Rev.*, 2nd ser., Vol. XXII (1949).

9. Farmer, 'Some Livestock Price Movements'.

10. The fullest exposition of this thesis will be found not in studies of fifteenth-century England, but in those of the 'price revolution' of the sixteenth century, particularly in Earl J. Hamilton, *War and Prices in Spain, 1651–1800* (1947).

11. Sir John Craig, *The Mint*, Cambridge (1953), pp. 25, 32-5; also appendices to the report of the *Royal Commission on the Constitution etc. of the Royal Mint, 1848*.

12. M. M. Postan, 'Credit in Medieval Trade', *Econ. Hist. Rev.*, Vol. IV (1935).

13. For the insensitivity of fourteenth- and fifteenth-century prices to the quantity of money, cf. A. E. Feaveryear, *The Pound Sterling*, p. 40.

14. Alfred Marshall, *Industry and Trade*, Vol. II, p. 432; see Appendix 5, page 248 below.

15. Lord Beveridge, 'Westminster Wages in the Manorial Era', *Econ. Hist. Rev.*, 2nd series, Vol. VII (1955–6).

16. M. M. Postan, 'Some Economic Evidence of Declining Population', *Econ. Hist. Rev.*, 2nd series (1959).

Appendices

1 Teamlands

In the past historians were inclined to disparage the relevance of the Domesday 'teamland' to agrarian reality; e.g. H. Round, 'Introduction to Somerset Domesday', *The Victoria County History of the County of Somerset*, Vol. I; and to a smaller extent F. W. Maitland, *Domesday Book and Beyond*, p. 453. But Maitland admitted the relation of teamland to real areas and assumed it in his computation of cultivated land in 1086. For a more recent reappraisal and a proper emphasis on underlying agrarian facts, more especially on the fertility of the soil, see J. S. Moore, 'The Domesday Teamland: a Reconsideration', *Trans. Roy. Hist. Soc.*, 5th ser, 14 (1964). But the clearest indication of the agrarian reality of teamlands, which escaped most Domesday scholars, is the part it was to play as a basis for the assessment of an aid in King John's time. S. K. Mitchell, *Taxation in Medieval England*, 2nd ed. (1951), p. 178.

2 Land Sales in the Thirteenth Century

The hypothesis about sales by smaller landowners has been countered by the argument that the evidence of thirteenth-century land sales may be biased against smaller men since the bulk of the evidence of land purchases comes from the records of large estates. This is, however, immaterial. The fact that the records of large estates record a large number of purchases from smaller men and hardly any sales to them is sufficient to support the contention that land transactions were reducing the smaller man's share in England's land.

3 Danegeld

In the course of the twelfth century Danegeld was levied with increasing frequency, but at decreasing rates. It was collected at 6*s.* per hide in 1084, and 4*s.* per hide in 1096; almost annually in Henry I's reign at 2*s.* per hide. But Henry II took it only twice at 2*s.* *Pipe Rolls, passim*; Painter, *English Feudal Barons*, pp. 76–8.

4 Fifteenth-Century Landlords

The information on the Hungerfords is mainly derived from an unpublished London thesis on Hungerford estates in the fifteenth century by Miss Richenda Payne (Mrs R. Scott). The information on Cardinal Beaufort is based partly on my own unpublished studies and on Dr J. Z. Titow's forthcoming study of the estates of the Bishops of Winchester in the late middle ages. The evidence of manorial profits of the Lancaster estates is based on my own unpublished studies, as are also the references to the Earl's non-manorial profits. The references to the Percy estates are based on M. W. Bean, *The Estates of the Percy Family;* the references to the Staffords are derived from the Earl of Stafford's records in the Staffordshire Records Society and from Ross and Pugh, 'Materials for the Study of Baronial Incomes', *loc. cit.*

5 Currency and Prices

There are additional reasons why the state of the currency and its bullion contents could not be accepted as principal causes of price change.

1. The quality of coinage was deteriorating at all times except in the years immediately following the successive recoinages. This might account for the steady rise in prices in the thirteenth century, but could not account for their stability and decline in the late fourteenth and fifteenth. What makes the latter all the more difficult to link with the currency hypothesis is that from the second half of the fourteenth century onwards the silver content was repeatedly reduced by royal prescription in 1344–5 and 1351. As a result of these reductions the legal silver content of a penny fell from the traditional 22.5 gr. troy to 18 gr. troy; yet throughout that period of successive devaluation prices were buoyant. (R. Ruding, *Annals of the Coinage of Great Britain and its Dependencies*, 3rd. ed. (1840); C. G. Crump, A. Hughes and C. Johnson, 'The Debase-

ment of Coinage under Edward III', *Economic Journal,* Vol. VIII; A. E. Feaveryear, *The Pound Sterling* (1931), pp. 10–26.)

2. The upsurge of prices which Mr Farmer noted in the years following some of the recoinages does not occur in the years following other recoinages. Between 1150 and 1300 recoinages occurred at least six times, in 1156–9, 1181, 1205, 1247, 1279, and 1299, yet some of these do not appear to have had any effect on prices, especially those of 1181, 1205, and 1299. (Ruding, *Annals of the Coinage.*)

Select Bibliography

I GENERAL

The Cambridge Economic History of Europe, Vol. I, 2nd ed. (1960), more particularly chapters by M. Bloch, Ch. Parain, M. Postan and L. Genicot; Vol. II (1952), more particularly chapters by E. Carus-Wilson and M. Postan; and Vol. III (1963), more particularly chapters by E. Miller and S. Thrupp.

W. Ashley, *An Introduction to English Economic History* (1909); old-fashioned, but in many ways still the best introduction.

E. M. Carus-Wilson (ed.), *Essays in Economic History*, Vols. I and II (1959 and 1962).

II AGRICULTURE AND RURAL SOCIETY

N. J. Hone, *The Manor and Manorial Records* (1906).

G. Duby, *Rural Life and Economy in the Medieval West* (1968), more particularly the sections dealing with England.

R. Lennard, *Rural England, 1086–1135* (1959).

F. W. Maitland, *The Domesday Book and Beyond* (1897).

P. Vinogradov, *The Growth of the Manor* (1905).

P. Vinogradov, *Villeinage in England* (1892).

R. H. Hilton, *A Medieval Society*, 1968.

J. Z. Titow, *English Rural Society* (1969).

E. A. Kosminsky, *Studies in the Agrarian History of England in the Thirteenth Century* (1956).

S. Painter, *Studies in the History of the English Feudal Barony* (1943).

III TRADE AND INDUSTRY

E. Lipson, *An Introduction to the Economic History of England*, Vol. I (1915), Chapters VI–XI.

E. E. Power, *The Wool Trade in English Medieval History* (1941).

M. Bateson, *Borough Customs* (1904).

C. Gross, *The Gild Merchant* (1890).

J. Toulmin Smith, *English Gilds* (1870).
S. Thrupp, *The Grocers of London* (1949).
E. E. Power and M. M. Postan, *Studies in English Trade in the Fifteenth Century* (1935).
E. M. Carus-Wilson, *Medieval Merchant Venturers* (1954).

Index